Making a Difference

Making a Difference

Fred Rosene

Library of Congress Control Number: 2010911581
ISBN: Hardcover   978-1-4535-5238-4
                 Softcover   978-1-4535-5237-7
                 Ebook   978-1-4535-5239-1

To order additional copies of this book, contact:
Xlibris Corporation
1-888-795-4274
www.Xlibris.com
Orders@Xlibris.com
82703

CONTENTS

In memory of my mother, who taught me,
by example, to always help others.

For these are all our children and we shall either profit by, or pay for, whatever they become.
—James Baldwin

PREFACE

This book is divided into three parts. The first part starts with the earliest things I could remember up to my retirement at age sixty, when I moved to Florida. It leaves out the part where I was involved and running a youth drop-in center called Beginnings. Part II covers the story of Beginnings. Finally, part III covers my retirement in Florida, which is primarily the story of twenty years of volunteering in the Palm Beach School District.

Part II was written first during the first ten years of my retirement, and parts I and III were written after nineteen years of volunteering. I spent many years working with a fourth-grade teacher, Bonnie Gomez, who was a great teacher of writing. Listening to her teach gave me confidence to try writing this book.

Thank you, all you wonderful children and youth
for letting me help you and being my friends.

Thank you, all those who helped me accomplish what I have.

PART I

Early Memories

Wow, look at this! I thought as I realized that when I slid out of my sunsuit, I was free of the rope that was tied to it. The fact that I was totally nude didn't bother me at all. I walked to the front of the house, found my sister's little doll carriage, and started wheeling it down the street. I guess a small nude boy pushing a doll carriage must have been a strange sight. When my mother left the house, she always walked down to the trolley tracks so I did too. It was only five or six blocks to the tracks so it didn't take me long. After a short wait that seemed forever, a car came along. I tried to get on the trolley, but the driver wouldn't let me, but I held my ground on the car steps. That's where my mother found me, and my little adventure was over. I was about three when this adventure took place. Yet I can clearly remember the thought process that went with my rope escape and the feeling I had when I solved the problem. If only all life's problems could be that easy.

I lived on Nonantum Street in Newton, a western suburb of Boston. If we had lived in the house next door, we would have been in Boston. It was during the Great Depression although I didn't know what it meant at that time. My father had lost his home-building business, and that made us very poor, but, of course, I had no idea what rich or poor meant. Most of my early years were spent on our front porch playing vegetable man. A truck would come by selling vegetables. He would get them out

13

of his truck, weigh them on a spring scale, and put them in bags. My vegetables were weeds and I had a bag but, alas, no scale. I never did get a spring scale until I was in my seventies. Oh well, better late than never.

I had a friend next door named Tommy, who died of leukemia before he ever got to school, and a friend up the street called Leonard, who had a ground hut and a tree house. I felt he was the luckiest kid in the world; we didn't even have a tree for a tree house. Life seemed fine until one day, my parents did something for which I have never forgiven them. They took me down to the children's library and had me tested to see if I could start kindergarten at four! The test lady sat me in her lap, accidentally struck me with her hatpin, and unfortunately, I passed!

You may be thinking, "So what? Isn't that good?" I didn't know what school was, and I was told that it was good that I was smart enough to start early. Wrong! Wrong! As I grew up, it became a major problem. I was, on average, more than a year and a half younger than my classmates. They would be joining scouts while I had to wait a year. They would make fun of me being little and not physically able to do what they did. I was always running to catch up but never did. We had a sex lecture at church and I had no idea what sex was and, hence, no idea what the man was talking about. I grew up thinking there was something wrong with me because I couldn't keep up. That plus being the poorest family in the neighborhood and being told I couldn't do things caused me to develop an inferiority complex.

I remember crying my first day of kindergarten and at Christmas, getting silver paint in my eye trying to paint pinecone tree decorations. In first grade, I ran home from school every day because a boy said he was going to beat me up. One day, I accidentally met him and he was very nice so I guess my fear was for nothing. My sister and I used to stop at an older girl's house every week to hear the latest chapter in the mystery she was writing. I remember looking forward to finding out what happens next. One night, the house directly behind us burned up. Watching the fire and seeing the damage from the fire was one of the scariest things that happened to me.

My father was selling pots and pans and fire alarms and shoveling snow to keep us going, but it wasn't enough. One day, a man came to auction off our house; somehow my mother talked him into delaying it. Before the Depression, my father had built a lot of English Tudor-style houses in Newton Highlands, one of the richer parts of Newton. The buyer of one of his houses couldn't pay his bills, and my father ended up with the house and everything in it. So we lost the little cheap house in one of the poor sections of Newton and moved to a rich section. What a change! A new school, new friends, and a new house.

Sagamore Road

The memory of walking into the new house was like walking into paradise. Our old house could have fit in the living room of this one. It was completely furnished with great stuff. There was a cast iron statue of a fisherman that stood by the biggest fireplace I had ever seen. There was a den with a yellow leather wastebasket with a painting of some dogs on it next to the desk and what seemed like the largest dining room and table in the world. For the first time, I had my own bedroom with a maple desk filled with all sorts of treasures of the son of the previous owner. The house had a maid's room and bath, a cedar closet, a back staircase, a two-car garage, and a big playroom in the cellar.

As amazing as the inside of the house was, the outside to me was even better. There was a wooded hill across the back of the backyard. To this day, I remember the feeling of excitement I had climbing up that hill and wondering what I would find at the other side. I found a huge sandpit that went almost as far as the eye can see. I didn't go any further at that time because I was afraid, and I had been told only to go to the top of the hill. I was riding a streetcar through Newton Highlands a few months ago, and as I looked at the woods going by, I had that same feeling of excitement as all those years ago.

We had moved at the end of the summer, and my sister and I soon started school. I was treated like royalty. Everyone was nice to me, and I was picked first for whatever was going on (I had never been picked first before). The school was next to a junior high school, and I often heard students talking about how hard algebra was. After that, I dreaded the thought that I would someday have to take algebra and wondered what it was. When I took algebra, it turned out to be the easiest and most fun of any class I would ever have. I guess I always worried about things I knew nothing about.

Wilton

We quickly made friends with kids in our neighborhood, and the sandpit became our playground. We ventured across the sandpit and came to a defunct tar pit. The older kids would crawl through pipes but I was chicken. Right near the tar pits was the city water tower. We all tried climbing up its ladder but I didn't get far. Best of all, right near the tower was the city hall. We ran around the halls, checked out the city museum, and usually ended up getting kicked out. We hadn't lived there very long before they started building two houses on the edge of the sandpits right behind our house. My mother said to stay away from the construction, but, of course, I didn't. It wasn't long before I came home crying with a board nailed to my foot. I stepped on a board with a nail sticking up, and it went right through my sneaker and foot. It hurt a lot and you would have thought I learned my lesson. Not quite! A few weeks later, I came home with another board nailed to my foot. Fortunately, that was the last one. I guess I learned the hard way.

We only lived at Sagamore Road for a year. My father had rented it out, and we moved back to the school district where I had spent kindergarten and first grade but into a very rich neighborhood! I know you are thinking how in the world we could afford a rich neighborhood. We had the only two-family house in the neighborhood. My father had got it for back taxes, and the rent from downstairs paid the carrying costs.

Sargent Street

To give you an idea of how rich some of the neighbors were, let me tell you about the house four houses down from ours. Its front yard was almost as big as a football field, and it had three to four times as much land behind it. The house was a large brick mansion of three stories. The downstairs of the house was all paneled in some kind of neat-looking wood. It had a secret room you could get to by pressing one of the flowers in the design around the fireplace. It had a secret panel over the couch that held the controls to the fountains outside, and it had a button on the floor that opened a panel to a small space which held a statue of a Hindu boy holding cigarettes and a lighter. The den was filled with secret panels around the windows and the shelves. I am sure there were more we never found.

What amazed me even more was that the garage was bigger than the house! The garage had a cellar and two floors. The first floor had a tiled area with places to work on six to eight cars. It had a rope-operated elevator that was big enough to take cars upstairs; it also had twenty-six brass-decorated horse stalls. The second floor was the chauffeur's apartment, grain bins for feeding the horses, and a room large enough to store at least ten cars. The cellar had a driveway down to it and could easily hold twenty to thirty cars. I remember there was a 1923 fire engine, a 1930 Ford convertible touring car, some trucks, and other old cars in it.

The first day at Sargent Street, I met two boys my age—Peter Reiman and Teddy Barker. They both lived in large houses and had live-in maids and landscapers. Teddy also had a chauffeur. We became good friends over the summer, but when school started, I was in the third grade and they were in the second. In spite of the grade difference, we remained good friends until I went on to junior high.

From that point on, our friendship kind of disappeared. My age difference didn't affect Cub Scouts. My friends and I were in the same den and became Webelos together. The thing I liked the most about Cub Scouts was making Indian war bonnets. That's why a Cherokee fire bonnet was the first thing I bought for my house when I moved to Florida.

The neighborhood had some unusual features. There was an area called "the Dell" where a drainage stream from the streets and land higher than where we were ran through. The stream ran in empty land and woods between two rows of houses. We played there a lot—things like kickball, Hide-and-Go-Seek, and trying to dam the stream. Some kids had large yards we used for football and baseball games, and there were even a couple empty houses with barns to explore or hide in. The best was going up to see Frank Day and getting to explore their garage, play Capture the Flag, shoot bow and arrows, and ride their pedal-powered merry-go-round. There was a small pond nearby, where we could skate in the winter, and a place called Cabot Woods, which had a bigger pond and lots of woods.

YMCA

My first contact with the Y was in the summer after third grade. My mother enrolled me in a special swimming instruction program. She told me that no one wore swimming suits at the Y. I didn't like that, but I didn't have a choice; I went. I was real scared when I walked from the locker room to the showers naked. Once I got into the pool area, I was relieved when I saw we all looked the same except one older boy. I thought there was something wrong with his genitals.

The next fall, I was enrolled in the Indian guide program for fourth graders at the Y. On Saturday mornings, about forty boys one year older than me, plus me, would go to gym classes then swimming and then go upstairs to the auditorium for the Indian part of the program. They divided us into eight tribes, each of which had a high school boy as a leader. Then each tribe chose a chief. I was chosen as chief! I couldn't figure it out. I was never chosen; why me? Then the Sachem was chosen from the eight chiefs. Oh my god, they chose me! The Sachem had to get up in front of all the tribes and start the meeting by putting out his arm and saying "how!" I was scared to death to get up, but I did it. I guess you could say that was my first class in public speaking. There were many things like being picked that should have improved my self-esteem and help me get over my inferiority complex. They didn't. I stayed in the Saturday morning program for three years (through the sixth grade). I next joined the Y again when I was in high school, and the Y became my life!

Polio

The summer after my fourth grade was a bad polio year. I was staying at my cousins' house with my mother and sister while my aunt and uncle were away when we heard that a friend of my cousins was severely paralyzed due to polio. We had planned to go to Crescent Park, a nearby amusement park, the next day. My mother wondered if we should go because it would be a good place to catch polio. I wanted to stay home, but my two cousins and my sister wanted to go, so we went. I kept saying I will catch polio and they said I was crazy. The next day, I woke up sick with a bad stiff neck. When we got home, I was still sick and guess what! I had polio! I was immediately put in Massachusetts General Hospital. I was in a single room (quarantined, but I didn't know it). What I also didn't know was that the kind of polio I had affected your lungs and speech, not your arms and legs, and if serious, it would kill me. All the time I was in the hospital, an iron lung was sitting outside my door. I sure am glad I didn't know. I couldn't figure out why no one understood me; I didn't realize how weird my voice had become. Also, my legs had become so weak I couldn't stand holding on to the sides of my crib. That scared me. I thought I was getting paralyzed.

They kept bringing me spinach and I hated it and wouldn't eat it. Then they said, "No spinach, no dessert." The next time I had spinach, I ate everything else on my tray, scooped the spinach in my hand, and hid it under the sheet. They came to check if I had eaten it and then gave me dessert. When I finished the desert, I put the spinach in the dessert dish. It didn't work; I had to eat it!

One day, a doctor asked me if I wanted something to read. I told him I didn't like to read. Next thing I knew, he showed up with a book (The Hardy Boys' *Mystery of Cabin Island*) and read me a few chapters and said he would come back tomorrow to read some more. By the time he got back, I had finished the book. From then on, I read a lot, including all the Hardy Boys books I could find. It's amazing how what seems like an insignificant thing can have such an impact on your life. A half-hour effort by someone whose name I don't even know got me reading and, by doing that, put so much joy into my life. I still tell students that can't read well to try the Hardy Boys mysteries. As I think back, I realize how often someone has done something for me that turned out to be a major plus in my life, and they don't even realize it.

Thank God I got better and never even saw the iron lung. When I got home, I quickly got my strength back and could walk again. However, my speech took a longer time to come back. I was told I could go out and play, but I couldn't go up or down the stairs. A few times, my friends carried me up and down, and then I started doing it on my own. Before I knew it, I was a normal nine-year-old boy running, climbing, and reading.

Dancing Class

Dancing class—ugh! Who ever came up with that idea? Mr. Champaign's ballroom dancing lessons were going to be held in the ballroom of the Huneywell Club that was a few blocks from my school. You had to dress in a suit and tie and black leather shoes and, worst of all, white gloves! Not me! No one could get me there. My parents had other ideas. Everyone important goes, it will make you more popular if you can dance, you won't get invited to parties if you can't dance, etc. It was a losing fight; I was going to dancing school.

I remember sitting in chairs that were placed around the ballroom. Mr. Champaign and his wife would demonstrate steps, and then they would dance with a few other kids, and then we would all dance. Most of it were steps like foxtrot and waltz. We had white gloves so we wouldn't get the girls dresses dirty. It was very boring at times, but all in all, it was a good thing for us to do. One very funny occurrence happened in one class. We were all sitting in a circle around the ballroom, listening to directions of how to ask a girl to dance. A friend of mine, David Eusden, had his eye on a girl across the hall. On the word "go" he jumped up, ran on the waxed floor, slipped on the wax, and slid on his butt to the girl's feet. Wow! What a first impression! It's always good to have a little humor. However, David didn't find it funny.

Monopoly

One day, I was at Peter Rieman's house, and he suggested we play Monopoly. I had no idea what it was, so he taught me the game. I fell in love with Monopoly. I wanted to play all the time but there was a slight problem. I didn't have a Monopoly set. In fact, all my friends who wanted to play didn't have a set either. On the other hand, those who had sets were sick of playing it and, hence, didn't want to play. In those days, Monopoly sets cost $1.79. That was a lot of money if you were poor, so the poor kids didn't have sets. Alas, I never got to play much Monopoly when I was young, but I made up for it when I was in high school. I finally got a set of my own. To my surprise, when we lived on Nonantum Street, my parents used to play a game with a rolled up paper board and lots of small pieces of paper. It was a Monopoly set made by my father; he also couldn't afford to buy a set.

Huts

My friend Leonard Allen had two huts—one on the ground and one in a tree. I got to play in them until we moved to Newton Highlands. When we moved back, I was looking forward to playing with Leonard again, but it wasn't in the cards. Leonard moved away right after we moved back. When he left, he gave me his ground hut that was to me the greatest present ever. Soon after we moved back, we went on a short vacation to the Cape (Cape Cod). When we got back, I found my hut was now a pile of kindling wood. The tenant downstairs, Sgt. McCullough, had chopped it up because he didn't like the looks of it. I never forgave my father for not making him get me wood so I could make a new one. In fact, the sergeant never even apologized.

During the summer after fifth grade, Teddy, Peter, and a few other friends decided to build a hut in Teddy's yard right over the underground hut we had built a couple years before. The underground wasn't a subway; it was a hole lined with rugs with a roof built over it and a trapdoor entrance. The underground became the cellar. The first part we built was about ten feet by six feet. It had a bed that folded up against the wall. The window had screens and plywood shutters. The walls were even wallpapered and the floor was linoleum. The only thing I didn't like was the roof. It was made of strips of thin wood and then covered with tar paper. The trouble was you couldn't climb onto it. (At that time, I climbed on anything I could.)

Next, we decided to add a kitchen. It was about six by six feet and had a glass window, a table, chairs, and an oil heater. The trapdoor to the cellar was in front of the exit door and the door to the kitchen. We had an old "For Sale" sign under the linoleum. I got the idea of removing the sign, and then if someone came in, they would fall into the cellar. After I fell in twice, I decided it wasn't such a good idea. Finally, Teddy talked his parents into getting us some wire that we strung from his house to the hut. Wow, we had lights. We played a lot in it that summer, and then it just sat there. A few years later, I went into the hut and fell through the rotten floor into the cellar. Oh well! The most fun was making it.

Junior High

Bigelow Junior High was just around the corner from my grade school, yet it was a whole different world. The students from four elementary schools came to Bigelow. I felt very uneasy in classes with all these new kids plus kind of sad that most of my friends were still back in grade school. For the first time, we had homework and report cards, and for the first time, we changed classes. There was a gym, a big park, and a gym teacher. We had gym classes and had to dress in gym clothes and take showers. The biggest difference of all was we started having boy-and-girl parties.

I was eleven a few weeks before sixth grade ended, and hallelujah, now I could join Boy Scouts. The first thing I did was to go on a weeklong camping trip to Nobscot, a scout camping area. Each troop in the council had a cabin in Nobscot. The trip consisted of the senior patrol leader, three older scouts, and two other neophytes like me. The assistant troop leader and the father of one of the scouts were the leaders.

Nobscot was about a half-hour drive from Newton. There was a mountain (albeit a small one) with a fire tower on top and lots of woods and trails. About one hundred yards from our cabin was a swimming hole that we made good use of. Our troop's cabin was really neat. Right in the middle of it was a huge stone fireplace. In the front area of the cabin were bunks and, in the back, a kitchen which consisted of a wood stove, a dry sink, a table, benches, and a cupboard. There was no water in the cabin; we had to walk about a half mile to get it. The bathroom was an outhouse. I was a little nervous being with people I didn't know very well in a strange place, but it sure looked like we were going to have fun.

The first day, we started building a picnic table and a flagpole. The father that was with us was a great woodsman and led the effort. We started by cutting down some trees. All day long, the older scouts keep pointing to birds in the air and saying, "There go some snipe!" Then they announced that we would go on a snipe hunt that night, and I was going to hold the bag! The way snipe are caught is one person is in the middle of a clearing in the woods holding a burlap bag, and everyone else makes a big circle around him and hits two sticks together. The noise is supposed to cause the snipe to run into the bag. Boy, was I scared. I kept asking, "Why me!" and they kept saying because the newest person always gets to hold the bag. The other kids spent a lot of time that day getting the right sticks to scare snipe; I spent a lot of time scared to death.

When it got dark, the senior patrol leader, Fred Allen, led us through the woods. I thought we would go on one of the trails, but no, we went right through heavy woods. Finally, we came to a trail, which led to a small cemetery. It was called the smallpox cemetery because the family buried there all died of small pox years ago. There was a small, treeless spot next to the cemetery that I was told to stay in with the bag and try to catch a snipe when I heard one running toward me.

Then everyone else disappeared. I could hear them talking as they moved away, and then they all started hitting their sticks together. Every noise I heard I thought was a snipe, but thank God, none came. All of a sudden, everything went silent—no sticks hitting each other, no voices, no animal, noises, nothing! What should I do? I didn't know the way back. They had made sure of that. Should I stay put? Should I go out to the trail? What? I took the only reasonable action; I started crying and yelling for Fred. After a while, Fred showed up, and slowly, the others followed. One of the older scouts pretended he had broken his leg to scare me, but only the assistant troop leader believed it and he got real scared.

The rest of the week, we finished the flagpole and the table and had some mock wars with a troop from Newton that had a cabin near us. There were a lot of pranks played on us new kids. One kid had all his clothes hoisted up the flagpole, a couple of us got wet playing Penny in the Funnel and became black bybeing hypnotized.

Penny in the Funnel Trick

Penny in the Funnel is a game where you get the pigeon to put a funnel in his belt and try to tip a coin balanced on his forehead into the funnel while blindfolded. As he tries, a glass of water is poured down the funnel!

Hypnotize Trick

The pigeon is hypnotized in a candlelit room while sitting at a table that holds a pan of water. The pigeon repeats what the swami sitting across from him is doing. That is to run his finger around the pan of water and then around his face. The inside of the pan is coated with the black from a candle. The swami knows not to touch the bottom; the pigeon does not. When the lights go back on, the pigeon's face and hands are black.

One of my best memories was lying in my bunk late at night watching a red aircraft light on one of the hills going round and round and round. My worst memory was when I got home, I found out the son of some friends of our family was killed while training for the air force. That was the first impact I felt of World War II.

World War II

The attack on Pearl Harbor on December 7 of my seventh grade changed a lot of things. A lot of things we used to get, like cars, were not made because the factories were making weapons like planes, ships, and tanks. A lot or products, we imported from the Caribbean and South America like sugar and bananas, which were almost impossible to get because U-boats were patrolling the sea-lanes from the south to the U.S. We used banana powder to make banana bread and milkshakes. Meat products were very scarce; I remember my mother would rush down to the store when she heard that meat was in to stand in line. Sometimes, she didn't get any. Gas was rationed, and tires were not available so not much driving was possible. We had blackout curtains on all our windows and a lot of canned goods stored under the eaves in the attic in case food stores were closed. My mother and father and the couple that lived on our first floor became air-raid wardens. They had gas masks, wooden noisemakers, white helmets, and armbands. We kids couldn't imagine our parents doing anything useful if there was an air raid, so we made a big joke of it. We never had an air raid, so their skills were never tested.

One day after school, I had gone to a movie with some friends. In those days, there were always two movies. The day we went, the first movie was *The Smiling Ghost* and the second was *The Maltese Falcon*. Partway through the second movie, my mother came down the aisle with an usher looking for me. She had heard there was an air raid warning and made me come home. There was no air raid, and I got kidded a lot about my overprotective mother. It was many years after before I got to see the rest of *The Maltese Falcon*.

We would get a chance every week at school to buy war savings stamps and, if we had enough money, war bonds. We started collecting newspapers and scrap iron. We had a paper and scrap drive so big we had a day off from school. VE Day came in the spring of my ninth grade. Some friends and I skipped class when it was announced; of course, we got caught. (That was the only time in all my school life that I skipped a class.) VJ Day was announced early on a summer evening in August. I was fishing out in the middle of Lake Wentworth in New Hampshire. All of a sudden, we heard bells and sirens and yelling. We got to shore as quickly as we could and went to Wolfboro, the nearest town. The streets were full of people marching, yelling, and crying for joy. The main thought I had was I would not have to go to war and not have to kill or be killed. I didn't know it then, but I was a pacifist and could never kill.

Dr. Carl Heath Koph

My parents had met at the Mount Vernon in Boston. I was baptized by Carl Heath Koph and attended Sunday school at Mount Vernon until I moved to Sargent Street. I clearly remember his wonderful voice and how he came sweeping into church. In later years, Bishop Fulton Shields started his TV program the same way. I even remember parts of his sermons. Dr. Koph had a radio program, *From My Window on Beacon Street*, which I used to listen to although I didn't understand much of what he was saying. I liked the sound of his voice. Carl Koph was called to the First Congregational Church in Washington DC. I remember my parents talking about it. They hated to see him leave. Many years later, the news came that Carl Koph had hung himself in the belfry of his church. As shocked as I was at the news, I still feel he was important while I was growing up. The minister that had replaced Koph declared he was a conscientious objector (CO). I didn't know what a CO was. However, the way my parents got upset about it and how they explained it to me sounded real bad. I never told anyone, but a CO seemed to be just the way I felt about war. That's why I was so glad the war was over; I wouldn't have to face the ridicule of being a CO. Little did I know something else would keep me out of future wars.

Chatham

My family usually went to Cape Cod or New Hampshire for two weeks in the summer. The summer after my eighth grade was very special. Some friends of my parents let us use their house in Chatham for the whole summer because they were travelling in Europe that summer. Chatham is at the bend in the Cape. North of the bend, the water is kind of cold, but south of the bend where we would be, the water is warm. The house was in an area called Stage Harbor. From what I had seen of the Cape, I expected a white cottage with a picket fence, flowers, and green grass with water behind it. What we pulled up to was about an acre of eel grass with a sand driveway down to a low, shabby-looking house on the water. Wow, was I wrong! This house turned out to be better than any little, white house with flowers. It was so close to the water the water came under the house at flood tides. It was wood paneled; it had three bedrooms, two of which had bunk beds, a large living/dining room with a big picture window looking over Stage Harbor, a small kitchen, and two baths. My bedroom had tile flooring with a big compass design made out of tiles. What was coming was the best summer I ever had! Swimming all the time, rowing a skiff, sailing, exploring Chatham, and reading. There was a small library in Chatham and I really enjoyed reading. The best one I read was *Blueberry Hill*. When it came time to go home, I wanted to stay, but as you might expect, I didn't get my way. It turned out to be a good thing; a hurricane hit that area a week after we left and took the whole house out to sea.

Sports

I was kind of average in sports if I was in my age group, but I wasn't. I was used to playing baseball, football, a little ice hockey in the parks, and the backyard games we played whenever we got a chance. I didn't even know what basketball was until they started teaching it in junior high school.

In the spring of my ninth grade year, all of my friends decided to go out for baseball. They talked me into coming to practice.

Things seem to go pretty well my first day; I even got a hit the one chance I got. At the end of the second day, the coach was going through his list and crossing out kids he was cutting. My name wasn't on the list because I had not come the first day, so he wrote my name down and immediately crossed it out. The kids that saw him do that laughed; I didn't and I never went out for sports again until I got to college. As I got older, I spent all my free time playing basketball at the Y.

Printing

Peter Reiman, one of the friends I first met when we moved to Sargent Street, had a small printing press. It was only big enough to print a ticket or a business card. I thought it was the greatest thing in the world, but, of course, I didn't have one. We kept trying to start a printing business with it but it never happened. When I started junior high, we had fine arts, which consisted of three things: woodworking, printing, and metal working. Woodworking was a new world to me, as the only tools in our house were a screwdriver, a rusty saw, a monkey wrench, and a paintbrush. We got to use planes, chisels, drills, and saws. If we did well, as I did, we got to use power tools like lathes in our eight-grade year. The end post of my sister's bed had been broken for a long time. It was broken because we were always sitting on it. I decided it would be a great project to do at school. I would get to use the lathe. It took more than half the year but it came out great. It had all the designs of the original one. The day I brought it home from school, I got in a fight with David Eusden and ended up hitting him over the head with it, and, of course, it broke in two. So much for woodworking. When it came to printing, I knew all about setting type and printing. However, the school had a press that was way bigger than the toy Peter had. A short time after that, a friend of mine, Ted Leonard, moved to a big house near us, and his parents (they were much richer than mine) bought him a foot-operated press that could print an eight-by-ten-inch page. They also got him lots of fonts of type, typesetting sticks, and all the other stuff needed to use the press. I finally had my wish; Ted and I started a real printing business. We got a lot of orders for tickets and business cards and even small flyers. We became well-known at Barker Press in Newton Corner; they were our source to buy stock and to get information about printing. About twenty-five years later, I made sure the youth drop in the program I was involved in had a printing press. I had never forgotten the fun Ted and I had.

Algebra

I wanted to take algebra. In spite of the things I had heard about it in the second grade, I was looking forward to taking it. Disaster! My math teacher told my parents I wasn't very good at math and should take business math instead. My parents expected me to be good in math because my father was, and math was the one thing they kept telling me I could do. Somehow, after a long conference with the teacher, Mr. Ring, I was allowed to take it. Boy, did he regret that decision.

Algebra turned out to be the easiest and most interesting course I have ever taken. I got A's on all my tests and homework and still had time to talk too much in class. Mr. Ring put me at a special desk in front of the class, but I went right on talking. I think one of the hardest things Mr. Ring had to do was give me an A. I often wonder what he would think if he found out I got two degrees in math from Massachusetts Institute of Technology.

Smoking

"I think you're crazy" was my response when I told my sister I didn't want to start smoking. She kept pressuring me by saying, "When you get to high school you won't be popular unless you smoke." Leon Avackhian was the only kid in my ninth grade class that smoked. The rest of the class kept saying he would have a heart attack, and I believed them. My sister kept after me, and I started smoking just a few cigarettes a month. Then it was a few a week and then a few a day; I was hooked! As I look back,

I don't think smoking did anything for my social life that was kind of meager anyway. I smoked a few a day to a pack a day, and I kept trying to quit without success. It was really tough. I quit about twelve years later after smoking only three cigarettes a day for about five years. It was one of the hardest and one of the best things I have ever done for myself. It was coffee break at work, and I had just bought a new pack of cigarettes. I opened the pack, took one out, put the pack in my desk, and, out of blue, threw away the cigarette in my hand and quit. A year later, that pack hadn't been touched and was also tossed out; I had finally done it!

Newton High School

Newton High School was composed of three three-story buildings. There were tunnels between the basements of the buildings, so it was possible to change class in bad weather without getting wet or cold. Four junior high schools fed into Newton High. Bigelow, the one I came from, was the smallest; it had about 350 students. Newton High had almost three thousand students. I have to admit that I was scared silly on my first day of high school, but somehow, I got through it. One thing scared me more than going to high school that turned out to be ridiculous. All through grade school and junior high, I had always walked north, and except for a few kids in my neighborhood, no one had seen my house. I was embarrassed to have anyone see the crummy house I lived in. Now we walked south so most of the kids would be walking by my house on the way to school; how embarrassing! In later years, I found out that most of them lived in worse houses than mine. It was a good example of creating nonproblems; I was good at that. It made me wonder a little bit more about my inferiority complex, but I had a long way to go before I would lose it.

Although I had all A's and B's in junior high school, I was having problems with English. It turned out my English teacher in Bigelow gave me good grades because she liked me, not because I earned them. I got away with a lot of things in her class because she thought I could do nothing wrong. As a result, in my sophomore year, I got a D in English and in Spanish. I couldn't understand the need for foreign languages when everyone in my world spoke English (I lived to regret not knowing more Spanish), and I couldn't understand why we needed more English when everybody already spoke it very well. The things I hated about English were the teacher seemed to me to read more things in a book than the author ever intended, and whatever we did there wasn't just one correct answer like in math. Also, math was so consistent and logical while English was so inconsistent and confusing.

Having two D's meant that I had to stay in a sophomore homeroom during my junior year but could conditionally take Spanish II and English III. If after the second marking period I was passing these courses, I would get credit for last year's D's. I ended up passing Spanish but still failing English. That meant I was put back into an English II class. Somehow, I passed English II the second time and ended up back in the same homeroom I had started in as a sophomore for my senior year. However, I would be taking English III again. This meant I would not take English IV and still be able to graduate with my class because my PE credits for three years were equal to one major class credit.

All during high school, I went from school to the YMCA and usually did not get home until about six thirty. I would play basketball if the gym was available (no classes going on), go swimming if the gym wasn't available and the pool was, or hang out in the weight-lifting or wrestling room if the pool was busy. I also played a lot of ping-pong. I had a job working at the locker room desk from five to six while the man running it went to supper. It was mainly selling towels and soap to men and boys going into the showers and, once in a while, gym equipment. I made $2.40 per week and that easily covered all my expenses. I also worked at both the youth and the men's departments' desks in the evenings. Another thing that kept me busy was running a Gray-Y Club[1],

---

[1.]   A club for fifth and sixth grade boys

for kids that were always hanging around the Y and getting into trouble. Last but not least, I ran the craft shop a few times a week.

On Saturdays, I was a counselor of the Indian Guide and Gray-Y programs the same ones I had gone to when I was in grade school. In the summer, I worked in one of the Y's day camps. I felt really rich then, for I was making $25.00 per week. The best summers of my life were working at the camp.

Camp Chickami

Camp Chickami was the best job ever and was a major influence on the rest of my life. I made $25 a week and I never felt richer. I ran the crafts program, organized Capture the Flag games, told stories, put on magic shows, made up treasure hunts, and taught swimming. In later years, I was in charge of the waterfront. For the first time, I felt I was not inferior! The campers would always crowd around me and ask me to tell them a story; it felt really great to have someone looking up to me and wanting to hear from me. I made up a treasure hunt every summer. The campers were divided into teams, and each team had to follow a series of clues. The team that got back first won the prize.

Here is an example of a clue:

> Like all the rest you won't get this,
> At first to you it will seem no assist,
> Stop and think and don't give in.
> To take some time is not a sin.
>
> First don't read this the English way,
> Instead do this without delay,
> Read this instead the Chinese way,
> Erase from your mind about going across,
> Place there instead without getting cross,
> Living in China the Pacific across,
> And so take some time to think it out,
> Careful now and don't you pout
> Enjoy the puzzle and don't let it out.

Can you tell where the next clue is?

Those were the greatest summers of my life and led me to want to go into social work instead of becoming an engineer like my father. This desire changed my life and had consequences I could have never imagined and that would have major effects on my life. The people I worked with at camp and at the Y became lifelong friends. I still am in touch with those that are still alive.

Eliot Congregational Church

The two boys I first met when we moved to Sargent Street, Peter and Teddy, introduced me to Eliot Church. I started going to

Sunday school at Eliot when I was in the third grade, and I joined when I was in junior high school and am still a member. My third-grade teacher was Isabel Conway. When we sang hymns in Sunday school, I was amazed at her voice; I had never heard anyone sing so well and so loud. Isabel always told things the way they were. She would not hesitate to speak her mind. She liked dramatics and was leader of the Eliot Art Skills Club. When the youth wanted to put on a play or something, we had to go through Isabel. In spite of giving each other a hard time, we always had a great time. The last time I saw Isabel was on a trip north. (I had moved to Florida by that time.) I took her to breakfast the last day I was there; it was the day before she was going to have a major operation. She gave me some keepsakes she had of the old Eliot (before it burned down) and a copy of the story of her life. She never really recovered from the operation and died a short while later. I will always miss her.

When I went to high school, I continued to go to Sunday school at Eliot Church, and as I got older, I was an usher in church. The church had a very tall bell tower with a clock. At that time, the sexton had gotten too old to climb the tower, so a few of us got the job to wind the bells and chimes. I also was active in the church's youth group program. Church introduced me to mission work and how great it felt to help someone else. When I was in junior high, we invited some children from an orphanage in Charlestown (a very poor section of Boston) to a Christmas party every year. Two of us would be paired with each child from Charlestown. We played games, sang carols, showed a movie, had a visit from Santa, and lots to eat. Then we would pack up a box of food for each child to take home. To me, that was the best part of Christmas. I realized much later the reason I liked the afternoon with the Charlestown Orphanage—I was giving, not getting.

There was a church basketball league, and playing in the league turned me into an avid fan of basketball. It also, in the future, became the key that saved my life. I liked all sorts of dancing including square dancing and folk dancing, and shy as I was and as nonmusical as I was, I liked taking part in musical shows that we did almost every year. The first time I went away from home alone was to a youth conference put on by a group of congregational churches. I always ended up in the drama groups at the conferences. It turned out to be a lot of fun and very important to my growing up. I always seemed to end up on stage trying to act. Later in this book, you will hear a lot more about Eliot Church.

Moving On

As my high school graduation came closer, so did the Korean War. With graduation came two choices—go to war or go to college. It was no choice for me. I was so afraid of going to war that my choice had to be college. During high school, I never took SAT exams. I was forced by my parents to take a navy ROTC exam that would pay for my college in return for two years in the navy after I graduated. I passed the exam but not high enough to get the scholarship. Deep down, I was glad, but I never told anyone. My father had gone to RPI (Rensselaer Polytechnic Institute), and it was always planned I would go there too. One of my father's classmates was registrar when I was applying. He struck a deal with my father that I had to take English IV and retake chemistry because I only got a C in it before, and I would be accepted. That decision gave me one the easiest and most fun years of my schooling. I got enrolled in Berkeley Preparatory School in Kenmore Square (Boston).

My weekday schedule was great. I would take a bus to Newton Corner (About five minutes) and then take the streetcar to Kenmore Square in Boston (About thirty minutes). I would usually sleep on the way to school. I had two forty-minute classes. I would do my homework on the streetcar on the way back to Newton Corner and spend the rest of the day at the Y. I also studied accounting at Newton High one night a week. I found Berkeley Prep really easy; I was getting A's with very little work. About a month after I started, they made all students take an IQ test. A few days later, the results were posted for all to see. Posting IQs was a surprise to me! Then I found out why it was so easy; my IQ was 130—the highest in the school. This really surprised me because I always considered myself as average, not the lower end of genius. Needless to say, I sailed through school that year, was waterfront director at the Y camp that summer, and was then off to RPI.

College

I was not looking forward to going to college, particularly RPI. I wanted to go to Springfield College, the YMCA college. I had picked management as my major because I thought that might be less technical than the other majors. It wasn't a good choice, but at least for the first time, I would be in a class of kids my age. My parents drove me to RPI, which was in Troy, New York.

We left the day before I had to be there and stayed overnight in western Massachusetts. The dorms for freshmen were ten-room Quonset huts with common facilities for each pair of huts. Most of my clothes had been sent in a big steamer trunk that had been sitting in my house as long as I could remember. An old Underwood typewriter, a desk lamp, radio, bedding, and some clothes came with us. When we got to the dorm, which would end up holding seventeen students that year, just four were there. Once I got my things in, my parents left, and there I was on my own. What a strange feeling! The five of us walked down to Troy for dinner and had a good time getting to know each other. We got along just fine. The next day, we all went off to Lake George to a freshman camp. At the camp, we were split up and didn't get to see much of each other until we got back. Once we got back, most of the rest of the guys that were in our dorm were there. Only two were not, one of which was my roommate. We went through the pulling of pranks on each other, and then things settled down. However, my roommate thought I had put his muddy boots in his bed and never quite forgave me. That was kind of sad because I had not done it.

The rules of being in class were very strict. There were only three reasons you could miss a class: you were in jail, in the hospital, or there was a death or marriage in your family. I had a chemistry lecture every week with Professor Fagenbaum, the scariest person on campus. His lectures were held in a building far away from where most of the classes were held. It was on the third floor. The only door was in the center of the front wall of the lecture hall. The seats were very much like a movie theater but not as comfortable. When his class was about to start, he would close the door and pull down the shade on the door's window. If the shade was down, you could not come in. You were never late to his class. I never was. Classes started as early as eight and were even held on Saturday mornings. I had an accounting class at eight o'clock in which I had to work real hard to stay awake. I fell asleep one morning as the professor was going over yesterday's test. He saw me sleeping, so he called on me. When a student next to me woke me up, he asked me what I got on the test. I told him 100 percent. He said, "Go back to sleep."

I felt that now that my parents were paying for college, I would work harder than I had in high school. I was in for a big surprise. A lot of the kids in my dorm were members of the National Honor

Society. I always felt National Honor students were way smarter than I was, and I found I was way ahead of all of them. (Now my inferiority complex was really losing ground.) I even started doing better in English. I ended up with mostly A's!

Snap, Crackle, and Pop

One of the guys in my dorm had a friend who was a Kellogg's cereals salesman that often dropped by our dorm. He had a car so he became our wheels. RPI was in New York State, where the drinking age was eighteen. This meant that along with college came alcohol. There was a bar in Troy named Gainors that was a hangout for RPI students. It was a strange experience to be able to walk into a bar and order a beer. I didn't do it too often because I didn't have much money. Though I guess I got used to it because the next summer, I walked into a pizza shop with a friend and ordered a beer and a pizza. Then I realized I was in Massachusetts, not New York. I ate that pizza and beer very fast and got out without getting caught. We were able to get to nearby girl colleges via our "Snap, Crackle, and Pop" friend. That provided most of our amusement during a lot of our freshmen year. When we went into bars, I would order rye and ginger because it was the only drink I knew other than beer. I grew to dislike them very fast.

In spite of the good times, there were times when I would start thinking about home and the Y. I would look up at the stars and think they're seeing the same stars back in Newton, but it seems so far away. One of the things RPI students were encouraged to do was to volunteer in some the youth programs in Troy. I checked it out and started teaching crafts in a YMCA. It was like being home for a while.

The Grease Rush

The Grease Rush was one of two freshmen-versus-upper-classmen contest held each year. The rush was held in a field at the top of the hill that the freshmen dorms were on. The contest consisted of a six-foot cane that started with three freshmen and three upper classmen laying on the ground and holding onto it. All of the other participants were standing around as close to the cane as they could get. When the whistle blew, every one tried to get a hand on the cane before it blew again (about five minutes later). There was only one catch; each participant wore nothing but a coat of grease! My roommate and I were the only ones from our dorm that took part.

We cheated in that we wore jock straps but so did about three quarters of the freshmen. It was kind of weird walking up the street dressed like that. There was a hill along the side of the field that made kind of a natural amphitheater, which was full of spectators of both sexes. When we got there, we had to take a handful of grease and rub it all over ourselves. When the whistle blew, I dove for the cane and got a hold of it. After a few minutes, I had to breathe and tried to fight my way out, which was impossible. When the whistle blew, the grand marshal (student-body leader)

started counting hands on the cane. Somehow it came out that the upper classmen won although there were at least ten freshmen to every upper classman. That's the way it always is. The grand marshal must count so the upper classmen win, and then the freshmen jump on him, rip his clothes off, and cover him with grease. We spent several hours in the shower getting the grease off, and I had greasy hair for a couple of weeks.

When my father went to RPI, there were several other rushes that were either stopped because someone got killed or watered down because someone got hurt. The Grease Rush and the Flag Rush were the only two left. I had seen many pictures of the Flag Rush when my father was there and had looked forward to it. However, it was so watered down it was a waste of time. However, the beanies were still in play. Every freshman had a red beanie with a white *R* on it. The rules were if we got caught by upper classmen, we had to get on our knees, reverse our jackets and beanie, and sing a song called "Ah Me, My Poor Freshie." If we got caught without our beanies, we would get our hair shaved off. I was scared to death of getting caught because I couldn't carry a tune.

One night, a few of us were wandering around downtown Troy when a bunch of upper classmen captured us. We had our beanies on, but we had to kneel down in the street and sing the song. Then they marched us through the streets to their apartment. We were scared we were going to lose our hair, but they turned out to be nice guys. At the end, they took us to their frat house (Sigma Xi) to meet some of their brothers and then let us go.

Fraternities

Unlike most colleges, the process of fraternity rushing was put off for the first two months of school. This was a good idea because it gave us time to become friends with the guys in our dorms and classes. Rushing consisted of the freshmen visiting fraternities of their choice for three or four Sundays. Then the frats that were interested in you would invite you back for dinner. A few of my dorm mates and I went to a few of them. I got invited back to two of them, one of which was the Sigma Xi, the one we were taken to the night we were caught by upper classmen. That was the one I wanted to join, so I didn't go to any others. After dinner, we were in a recreation room with, among other things, a ping-pong table. I was very surprised to find that Dick Barker, the big brother of Teddy Barker, one of the boys I met my first day at Sargent Street, was a member of this fraternity.

Dick Barker had been my bully as I was growing up. The Sunday I was given my Bible at Eliot Church (fourth grade), he beat me up on the way home. For some reason, he put a rope around my neck and gave me a rope burn necklace and, in the process, scraped up my new Bible. When I got home, I told my parents about it. They said they would call his parents, but I don't think they ever did. Another thing he and others did was to continually tease me by yelling, "He's going to Rinse-Her-Rear College." I rued the day I had told them I was going to Rensselaer. Many years later, Dick Barker's father asked my father if he would help Dick get into RPI. I was outraged that after all Dick had done to me and all the kidding he had done about the school, he would ask for my father's help! What was worse was my father got him in!

Dick and I talked for a while after dinner, and then he asked me to play ping-pong with him. At that point, a few other brothers came over and asked me if I wanted to come talk with them. My response was, "Well, Dick just asked me to play ping-pong." They said, "Okay, we'll talk later." But we never did. I was pretty naïve and didn't realize I had blown my chance to be a member of Sigma Xi. After that, I didn't go to any other frats, and when the day came for the requests to join to show up, I didn't get one while most of my other friends had received invitations. Later, when I thought about what had gone on, I realized Dick had got me again in spite of the fact that he wouldn't even have been there without my father's help. All he needed to do was say, "We can play later."

I went home at Thanksgiving very embarrassed that I wasn't asked to join a fraternity; it was my inferiority complex taking over again. A few months later, I was asked to join Sigma Psi Epsilon. There was a pledge class of about ten; the first thing we were asked to do was elect a leader. I was one of two boys nominated, which really surprised me. I told a friend of mine in the class not to vote for me, and I lost by one vote. Afterwards, I regretted my decision, but it was too late to change it.

When the Rubber Meets the Road

A semester at RPI consisted of three parts: advance, review, and finals. Advance was the part where we learned new stuff. It consisted of lectures, recitations, and quizzes. Reviews were a week of tests—one in each class, each day. If we got 85 percent or more on all the tests of a subject, we did not have to take the final. My first semester, I only had to take finals in engineering drawing and English. I had A's in all my engineering drawing tests, but my plates (drawings) were too messy. I had a C in English, my old nemesis. Finals took about a week and a half. I had my engineering drawing final on the first day and my English on the last. Needless to say, my parents were very pleased with my progress.

Sports

My roommate, Jack, announced he was going to try out for lacrosse. Most of the kids that played lacrosse were from private schools; public schools like mine didn't play it. Jack had never played it but thought it would be fun to try. He convinced me and we both tried out. The practices started in January and were held in the arena directly across from our dorm. Jack and I would get up about 4:30 AM to get to practice at 5:00 AM. It was very cold in Troy (upper NY), and getting up at that time was painful in the cold. I rigged up my alarm clock to turn on the heat. Most of the practice in the beginning was running to get in condition. We would run up the stairs at one side of the arena, across the top aisle, and down the stairs at the other end to the floor. Then we would cross to the other side and then run up and down again. I was surprised at how well I did; I could keep up with any kid that was there. Then we were given lacrosse sticks and began to learn how to throw and catch the ball. Lacrosse balls are weird; when one bounces, it takes off on the second bounce and goes faster and further than the first bounce. Also, they are very hard, so you don't want to get hit with one. When the weather got warmer, we started practicing outside. The coach handed out equipment: helmets, gloves, body pads, etc. The only problem was he only gave it to the kids that had played before. There were about ten of us that had never played. Day after day, the kids with equipment scrimmaged while we watched. We asked when we were going to get a chance, he kept saying later. Then one day, our turn came, but he wanted us to play against the prep-school guys without equipment! We all quit on the spot thus ending my lacrosse career.

It was more of the same to me. When I went out for baseball, I got cut without a chance; when I played church basketball, the coach never taught me anything but, at least, let me play. Now in lacrosse, I got taught next to nothing and didn't get to play. Who would ever think that I would someday do a lot of coaching?

Race Awareness

There was a far greater diversity of races at RPI than I was used to in my little "white" town of Newton. I had no trouble getting along with other races; in fact, I enjoyed meeting and associating with them. We particularly had a large number of students from Central and South America and Asia. It seemed to me to be one on the neat parts of college life. There was a much bigger difference between the public school students and the private schools ones. I never felt comfortable with the rich ones.

Second Semester

One of my classmates from the Boston area and I decided we would hitchhike home for spring break. We had a good time and no problems and got home in pretty good time. I would never let my son do that today. When I came back, I had my father's old Nash (1940). He had just gotten a new Nash and I got the old one. Boy, did I feel important as I pulled up in front of the dorm until I couldn't get the key out of the ignition. One of the guys came out and showed me how to get the key out. The problem was our dorm was on a hill, and that causes the wheels to turn enough to lock up and stop the key from coming out. I never again had that key problem again.

I was the only one in the dorm with a car. All of a sudden, I had a lot more friends. The second semester went pretty well. I had to go to meetings at the fraternity and went to some parties there, but I still spent a lot of time with my friends in the dorm. In April, for the first time, I met our dorm monitor, who was supposed to be keeping tabs on us all year. When he showed up, we were in the middle of a big water fight, and several inches of water were flowing down the corridor. That gives you a feeling of how free we were.

I did the same thing again with finals; I had one the first day and one the last. I had to take a descriptive geometry and English finals. I was upset at taking the descriptive geometry final. Descriptive geometry is solving problems by engineering drawings. During the semester, we had four tests. Each test consisted of four problems. If you got three right, that was 100 percent; if you got four, you got extra credit. I got four right on all the tests, but again, my plates were not neat enough.

Sophomore

I had the greatest summer of my life. I went to Springfield College to get my leader examiner badge. This was the top swimming badge in the YMCA. It meant I was qualified to teach up through senior lifesaving and to run a waterfront. I felt great. I was going to be completely in charge of the waterfront, I would oversee the craft program that one of the junior counselors would run, and I would still get to play Capture the Flag, run a treasure hunt, and tell stories to the campers. That summer went way too quickly, and before I knew it, it was time to go back to RPI. My sister had the old Nash and I was back to being carless. The mother of a close friend of mine was going to drive me to school (my mother never learned to drive). It was real nice of her because it was about two hundred miles. She came to pick me up, and as I came out to get in the car, I fell apart. I started sobbing and couldn't stop. I just did not want to go. I just couldn't face leaving behind all the great times and all my friends to go back to something I didn't want to do. It took a couple hours and a promise that I could switch schools at the end of the semester for me to settle down. I finally realized I had no option but to go.

The sophomore dorms were on the campus so no more long cold treks to class. The dorms were four-story brick building. Each floor had two suites that consisted of a large room for desks and two small rooms, each with two bunks in them. I was rooming with my best friend from the dorm the year before and two other guys from last year's dorm were in the other suite on our floor. Since I knew I was leaving at the end of the semester, I cut off my pledging activities and settled down to classes.

I found out that Sergeant McCoullgh, the tenant that chopped up my hut, and his family lived in Albany that was just a short bus ride away. I contacted them and one Saturday went over to spend the day. I took the bus to Albany, and then Sergeant McCoullgh picked me up. As we were driving to his house, I experienced my first incident of racial bigotry. As we were driving along, he spied a group of African boys and started swearing about them and how awful they were and that they shouldn't be on the streets. I have never seen anyone show so much anger, and it was at people he didn't even know. Needless to say, he grew up in the South. I never went back to his house. His outburst made me remember that my mother would go out of her way to help black people. I thought it was because there were so few of them around, but I began to see it was a lot more than that.

Before I knew it, the rest of the semester was over. When I was home at Christmas, my parents had me scheduled to take some tests to see what kind of a career would be best for me. Once I got back to RPI, it wasn't long before finals. I did well as I always had at college. Before I knew it, I was getting ready to go home! My father drove out in his new Nash, the model I used to think of as an upside down bathtub. I said my good-byes and we were off. It started to snow just as we left. The first part of our trip was through the Taconic Mountains. By the time we got up in the mountains, the snow turned into a blizzard. It was slow, tedious driving. My father asked me to take over driving, and he crawled into the backseat and went to sleep. I wasn't real used to driving in snow, but I knew I had to go slow and, if I started to skid, turn into the direction of the skid. When I took driving training, the instructor made the skid thing sound very important. I was always puzzled about it. It seemed to me if I was skidding to the left I should turn to the right! As you might expect, I got to test the skid thing out that night on the mountain. I was going along very slowly, and suddenly, I was in a skid (my front wheels were moving left). I followed the directions: I turned to the left. The skid increased, I did a 360, and went off the road. My left front wheel hit a boulder under the snow, and before I knew, it the car was upside down. At this point, my father woke up and asked, "What are you doing?" I answered, "Shutting off the motor." Within a few minutes, some cars stopped to help us get out. It isn't easy when the car is upside down and buried in snow! Somehow we got out and got to a motel nearby and made plans for a garage to tow our car out in the morning. Needless to say, my father was not a happy camper. He didn't like me leaving RPI, and he sure didn't like having his new car totaled. That night was when I learned that "turn in the direction of the skid" meant the direction the rear wheels are going. I have driven about sixty years since then and never had an accident and only have had one ticket, so I guess I learned my lesson well that night. The next day, we got the car turned over, and we were able to drive it home although, because of the dent in the roof, my father couldn't wear his hat.

Tufts University

My parents had enrolled me at Tufts University in Medford, a suburb of Boston. It was about an hour ride on streetcars and buses to get me home to Newton. It is not easy switching schools, particularly at midterm. All my dorm mates were from Siam. It turned out to be fun rooming with people so different than I; we got along fine. I played squash with Sueki, and although he was better than I, it was a lot of fun. I hated my classes. They were general engineering stuff like learning to use a metal lathe and absolutely not what I wanted. I had only been at Tufts a few weeks when along came Washington's Birthday, a three-day weekend. When I left Tufts that weekend, I had no idea I would never come back!

Fate Was Waiting

I had signed up to go with a young adult group from several Newton churches on a skiing trip to North Conway, New Hampshire. I looked forward to the trip because I would get away from Tufts and see a lot of old friends. I didn't give much thought to the fact that I was a terrible skier. We arrived at the ski lodge late Friday evening and, after talking for a while, went to bed.

I woke up real early Saturday morning along with two very close friends of mine. We got dressed warmly and went out to explore where we were. In the back of the lodge was a big hill and, leaning against the lodge at the bottom of it, was a toboggan. We put two and two together and decided to go for a toboggan ride. I always felt a lot safer on toboggans than skis, so it felt good to do something safe instead of worrying how I would make out on the slopes later. When we got to the top of the very icy hill, Les got on first, I was in the middle, and Joe was at the back. I remember feeling a little scared as we got ready to go although I had been on toboggans many times. None the less, down we went! As we went over the first bump, my legs went dead and I slid off the toboggan. The first thing that came to my mind was, "So this is what it feels like to be paralyzed."

Oh My God, What Next?

As I think back to that fateful day, it amazes me to think how a simple little action can completely change the rest of your life and how unexpected the outcome can be. The only thing I was pleased about was I wasn't going back to Tufts. When I told Joe and Les I was paralyzed, they ran to get help. The lodge manager talked with the North Conway Hospital; they slid the toboggan under me keeping me flat, put me in a vehicle that would keep me flat (the lodge station wagon.), and off we went to the hospital. That ride has to be one of the worst experiences of my life. Although when the accident happened I didn't feel any pain, as we drove over the mountain road, each bump caused me more pain. By the time I got to the hospital, I was screaming, "Give me something for the pain, quick, give me something."

They must have given me morphine because I don't remember much at the hospital. I later found out they took X-rays and then made plans to ship me back to the Massachusetts General Hospital in Boston. I was put in an ambulance with a nurse who kept me doped up, and off we went to Boston. When I arrived at Massachusetts General, I was wheeled on a gurney up a ramp that was lined with people. The only person I saw that I knew was the minister of my church, Dr. Eusden. It was a wonderfully calming feeling to see him. They took more X-rays, and I got to see my parents and Dr. Eusden again. I kept saying to the doctors and nurses, "Do something to stop the pain, please operate." The last thing I remember was the mask going over my face. All I thought was, "Thank God, they are doing something." I don't think I ever gave a thought of whether I would ever wake up. As I think back, I never thought of what was going to happen to me next and what my future might be. All I thought of was how to get them to stop the pain.

Baker Five

I woke up with a lot of strangers in white standing around me saying my name. I have never in my whole life felt so bad. If you could imagine every part of your body feeling awful plus aches and pains all over and you are unable to move and do not know where you are, you would feel a little like I felt. I was in an almost full body cast so it's no wonder I couldn't move. There was only one thing you could do in a situation like that. I asked, "May I have a cigarette, please?" I guess that gave them a feeling I might make it. In those days, you were allowed to smoke in hospitals so the answer was yes. They also pointed out that I couldn't smoke if a nurse wasn't with me. I am not sure why they said that; I couldn't even reach the cigarettes, and a nurse had to light it and catch the ashes while I smoked. The pain at the time I woke up wasn't the severe pain I had right after the accident; it was more of a sick ache, unless I tried to move and then it hurt like hell. It hurt so much I was given more drugs and quickly went back to sleep.

I was in a single room for a few days and then put into a four-bed ward. I was on the fifth floor of Baker Memorial, one of three buildings that made up Massachusetts General Hospital. Next, they put me in a Stryker frame. A Stryker frame is like two cots that can be strapped together with me in between, like the filling to a sandwich and on a frame that rotated. All my life, I loved sandwiches, but I never dreamed of being one.

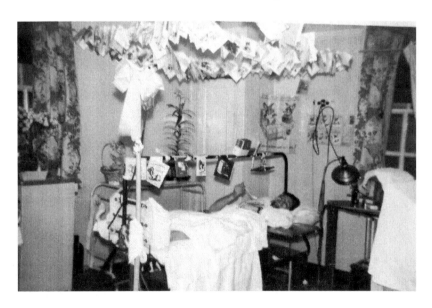

This way, they could keep turning me so I wouldn't get bedsores. At that time, I had no idea what bedsores were, but boy, would I find out! In a few days, they were able to put me in another cast. The one I had was slapped together quickly in the OR and had to be replaced by a stronger, firmer one. They promised me it would make me more comfortable, but it really didn't help much. I had two special nurses—one during the day (7:00 AM-3:00 PM), another during the night (11:00 PM-7:00 AM). Every day, the doctors would come in and stick me with pins to see if I was regaining any feeling; alas, I wasn't. The nurse told me my spinal cord wasn't cut, but it was just squeezed together. I knew she was trying to give me hope so I would get better. It helped a little, but down deep, I knew it wasn't true. It seems strange to me now, but at this time, I never thought of what was going to happen to me or what kind of a life, if any, I would have. The thing that worried me the most was the cost of being in the hospital. It cost $14 a day for my room plus $14 a day for each nurse. In those days, that was a lot of money. When I left RPI, my school health insurance was terminated, and I was too old to be covered by my father's, so I had no insurance.

I was in a room with three other patients, but I could only see two of them. The other one, Michael, also had to stay lying down and was positioned such that we couldn't see each other. We were feet to feet, about thirty feet apart. Since my Stryker frame was lower than the normal hospital bed, I couldn't see up over the edge of Michael's bed, and he couldn't see down to mine. I talked to Michael for three months before he got up, and we finally saw each other. Believe me, it is very strange to get to know someone very well without knowing what he looks like. The daily routine started with my day nurse getting me breakfast and letting me have a cigarette with my coffee. She was able to cook my eggs the way I liked them and also get me bacon. That made breakfast the only meal I liked. I got in the habit of falling to sleep at lunch and dinner to avoid eating. In those days, hospitals never served sandwiches, hamburgers, or Italian food or for that matter, nothing I liked. The chicken was so dry I couldn't eat it, as was the pork, the roast beef, the veal, and the lamb. Besides, I just wasn't hungry. During the morning was the routine of a bath, doctor visits, medicines, and the care of all the tubes I had going in and out of me. It seemed to me they were trying new things and giving me new medicines every day or two. At one point, they gave me testosterone, which caused me to very frequently have erections which was embarrassing when I had visitors. The afternoons were quieter and a time for visitors and a time to read and sleep. My mother didn't drive, but she came in every day to see me by a combination of bus and streetcars. I kept telling her she didn't have to come every day, but she kept coming. After visitors at night, I would be turned on my stomach, given some codeine, and quickly, I went to sleep. I would usually wake up about 4:00 AM in great pain caused by my anterior and superior spines (these are the bones that stick out at the top of your legs) pressing against my cast. My special nurse would flip me over, and I usually went back to sleep for a couple of hours.

I never even gave any thought to what my future would be like. I guess because I didn't see how I could ever have a future. I was totally helpless when I was in the cast. I had no control of any of my bodily function; I couldn't imagine ever leaving the hospital or ever being independent again. One morning, I was looking out the window by my bed that looked out at the Charles River, at MIT across the river, and Storrow Drive on my side. What got my interest were the people on the sidewalks. I suddenly realized I was a prisoner. I couldn't get out of here, I couldn't walk, I couldn't take care of myself. I was in jail! What was worse was there was nothing I could do about it. It was about that time that some of my friends from Rensselaer came to see me. I was pleased they made the effort to come two hundred miles to visit me. However, I was ashamed for them to see what an awful mess I had made of my life. I could read their thoughts as they looked at me and realized I had nothing left to live for. It really, really hurt. I never expected to see any of them again, but lo and behold, one of them ended up working in the same company I did.

My day nurse used to take me up on the roof often so I could get some sun. I kind of accepted that it was about the only outdoors I would ever again experience. It was better than staying in the room, even if it was only a once-in-a-while experience. The doctors kept trying to get me to eat more, especially meat, but I just couldn't. Before I was hurt, my favorite meat was lamb. My mother always cooked it well done. I had never seen a piece of rare lamb until I was in the hospital. It almost made me throw up to try and eat red lamb. My mother always got rib lamb chops and cooked them well, not kidney chops. Of course, in the hospital, they had nothing but rare kidney chops. To this day, I cannot eat a kidney lamb chop, but I still love rib chops. The doctor kept telling me I had to eat more protein. I said, "Beer has protein in it. How about letting me have some beer?" His answer was okay. From then on, I had a case of beer under my bed.

Bob and Ray were a popular comedy team on Boston radio when I was in the hospital. They would later become known nationwide. It turned out that Bob's wife was on the fifth floor of Baker at the same time I was. The nurses told us about each other because she had a closetful of liquor in her room, and I had beer under my bed. Bob and Ray would sometimes visit me when they came to see her.

I was in the cast on the Stryker frame for three months and then put back in a regular bed, but I still could not sit up. All they would allow was for my bed to be slightly cranked up. Still, it was a lot more comfortable than the Stryker. After a few more weeks, the big day came; I was going to sit up, but I had to wear a steel corset. Sitting up after all that time was weird; at first, I got very dizzy and then I was okay.

The first time I was allowed to get in a wheelchair, I went to Bob's wife's room and had a cocktail with her. I then came back to my room and threw up. Until the time she left the hospital, my first stop whenever I got up was her room. We had a good time. When she went home, she left her liquor supply to me.

Once I was back in a real bed, they starting me lifting weights. The therapist brought in a barbell with about five pounds of weight on it. I would lift it about ten times with each arm while I was flat on my back. Slowly, she would increase the weight until it got so heavy she couldn't lift it up to my bed without getting help. While the weight lifting was going on, they fitted me for full leg braces. This reminded me when I was younger, seeing kids who had had polio, struggling to walk with crutches and braces. It scared me to death to realize I was going to end up like that! Then each day, I was taken to a room that had a set of parallel bars, and I began to learn how to walk. It wasn't easy; a lot of energy was spent to go just a few yards. I realized then that if this was the way I was going to get around, I wouldn't be going far. The walking lessons went on for about two weeks, and then they noticed my shoe had caused a blister on my foot. This caused them to stop the walking for a couple of weeks. It also caused me to spend five more months in the hospital.

Bedsores

Once I was getting up and moving, they canceled my night nurse and then my day nurse. One of their most important jobs was to keep turning me to make sure I didn't get bedsores. Bedsores are caused by a bony prominence pushing against your skin while you are lying in bed. Normally, someone feels the discomfort from it and turns over; in my case, since I didn't feel them, I didn't know when to turn over. In the next couple weeks, I had bedsores on the base of my spine, my right hip, my knees, and my ankles. I was a mess.

At this time, I met Dr. Cannon[2], a plastic surgeon, the man that saved my life! I really believe that without Dr. Cannon I would have never left the hospital. He bawled out the staff, he gave me a hard time for letting it happen, and essentially took control of my care. The first thing he did was to make sure I got better care, and then he attacked the worst sore, the one on the base of my spine. The procedure was to first smooth down the bony prominence that was causing it, then to move a flap of flesh to cover it, and then take some skin from my leg to cover where the flesh came from. They didn't put me under or give me a painkiller because

---

[2.]   His assistant was Dr. F. J. Murray, who many years later won the Nobel Prize for medicine for his work on kidney transplants

I didn't have feeling where the sore was. I was on the operating table, lying on my stomach with a stool at the end of the operating table on which I rested the book I was reading, and they gave me a gas mask that I could breathe through if I felt any discomfort. It was kind of amusing watching the looks on people's faces as they walked by the OR door and saw someone reading a book while under the knife. However, it was anything but amusing, having someone using a hammer and chisel on your bones while you were awake. It was a long operation, and I had to take the gas a few times to get through it.

The worst part was what came next; I had to spend three weeks on my stomach. Wow, how could I ever survive that! I woke up the morning after the operation feeling very weak. It turned out I had been bleeding all night. They quickly gave me some warm blood that saved my life. Warm blood is blood that is taken from the donor and immediately given to the patient. Warm blood clots faster than cold blood, and thank God it stopped my bleeding. It turned out that about fifty years later, the spot where they had taken the flesh from for the operation started giving me trouble and would probably never heal.

In the middle of my weeks on my stomach, a funny thing happened. A young man, who had cut his hand real bad, was brought from the OR to our room. It was a hot summer day and in those days there was no AC. The man was only covered with a sheet. He was still under the effect of the anesthesia, and that kept him tossing around in bed, and, of course, the sheet would quickly come off. The nurses were keeping a close eye on him as they do with all patients coming from the OR. The strange thing was that every few minutes, a different nurse would come to cover him. Usually, one nurse per shift is assigned to a patient. We saw all the nurses on our floor plus lots more from other floors. The three of us in the room were wondering why so many nurses! Including many that we had never seen before. One of the guys in our room who was ambulatory walked over to the young man's bed to check out what was going on. His comment was, "They are all coming to see him because he is very well hung!" Even nurses need some amusement.

When I was on my stomach, I had a Foley catheter in my bladder. Foleys have a little balloon inside that can be inflated with sterile water once the catheter is inserted. This keeps the catheter in the bladder. Each day, an orderly would come around and irrigate my bladder. There was a gallon jug of some kind of disinfectant liquid by my bed. The orderly would take a syringe full of the liquid and run it into my bladder, leave it there for a few minutes, and then let in run out. One day, the orderly came and filled the syringe and put it in my bladder. My bladder started to sting, and a white foamy liquid started coming out. What had happened was the orderly filled the syringe from a bottle of Dazzle cleaning liquid by mistake. I have had bladder problems all of my life, and I never will know if they were due to that mistake. His mistake did save my father a lot of money; Massachusetts General cut a lot off the bill to avoid a suit.

The next operation was on my hip and involved the same steps. In this one, I didn't have to use as much gas, and I didn't have the bleeding problems. The rest were bone smoothing followed by sewing me up and, sometimes, a skin graft. By October, I was ready to go home for a day visit. I was so nervous I couldn't wait to get back to the hospital. Several weeks later, the time I was dreading was here; I was going home! I didn't think there was any way I could manage outside the hospital. One of the orderlies who had taken care of me since the beginning came home with me. A hospital bed was put in the living room (my old bedroom was upstairs). I was afraid I wouldn't be able to manage, but I had to try. After nine months, a lot of pain, a lot of discomforts, and some fun, I was going home. The hospital staff had a party for me, and I was off. As I look back, I was glad I didn't know all of the problems ahead. On the other hand, I could never have imagined what a great life was ahead.

Home at Last

I was home lying in a hospital bed in the living room; I would never be in my old bedroom again.

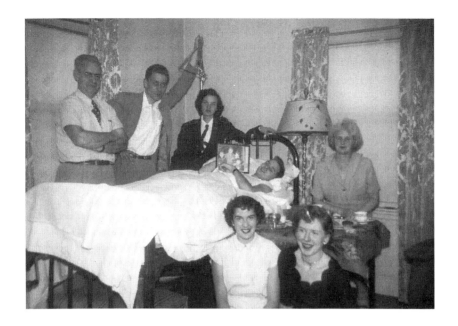

I could hear sounds from the dining room. However, they were not the hospital noises I was used to. It really felt good to hear familiar voices. My world now consisted of the living room, dining room, and kitchen. It was not going to be much fun. My favorite high school teacher, Tom Walters, surprised me by coming over to visit with his wife, Audrey. We talked for a while about how I was and what I was doing to keep busy. This led to their suggestion that I make candles. They brought over a candle mold they had for making candles with a base about three inches in diameter and a top about 1.5 inches in diameter and the height of as much as a foot. Then Audrey showed us a way to decorate candles by using a table knife to applying wax to them. To make a long story short, my sister came up with some good Christmas designs, and her husband got several department stores in Boston to sell them. It kept me busy, but once Christmas was over, so was our business.

Another surprise I had was when some of the members of the Gray-Y club I started about five years ago came to visit me. It always felt uncomfortable when old friends saw me in the sorry state I was in. I could just hear them thinking, *How sad, his life is totally wasted. How awful it is to see him this way.* These kind of feelings were painful to deal with even though it was great to see old friends. Many years later, one of the boy's daughter was in a youth program I was running called Beginnings[3].

When spring came, I started sitting outside to get some fresh air and sun. While I was at college, a new family moved in next to us. They had a son, Tommy, who was in the sixth grade at this time. During the winter, he and his family came over to meet me. My thoughts were, *why*? They sure don't want to be friends with me. Tommy started coming over to talk to me when he saw me outside, and soon, we became good friends. I'm sure he didn't realize it. In fact, I didn't either, but he played an important part in my recovery. I found out I could still make friends and help them in whatever was bothering them at the moment. Later that spring, I was back in the hospital again; however, this time I was in the Mount Auburn Hospital in Cambridge. We changed hospitals because of the catheter incident that cost Massachusetts General some money. We picked Mount Auburn because Dr. Cannon was on staff there. I had a new pressure sore on my butt and had to have some more bone smoothed off. I was there for about four weeks. Mount Auburn was on the Charles River in Cambridge. I got to know a few of the student nurses pretty well. In the evenings, they took me for walks on the path along the Charles River down to Harvard Square. We had a good time, and it was a great break from hospital life.

Soon after I came home, we moved to a house that would make things easier for me. It was about a half a mile away from our former house. All summerlong, Tommy rode his bike over almost every day, and he made my summer bearable just by being there. I would have much rather been at camp Chickami like the past years, but you have to do what you can. The camp had moved to a new site. I was taken out there to see if I could manage to run their craft program, but I realized it was hopeless and never attempted it.

---

3.   See part II, Beginnings.

Right after we moved, I had a visit from Sumner Dodge, one of my very best friends from junior and senior high school. Sumner had moved to New Hampshire right after high school, so I hadn't seen him in a long time. It was a very tough visit for me. I was surprised and happy he had come to see me, but I didn't like to have him see me the way I was. I had always looked up to Sumner and tried to be like him. It was impossible. He was handsome; I was not. He was popular; I was not. He was a great athlete; I was not. He didn't stay long; he was as uneasy talking to me as I was talking to him. I knew when he left I would never see him again

I was wrong! I had no contact with him for about forty-five years. Then I traced him down on the Internet and called him. He had moved to New Hampshire and married a girl whose father ran a hardware business. He spent his life in his father-in-law's business. A couple of winters after our talk, he was on vacation in Florida and stopped in to see me. This time, I had a lot to say and so did he! When he left, I felt good because in spite of my problems, I felt that in my life, I had made a big difference, and that made me feel pretty good. Also, this time, I felt he went away surprised and impressed with what I had been able to do with my life, not sad because I could do nothing.

Kidneys and Bladder

One of the greatest threats to paraplegics like me was dying from kidney problems. When I came home from the hospital, I had no control of my bladder. When it got full, it emptied, and I had no idea if it was full and no way to stop it. If I was careful and urinated frequently, I still had a problem. I couldn't empty my bladder completely; residue urine caused me to have urinary infections, and infections made me lose all control. They fitted me out with a rubber urinal that fit you like tight briefs, with a rubber tube around your penis that was connected to a tube going to a bag that was tied to one of my leg braces. It was not very good; it kept leaking.

I was taken to some kind of a rehab place for spinal injuries. They had a better model consisting of a small plastic button with a hole in it and some special body cement. You pushed the plastic button into a condom and poked a pin through the button to make a hole in the condom. Next, the button fit the rubber tube that came with urinal bags. You used the body cement to glue the condom to you penis. It worked a lot better than the rubber urinal because it didn't leak, but it was still a pain. There was one more major problem; you had to find a bathroom that was accessible to wheelchairs. Back in the fifties, it wasn't always easy. I struggled with the condom urinal and urinary infections for several years before I found a better solution.

Madison Avenue

We moved to Madison Avenue shortly after I got out of Mount Auburn Hospital, and I had a good summer, thanks to Tommy, who I told you about before.

The Madison Avenue house was a two-family house with a small apartment on the third floor. My father had bought this house as an investment several years ago. At this time, the second floor was empty, so he got the first floor tenants to move upstairs. Then he added a half bath to the room that would be my bedroom and repainted and updated the first floor. There was one major problem. There were about six steps up to the front porch plus another step into the house. My father put a railing up one side of the stairs that was the right height for me when I used my crutches and braces. And he made a ramp, but it was much too steep for me to use without help, a lot of help.

During the first summer we lived there, Tommy would help me up and down the ramp, and he talked me into letting him push me up to Newtonville just four or five blocks away. That was my first sortie into the real world since I had been hurt. We got kicked out of the five-and-dime because I was spending too much time talking to one of the pretty sales clerks. We went in Friendly's for ice cream and just hung around. It was a step up for me to be in a store again, but it felt weird when people kept staring at me. That was something I was going to have to learn to handle. Later on, I learned to stare back and smile.

Hand Controls

That fall, my father took me out to look for a car with hand controls. A friend of his was an automobile salesman, so we went to visit him. We found a two-door Oldsmobile sedan that I could get into and where I could drag my wheelchair into the backseat. The salesman did some research and found a place that would install hand controls. I vividly remember the first ride in the car. My father was in the backseat; I was in the passenger seat, and the salesman was showing us how to drive it by hand. When he first pushed the breaks, I almost went through the windshield and my father ended up in the front seat.

You have to remember in the '50s, hand controls and power brakes were not very common. The controls we got were designed and made by someone that didn't really know what he was doing. There was a pneumatic cylinder mounted under the hood, which activated the breaks when the hand control was pushed down (toward the floor). When it was pulled up, it activated the gas. There was one glitch! When the control was pushed down to break, it stuck a little as it went from gas to brakes. That meant it was easy to jam the breaks, causing a sudden stop and passenger displacement. It took a lot of practice to break smoothly, but I mastered it, I thought, and set out to get my license. I did fine, except at one point, I almost put the inspector through the windshield. He was nice to me; he gave me my license.

I was getting close to returning to school, something I thought I would never do. I was accepted at MIT. I could only get into the main building by driving around back and parking by a ramp that was used to take big stuff in and take trash out. Once inside, I went through a maze of corridors to get to the elevator. I passed by some rooms with interesting names like "Constant Temperature Room." I pictured professors in there in bathing suits, lying back on beach chairs under sun lamps, drinking high balls. Once I got to the elevator, I had access to almost all of the classrooms. I had no problems reaching my classrooms until the last year I was there. I had one class in a building with stairs.

I started school at the beginning of the second semester. I was majoring in physics. The accident had made me give up the thought of working with children. I now pictured myself hidden away in some lab doing research. When I got to my classes the first day, there were about thirty students in each one. When I got to my classes the second day, there were about eight. When it came time for a test, there would be about thirty again. I figured if my parents were paying for me to be here, I would be here every day. It felt kind of good to be able to go to school, but it didn't last long. Halfway through the semester, I had a pressure sore problem and was back in the hospital. Sometimes, you can't win.

During the part of that semester, I did attend a small event that had a major effect on my life. The husband of the daughter of some good friends of my parents was getting a master's degree at MIT. He was also working at Sylvania Electronics System, a company in a town next to Newton. He told me about what he was doing and showed me the computer he was working on in connection with his masters. Computers! I didn't know there was such a thing as computers! I knew instantly what I was going to do. I would switch to a math major and take all courses I could take dealing with computer programming and take electrical engineering courses dealing with computers. Then I would get a job at Sylvania. That's exactly what I did.[4] Wow, all because of looking at what someone was doing, I suddenly had a goal again. That was a big step from thinking I was going nowhere. As I look back, I realize that the act of a friend showing me a computer turned my life around and gave me something to work for. I hadn't realized that before that, I had no directions and expected nothing from life.

That was the first year Eisenhower ran for president. One nurse on the floor was really nice and I enjoyed talking to her. She was a Democrat and I was a Republican, and we had a great time arguing politics even though at that time in my life I knew nothing about politics. I was home by late spring, again wishing I could work at Chickami but knew I couldn't.

Working Again

A friend of my father's had a DeSoto Plymouth car dealership right near where we lived. My father got me a job working in the office of the dealership. I would sort and file repair invoices and found them when needed. It was boring, but for the first time in a long time, I was making money. The only problem with the job was the bathroom door was too narrow for my wheelchair. I had to use my crutches, which was a very hard thing for me to do. Somehow, I managed to keep the job for the summer break, not fall when trying to use the bathroom, and not wet my pants. It had been a long time since I felt I was able to do something real.

[4.] Sadly, my friend who showed me the computer had one kidney, and that one failed. He died a short while before I got to Sylvania.

Computers

My parents applied to the state for a disability scholarship to help with my college expenses. At that time, tuition at MIT was $450 per semester. I got a scholarship for $300. I was again starting my second semester of my second year, so I had two and a half years to go. All I had to do was keep my grades up. I got mostly A's, so by my senior year, the state paid $450 for each semester.

I was right at home with the courses I was taking, mostly math, but I had to take some nontechnical electives. I took psychology and history courses and German. You know what? In high school, I hated history and language, but now I was old enough to enjoy them.

At the time I was restarting at MIT, computers were quite different than now. MIT had one mainframe computer called Whirlwind. It completely filled a three-story building built for it. It was at least 100,000 times slower than desktop computers we have today and had at least 100 billion less bytes of memory. The only computer language was assembly language that required thousands of commands to do very little. I think at that time, there were only two other computers like Whirlwind in the world. One was in England and was called the EDSAC and the other was the ENIAC in America.

The programming I was learning was very basic and could be used for mainframes and for what was known as minicomputers. Minicomputers cost hundreds of thousands, not millions. I loved it; I couldn't get enough of it. I was also taking a lot of math that I thought would help me in the future in programming. My junior year went real well as far as my courses were concerned, but I had to spend some time in the hospital because of pressure sore problems.

That summer, I got a job at the supersonic wind tunnel lab at MIT. They had just bought a Bendix G15 minicomputer to use to reduce the data generated by the wind tunnel. The G15 had a magnetic drum memory. In order to get the calculations done in real time, we had to plan our data accesses so we didn't have to wait for the drum to come around each time we accessed data. It was a great summer for me. I was doing my first real programming job right in the middle of a real lab. The wind tunnel made so much noise we could only run it at night. Therefore, I also had my first experience of working nights. Before I knew it, I was a senior, a place I never thought I would be.

Bridge and Stairs and Fire

My social life was very limited during this part of my life. The only thing I did at MIT other than attend class was go to the MIT Duplicate Bridge Club on Saturday afternoons. My mother had taught me how to play bridge when I was in junior high. It was very common back then for kids to play bridge. After we moved to Madison Avenue, my father and I started playing duplicate bridge with the two sisters upstairs. I had forty-eight duplicate boards (the things that held the hands) that a friend of my parents gave me so I could play Duplicate at home. When you play Duplicate, each bridge hand is played by several pairs, and the scores are compared to see who did best. In our case, each hand was played twice.

My father had played in a neighborhood bridge league for years. There were eight teams from men's clubs all around Boston. I began to play for my father's team, the Huneywell Club. Yes, you are right—the same place I took dancing lessons years ago. That league was great fun, and it made a bridge addict out of me. I later on got to play against Stayman, the man who invented the Stayman convention, one of the most common bidding conventions today.

My mother talked me into going to a wheelchair square dancing group, which was run by the indoor sports club. I resisted at first, but I finally gave in. It just didn't compare to the square dancing I used to do. I got pushed into going to a lot of indoor sports activities. Then my mother and a few of her friends started an indoor sports chapter in Newton. Of course, I had to go. This whole experience with indoor sports taught me that one thing I didn't want to do was spend the rest of my life with handicapped people. I realized that I could do a lot more if I was with nonhandicapped people and that I didn't just want to be put off in a place where others wouldn't have to deal with me. At that time, I no idea how I could accomplish a life in the mainstream.

Since my accident, I didn't go to church much because my church was not accessible. There were six steps at every entrance, there was no bathroom I could get into, and once inside, I couldn't get downstairs where most things went on. I remember the first day I went to church after leaving the hospital. I was in the back of the sanctuary, sitting in the aisle. I had tears of joy running down my face as I came in. The minister recognized my presence, and everyone turned around and clapped. Then I was really crying. After the service, people crowded around me and I felt very important. For a while, I felt really good, but it also made me feel sad. I felt that I was being greeted because of what I couldn't do, not what I might do. At Christmas, carolers from church came to sing and bring me a poinsettia, and at Easter, they would bring me a lily. I was always reminded that instead of being one of the ones visiting, I was now one of the ones visited. That was hard to accept. Somehow, I turned that around and again became a giver.

One Saturday night, I was driving a girl I met at indoor sports home. We were driving down a road that intersected the road my church was on. As the church came into view, I realized it was on fire. Fire was flaring out all the windows that used to be stained glass, flames were coming out of the clocks in the steeple (the one I use to climb to wind the clocks and chimes), and then the roof caved in. I have never felt such a loss, not even when I lost the use of my legs. When the church leaders decided to rebuild, I didn't even think of the fact that I now might be able to go to church. My father was helping them with the plans and making suggestions to make it accessible. Unfortunately, they all goofed.

When I went to the first service at the new church, I parked in parallel parking in the front since the only accessible entrance was in the front. I got in my wheelchair and started up the walk. I was a little bit nervous because I was faced with about six stairs. There was a ramp that had the same slant as the stairs (forty-five degrees) with a wrought iron railing on one side. The first few times I used it, I had someone helping me. After that, I found I could do it alone, but it wasn't easy. The main problems with the ramp was I had to park in front where there was very often not a parking space, and in the winter, ice and snow made it unusable. The main floor of the church contained the sanctuary, the parlor, the chapel, the offices, and the nursery. The ladies' restrooms were on the first floor, the men's were downstairs. Several weeks later, I found that the nursery bathroom on the first floor was accessible to me.

A few weeks later, I came to a church meeting that was downstairs. I had been told that they had made the basement accessible for me. Oh boy, what a surprise. I parked in the lot behind the church near the back door that led in at a level halfway between the main floor and the basement. Some of the men said, "Just wait a minute, we got this all planned out." If I had known then how many times I would be helped up and down those stairs and how much time I would spend waiting outside for help to come along, I would have given up trying. I waited about twenty minutes for them to assemble the longest, most complicated ramp I have ever seen. When they took me down it, I was more scared than the time I went on the Cyclone roller coaster at Coney Island. I think that ramp was used twice, and then it was turned back into a pile of wood. When I finally got downstairs, there was a slanted corridor with Sunday school rooms off of it that led down to the fellowship hall. However, at the end of the corridor, there were about four more steps. Also, to top it off, the men's room downstairs was inaccessible as well. In the eighties, I was chairman of the mayor's committee to improve the access for handicapped to public places in the city. One thing I got done was making Eliot Church more accessible. It wasn't completely finished until 2008, when the job was completely finished by adding an elevator.

At that time, there were no public buildings other than hospitals and most stores that were accessible. Moreover, there were almost no homes I could get into without help. Slowly through the years, some buildings were made accessible but not the ones I used the most. Back then, I would have loved to have a cell phone so that when I arrived someplace, I could call to let them know I was out front. There were stickers for cars that had a right to use handicapped parking spaces, but there were very few handicapped parking places. The sticker also allowed me to park free at meters. People who abuse the use of handicapped parking became my pet peeve. Several years later, I pulled into a McDonald's and found the only handicapped place had a car in it without the required plate or sticker. Since there was no other place wide enough for me to park and be able to get my wheelchair out, I waited next to the car. In about fifteen minutes, a young woman came out with two young kids. I pointed out to her; she was parked in a handicapped place. Her response was, "I'm handicapped. I have kids." I should have answered, "I'm sorry. I didn't know you were retarded." Instead, I just smiled and waited for her to free up the space. Another time, I pulled into a bank parking lot with a friend. There was only one handicapped place, and a car without handicapped plates was in it. I parked next to the car and waited while my friend went in to do his banking. In a few minutes, a young woman came out and hopped in her car. She sat waiting for me to move; I didn't. Then she got out of her car and came over and asked me to move. My answer was, "If you were inconsiderate enough to park in a handicapped place, I will be just as inconsiderate and make you wait." And I did!

Driving gave me a freedom I never thought I would have. As I said before, there were stairs into and out of my house. It was hard at any time for me to maneuver those stairs on crutches, but it was frightening when there was snow and ice! As I look back, I don't see how I did it. I never fell no matter how much snow, ice, or rain slowed me down. What amazes me as I look back is I never even worried about falling.

Senior Year

My senior year was not much different than my junior year, except that I had completed most of my humanities and could take mostly math. One thing different was I had to write a senior thesis that was equivalent to a one-semester course. My thesis advisor suggested I write some math subroutines for the EDSAC computer in England. Subroutines are programs that are called to perform frequently used functions so they don't need to be reprogrammed with each use. For example, the square-root function. If the input were 169, the output would be 13. Since the EDSAC was new, it didn't have many of the math functions. I wrote programs for the hyperbolic trigonometric functions. It was fun. However, I didn't get to go to England to check them out.

I met a math student from Kansas City who was in a wheelchair; we were bridge partners at the bridge club most of the time. We had a great time experimenting with exotic conventions like the Roth-Stone bidding system and the Forcing Pass. We often won playing these conventions.

I had one trip to the hospital that year. I got a bad urinary infection and was rushed to the hospital with a temperature of 104. One of the student nurses on duty was a student I had dated. She came in my room and gave me a hug and a passionate kiss. If you have ever had a temperature of 104, you will know why I couldn't respond. We never dated after that. The nurse on duty that night asked me why I hadn't had my legs amputated since they were no use to me. Believe me, that is not the kind of question you want to hear when you are well and certainly not when you are as sick as I was that night. Sometimes people can cause a lot of pain and not realize it.

By the time I was in my senior year, I was able to be on my own. The orderly that had come home with me from the hospital had long since left. I had come to take it for granted. However, I realized wherever I went, I needed lots of help. I still had a long way to go.

Basketball

One night during my senior year of college, I was asked this question. Would you consider coaching our church basketball teams? The person who called was the director of religious education, Ruth Salinger, at my church, Eliot Church in Newton. I didn't know it at the time, but this was another of those simple things that turn out to be a major turning point. My first thoughts were, *How in the world would a person in a wheelchair be able to coach basketball?* The church leagues were at the YMCA where there were about twenty outside steps just to get in. Also, I wasn't sure if there was enough room on the sidelines for me to be in the gym during a game. I've never coached before; I wouldn't know where to begin. Ruth went on to tell me that David Lee, a long time friend of mine, had agreed to coach the junior high team and help me with the senior high team if I would coach the senior high team and help him with the junior high team. I said yes! I said yes quickly and then worried how I could ever manage to be a coach. If I had thought about it very much, I probably would have said no. The league games were January through March; practice would start in December. We got use of the Bigelow gym, my junior high, one night a week for a couple of hours. All we needed to do was to pay the custodian.

This was a big step for me. Instead of just worrying about how I would manage, I had to watch out for about ten teenagers. I went to our first practice very uncertain. My first problem of how to get in was solved when I was greeted by some of the players, and they helped me out of my car and into the gym. I remember exercises from when I played basketball, so I started them doing drills and then we had a scrimmage. It was not easy to officiate from a wheelchair. At the same time, Dave was at the other end of the gym doing the same with the junior high. Then we alternated use of the gym for full-court scrimmages. I was pleased that the practice went well and went home thinking, *Maybe I could be a coach.* I bought a couple books on basketball the next day and started doing my homework.

When the league started, we seemed ready. The teams helped me up the steps at the Y, and there I was again, in the gym I used to know so well. We had a good season that year. We didn't win the league, but we won more than we lost. At the final banquet, when the winners got their trophies, my team gave me a "Coach of the Year" trophy. It was one of those times you never forget. I COULD FUNCTION WITH NONHANDICAPPED PEOPLE; IN FACT, I COULD LEAD! I cry when I think back at what that year and that trophy meant to me.

We played games on Friday and Saturday nights, and most of the parents came to watch, as well as other members of the church. After the games, the kids and their friends would have a party, and the adults would have a party. Those parties were great for all of us. The kids became a tight-knit group that became a tight-knit church youth group. The parents became a tight-knit group too. I suddenly realized I was beginning to have a social life again; I was beginning to have fun! A few years later, I was picked to be one of the Men of the Year selected by the Newton Chamber of Commerce. I later found out one of the referees nominated me for the award. I guess I didn't yell at him as much as the other coaches. Before I knew it, I was asked to take over the youth group. I remembered the activities I liked when I was in the youth group. I read lots of books and I used my imagination. Before I knew it, I was also teaching the high school Sunday school class. Within a few years, I was elected president of the committee that ran the league. As I look back, I realized that everything I got into, I seemed to end up running. Year by year, we kept doing better, and finally, we won the league. That year, we had an all-star game with the winning team against the all-stars from the rest of the teams. Everybody thought we would get killed. By halftime, we were so far ahead, the game was called. It proved once again that teamwork is the secret to winning at basketball.

God Was There

I always looked forward to basketball season. One year, we were about ready to start our first game when suddenly I had an infection in one of my skin grafts. There I was back in Mount Auburn hospital. Then my temperature started to rise, and I developed a bad bladder infection. Next, they did some blood tests and told me they were going to do a bone marrow test in the morning. Here I was in the hospital for a long stay; I would miss a lot of the basketball season, my temperature was way up, and I was going to have a bone marrow test, which meant I probably had leukemia. It seemed that whenever things got going good, I ended up in the hospital. To make things worse, a new patient came into our four-bed room with some kind of intestinal problem. He was kind of in a daze. The nurses kept telling him to stay in bed, but he kept getting up, wandering around, going to the bathroom all around, and continually yelling and screaming. It got so bad they moved the other two patients and me out into the hall and cleaned and aerated the room. We were moved back in, and the new patient was at it again.

Meanwhile, they started giving me an alcohol-ice bath to try and bring down my temperature. An ice bath is very painful, so I was in great pain as well as all the other things. I was praying, "Why me, Lord, why me?" when suddenly I realized the problem was I was feeling anger and hate directed at this guy messing up our room. I stopped praying and then prayed for him and forgave him for the unpleasantness he was causing until finally the ice bath was over and I fell asleep. When I woke in the morning, my temperature was gone, and they found that the white blood count problem was because of a new urinary drug they were giving me. Within two more days, my skin graft problem was healed and I was back coaching.

A short while later, they asked me to go through a test of the new medicine they had used. Once a month, I had to go to a research hospital and take a pill, and then for the next few hours, they would do blood tests every fifteen minutes. The result was the medicine raised my white blood count, and I had a bunch of needle holes to heal.

I never doubted after that that when you need him, God is there, but you have to take care of your non-Christian actions first.

I ended up coaching and running the youth group and teaching Sunday school for more than twenty years. That simple yes many years ago gave me many, many wonderful years and the good feeling of making a difference.

Graduation and Graduate School

I graduated! I can't believe it; I finally made it. I was then put in an interesting dilemma—should I quit or continue and get a master's or a PhD. A PhD would take me at least three years; a master's would only take one because I had already taken most of the required courses as part of my bachelor's degree. I decided three years was too long. MIT awarded me a full scholarship for my master's degree, and I found it hard to turn it down, so I signed up for one more year.

I continued my youth group and coaching activities, bridge club, and, of course, studying. The high point of my year at school was my master's thesis[5]. I had a great thesis advisor, and he gave me the idea of programming a computer to play chess. A new building was almost built that would hold a new mainframe, an IBM 407. This computer was considerably faster than the Whirlwind and the EDVAC. It was supposed to be available in March thus giving me time to check out my program. I was ending my schooling with the best year ever.

Some of the things I had to consider in making the chess program were the following:

1. How to represent the board in the computer so I could tell if a move was valid.
2. How to evaluate the status of a board position, considering the position of the pieces as well as the value of the pieces still on the board.
3. How to look ahead a number of moves or until the game would be over.

[5.] A master's thesis was equivalent to two semesters of courses.

4. How the set parameters that would affect the evaluation.

I had a great time designing and writing this program and was looking forward to getting it to work when the bad news hit. The ceiling of the computer room had fallen in on the new computer. The plaster from the ceiling made a mess of everything. All the equipment had fans for cooling, and they drew the plaster dust into everything. The computer didn't get running until long after I left MIT, but fortunately, I still got my diploma on time.

One very unusual thing happened to me during my graduate year at MIT. Professor Norbert Wiener was known worldwide as the father of cyberspace. He was responsible for a lot of the initial research that eventually became the Internet. When he walked down the hall, he was known for keeping his thumb on the wall as a guide because his mind was always way off on some science project that he was working on. When he came to an open door, he was even known to walk completely around the room and back out the door. He was kind of like MIT's Einstein. One day, I was eating my bag lunch as usual in the math commons room when in walked Professor Wiener and asked me if I played chess. I said yes and we started playing a game. I could tell his mind was mostly off somewhere else because he moved so quickly. I was being very careful and giving a lot of thought to each move. All of a sudden, I realized I was going to get his queen! He suddenly came back to life and started playing real hard. It was too late; I beat him! I became one of the very few people in the world who can say, "I beat Norbert Wiener at chess."

During the spring of my graduate year, companies came to the campus to interview; I signed up for just one company—Sylvania Electronics. I knew where I wanted to be. The interview went okay, I guess, but I had a feeling I wasn't doing very well. Near the end, I mentioned I wanted to program computers; the interviewer's eyes lit up, and I knew I had the job. He described to me that they had two lines of promotions: technical and management. I was asked which one I wanted and I quickly answered technical.

I didn't see how anyone in a wheelchair could be a boss. Wrong again!

I got the job! I would be a senior engineer with a starting yearly salary of $5900. This was a big surprise to me. I had a friend that was getting a PhD and he was ecstatic at getting $7000. I figured that would mean I would get around $4000. I was also told that the top rung of the technical ladder paid $20,000. My God, I thought, I would never make that much. The last semester of my graduate year, I had all A's! That was the first time in my entire school life I got all A's. I would never have believed that average little me would ever get all A's. I did it at the top engineering college in the world!

Catching Up With Family

Finally, I had made it; I was out of school. I had a couple of weeks before I started at Sylvania, so I went to visit the family of the first man I worked for at the Y—Dwight Robison. I flew to Baltimore, Maryland—my first flight. In those days, there were no Jetways; passengers had to climb about thirty steps to get on the plane. I was still wearing full leg braces and using crutches that made it possible but really hard. Somehow, I made it. As I sailed through the air for the first time, I couldn't help thinking I had come a long way from that day I looked out my window at Baker Memorial and felt so helpless. I knew then I could make it, but it wouldn't be easy.

My friends lived in Easton, Maryland, on the eastern shore of the Chesapeake Bay. He was the general secretary of the Easton Y. I had a great visit with them. The only difficulty was that their bathroom was on the second floor. That meant I had to get driven to a gas station to use the bathroom. What a pain! Also, I had to sit my way upstairs at night. In spite of all that, it was a great visit, and then I flew to Cleveland to visit another old friend from the Y, John E. Danielson. He was the general secretary of one of the Greater Cleveland Ys. John Danielson became the assistant national general secretary of all the YMCAs in the United States. I stayed with his family for a few days and then came home. Both of these families have been and still are close friends. Sadly, Dwight died a couple of years ago. Both of these families have been family to me my whole life.

Sylvania/GTE

Before I knew it, I was starting work. It was kind of scary getting up to go to work that first day. Would I be able to do it? Would everything be accessible? Would I stand out and be felt sorry for because I was in a wheelchair? Would I dislike work? I got up; I went; I was successful.

The building we were in was divided into cubicles. The department managers had private offices; the section heads and senior technical staff had private cubicles; the rest of us were in five—to eight-person cubicles. I was in a five-man cubicle. The second day on the job, I ran into a boy who used to live behind me when I was in high school. That was a surprise; I thought he had moved away. When I started working, I had to get a secret security clearance. I thought it was neat to have a clearance, but it turned out to be a pain in the neck.

The department I was in was the fire control department, whose main job at that time was designing and building the Phoenix antimissile system. There were three main parts of the system: a long-range surveillance radar that was supposed to detect incoming targets, a tracking radar to lock onto detected targets, and missiles that were guided by the data from the tracking radar to destroy the target. I was assigned to work on processing the data from the surveillance radar. Our program had to compare returns from several scans to determine if any tracks could be missiles heading for the targets we were protecting. It wasn't an easy task, but it was further bogged down because the computer we were using to test it was in an IBM service center in New York. They had the IBM card deck that was our program, and we would call down changes or additions. They would run it that night and mail us the results the next day. It wasn't what you would call fast turnaround.

The problem in those days was that the threat kept changing. For example, we could have a system that worked perfectly, and the enemy could do something simple like having a packet of aluminum foil pieces that they could disperse in midflight. Then we had no chance of detecting tracks that were real. After a lot of changes and writing new proposals, we finally won a contract to build a portable system for detecting the source of mortar fire in combat and destroying their source. It was called the MPQ32. While I was working on the proposal, I had to have an operation on my ankle and had a cast on my foot for a few weeks. I spent the time at home (about four weeks) learning all about the MPQ32 and writing some of the proposal. The MPQ32 was delivered to the army but was not much use because it was so big it couldn't fit down an eight-lane highway.

Public Speaking

During the years I worked on these systems, we had a consultant from Columbia University that would come up monthly to review what we were doing. His name was Professor F.J. Murray, and he was great in reviewing our work and in leading us in better ways. He stuttered so we used to think of him as a high-speed computer with a jammed online printer. The trouble was that when he came, we had to make presentations describing our work. I thought once I was out of school, I would never have to make an oral report again. How wrong was I. I was told I was going to take a speaking course held at our plant. It was going to be 4:00 to 5:30 PM, two days a week for eight weeks. I dreaded the thought of going, but I didn't have much choice. The teacher was from a nearby prep school; his name was Buster Nevile. He had to be the best instructor I ever had. By the end of the course, I was sorry it was over, and instead of dreading public speaking, I actually enjoyed it. I realized that in junior high, senior high, RPI, and MIT, I never was taught a thing about public speaking. Looking back, that course was the best thing that could have happened because as things turned out, I ended up speaking often for the next thirty-four years. Professor Murray planted ideas for me that later on guided my work and were the basis for a program design technique, which I developed that was adopted by our whole company. I wrote a paper about my first try at software architecture that got accepted for a large technical conference that was going to meet in San Francisco. Suddenly, here I was at the top of the Mark Hotel, giving my paper to more than one thousand people. Wow, is this really I! I was too scared to worry about being in a wheelchair. I think I did pretty good job. It was the first of several papers I wrote, had accepted for presentation, and then publication in various journals.

My House on Highland Lake

Two months after starting to work, I realized I could now buy my own house. What I really wanted, however, was a house on water that I could make accessible for me to swim and boat. I decided to get the vacation house first, much to the pleasure of my mother. She still didn't think I could do anything. I went off one Saturday with my father to look for a house. A divided highway existed that went north as far as Concord, New Hampshire, so I decided to look in a twenty-five-mile circle around Concord. We found a house in East Andover on a 450-acre lake called Highland Lake.

The lake was crystal clear, and looking across the lake from my house, you could see Mount Kersarge and Ragged Mountain. The house had two floors, which I didn't like, but had a bedroom and bath on the first floor. It was mostly pine paneled, had a big stone fireplace, a one-car garage, and about three quarters of an acre of land.

It was perfect. All I needed to add was a walk from the back door around the house to the lake. It also had hot-air heating so it was usable in the winter. I bought my first house!

I went up to Highland Lake every weekend from Memorial Day to Halloween; I spent one week of my vacation there with the Robisons and one week with the Danielsons. I even spent a Christmas there; it was great even if it was twenty below zero. My basketball teams helped me open it in the spring and close it in the fall. I had the youth group up for a weekend in the summer and let friends use it when I couldn't be there. Of course, my parents came up whenever I didn't have other visitors planned. Since I was missing a lot of church, I started going to a little congregational church that was across the street from my house. My neighbors were a couple about my parent's age, and whenever my parents were there, they had happy hour together. During those years, I didn't drink. They also went to the little church. The church had a small pump organ that left a lot to be desired. When they asked my neighbor if he would pledge, he said, "I pledge at my home church. How about if I pay to have the organ tuned?" The response was, "We just had it tuned." He then said, "Oh, I guess it's how it's played." The pastor's response was, "My wife is the organist!"

I went to the boat show with my father the next spring, and we bought a thirteen-foot speedboat with a 35-hp motor. We soon tired of cruising around the lake; after all, there is just so much to see on a 450-acre lake. It was mostly used to show visitors the lake or to go to the store. The next year, I bought a Sunfish. I didn't know how to sail, so I bought a book on how to sail. When sailing a Sunfish, you are supposed to sit on the deck and put your feet in its small cockpit. I put a couple of boat pillows in the cockpit and then sat in it. This gave me a place to lean against so my back wouldn't ache. I would sail the boat on a reach that caused the boat to heel (tip), and then I would haul the sail in as much as I could to go as fast as possible until it turned over. The best part of sailing a Sunfish was that if it turned over, I could turn it back over and climb in without help. I also had a rowboat that came with the house and repaired a canoe my sister gave me.

My best times at Highland Lake were when the Robisons or Danielsons came up. We always had a great time. One year, Ginny Robison was into braided rugs, so we decided to go to one of the many mills in the area to see if we could get some scrap wool. The first mill we went to, Ginny and her son, Robby, went in while the rest of us waited in the car. She was in there a very long time. It turned out the owner of the mill was a director of the local Y, and when he saw that Robby was wearing a Y T-shirt, he couldn't do enough for us. I was driving a two-door station wagon with a luggage rack on top. We pulled up to the loading dock, and they used a crane to swing a big bale of scraps over my car and then dropped it. I swear my car went down several inches when the bale landed. When we got back to Highland Lake, we had a hard time dragging the bale into the house, but the big surprise was still to come. We cut the strap that held it together and *wham*, the house was full of wool. I couldn't move until they dug me out. We spent the rest of the week rolling up wool scraps and had a great time doing it.

UFO Sighting

There was a mountain in New Hampshire about twenty to thirty miles north of my house known for UFO sightings. Every ten years, there would be a lot of sightings. One of those special years, I was at my house with a friend. We were making ice cream with an electric icemaker in my garage. One of us would come out every fifteen minutes to add salt and ice as needed. One time when I came out, I heard a strange noise. I looked across the lake and saw a spinning disc with a spiral pattern on it, making a sound of something spinning fast. It came up from behind the mountain across the lake and disappeared over the hills behind me. The noise was loud enough to wake up my neighbor who had gone to bed and to make my friend come running out. The speed with which it crossed overhead was too fast to be a plane or helicopter and too low to be a jet or anything I'd ever seen or heard about. I never saw anything like it again.

Meanwhile at Sylvania

My first few years at Sylvania were spent working on simulating parts of antimissile systems, writing proposals for antimissile systems, and designing new ways to process data as the threats changed. After my first year, I was made a group leader, the first rung on the management scale. When I was hired, I said technical because I felt management was no place for wheelchairs. Wrong again; I was on the management ladder just about all of my working life. A couple of years after I started at Sylvania, it was bought by General Telephone and the name became General Telephone and Electronics. Later on, it got abbreviated to GTE. A few years later, I was made a section head. When the MPQ32 was finished, I was put on a job whose code name was "Crispy". This was a super secret project for the National Security Administration. I had to get a top-secret clearance plus some special clearance above that. I went to DC and took a lie detector test and they investigated my whole life. I made several trips to NSA that was in Fort Meade outside of Washington. Wherever we went in the fort, there were marine guards. We wore a badge with our picture on it around our necks. When we passed a guard, we had to hold our badge up to our chins so the marine could compare our picture with our face. While I had that special clearance, I could not leave the United States and had to get permission to travel in the States. When leaving the fort, there was a cement ramp that went down to get under a passageway and then back up. I used to try and go fast going down so I would have speed to go back up. One day, I did the dumbest thing I could do. I was going down the ramp kind of fast when I noticed a small piece of paper on my shoe.

Without thinking, I reached down to pick it off. My wheelchair tipped just enough for the footrests to hit the concrete. The chair stopped but I kept going. I felt so stupid lying on the concrete; I was immediately helped back into the chair and was not seriously hurt, but boy, did I feel like a jerk. That was the first of several falls during my lifetime.

When I was back at GTE, I had an office in a special area when I was working on Crispy and my desk in a cubicle when I was working on other projects. I hated working on Crispy because of the security and was very glad when it was over.

Time-out for Another Operation

Around that time, my urologist found that I had a slight blockage where my urethra entered my bladder, I was back in the hospital again for an operation. They used a cystoscope so the only cutting was around the entrance to my bladder. I had sodium pentothal to put me to sleep and—*bang!*—the operation was over. I was then back in my hospital room for a day so they could make sure everything was okay. It wasn't! I was rushed back to the OR because my blood pressure had suddenly dropped. The second time, they got it right. I then found I could hold a lot more in my bladder before I had to go and could tell when I was getting full and I now could empty my bladder. I'll never forget going to work the first day without the rubber urinal. I was scared all day I would wet myself, but everything went well. That day was a major milestone for me; I never again wore a urinal of any kind!

Back to Work

A little while after I made a section head at GTE, I was given the task of managing the design and programming of a small telephone switch called the DDM (December Demonstration Model). In December, all of the vice presidents of GTE met in

Florida to review new directions that were being proposed for the company. The DDM was a two-hundred line switch with all of the features required by the military. Features like six-party conferencing, call waiting, hot lines are common today but were not in the early '60s. Others like four levels of call preemption are not as well-known and are still just available for government switching systems. It was the first computer-program-controlled switching system made by GTE. I was assigned this job in September. We not only delivered a working switch by December, but we also developed a new program architecture which eliminated multiple interruptions that, at that time, was the main cause of programming bugs.

We then bid on and got a contract to make a similar switch for the United States Marines. I ran the programming part of that contract. I learned a lot about telephone switches very fast; they turned out to be one of the most enjoyable things I did at GTE. As time went on, I was travelling more and more. New York, Washington, Huntsville, San Francisco, Los Angeles, Chicago, Arizona, and Canada were ports of call.

During this time, the peace movement was going strong, and I was very much involved in it. I even had peace posters in my office. It led to some amazing times in my life that are discussed later.

Charlie

A few years after I started working, we moved to Mount Vernon Street in West Newton. We moved into a beautiful brick house on top of West Newton Hill, a really nice part of Newton. The best part was no steps into or out of the new house, hence, no more braces and crutches. It was so nice to not have to face the stairs into and out of the house every day, and it was great not to have the heavy braces on my legs. Once we moved, I never wore the braces again except to get down to the cellar. The cellar had a beautiful playroom and a super shop. The only way I could get down to it was to keep one wheelchair downstairs and one upstairs. That way, I could get down and up, albeit with a lot of effort.

At this time, I had a German shepherd puppy named Lobo that was the pick of the litter that my friends, the Robisons, got when they mated their shepherd. I used to often take Lobo out for walks and met two teenage boys, Charlie and Billy, who lived nearby. Before long, they joined my church youth group and played on our basketball team. I was kind of a pied piper back then too.

After couple of years, I decided it was time for me to get my own house. I had to hide the fact from my mother because she would get so upset at me moving out. I found a house in West Newton that was perfect for me and made plans to move. My mother, at this time, was beginning to act strange; it turned out she had Alzheimer's disease. My father took my mother out some place so she would not interfere with my moving. It was hard to leave, but it was time. Another milestone for me; I didn't think I would ever be on my own. My father, at that time, felt my mother got Alzheimer's from worrying about me. I don't think anything in my life made me feel so bad. She was in the hospital for a while when they diagnosed she had Alzheimer's. I went in to see her. I sat by her bed and cried as I said good-bye to her, for I realized the mother I loved was gone. She died about eight years later.

The first day I came home from work to my new house, Billy was sitting on my doorstep. It turned out I was seldom alone. Billy and Charlie and many members of my youth group would frequently drop in to see me. It wasn't only that they wanted to see me, they also liked the pool table I had in my dining room. I had always wanted a pool table, so I bought a pool table instead of a dining table. After I moved, my house became the party place after basketball games. A couple years after that, I got a call one night from Charlie's mother with an unexpected request. She asked me if I would take Charlie in before his father killed him.

I asked her to give me a few days to think about it. Primarily, I wanted to talk to my minister about it. However, the next day when I came home, Charlie was sitting in my yard with all his stuff. I ended up bringing up Charlie for the next seven years. After he left my house, he made peace with his father, and they became good friends. Charlie has become an outstanding mechanical engineer, and he is now a millionaire. We have always kept in touch, and he and his family always visit me on Christmas. Charlie thanks me every time he sees me for helping him when he really needed it. I had made a difference and gained a son.

Fernald School for Retarded People

One Saturday in March, my youth group was sitting around, trying to come up with program ideas for the spring. One of the members, Paris, told us he had seen an article in the newspaper that the Fernald School needed help taking the boys at Lavers

Hall for walks. Paris had gone out to see what it was like and suggested we all go. The next Saturday, the whole group went to Fernald School. Lavers Hall was a building for severely retarded young boys (ages about seven to twelve.). The building smelled like a giant sewer, so we quickly got some boys dressed for the outside and got out into fresh air. We walked and played with them in the snow and then brought them back. A few days later, I got a call from Fernald that hepatitis had broken out in Lavers Hall, and they suggested we all get gamma globulin shots. We got shots and kind of wrote off Fernald School as a program possibility.

At the end of May, I got a call from Fernald that the hepatitis was over and they would like us to come back. Normally, our youth group would shut down for the summer. Kids would go off on vacations or whatever, so very few kids were around. Right after that call, we had our final meeting until fall. I told them about the call and that David Eusden, a theology student that had been helping with the group, and I were planning to meet every Tuesday at five o'clock at the church to go out to Fernald School. We invited anyone who wanted to meet us at church when they could. We had no idea what we would do but we're going to try.

The next Tuesday, one youth—Bobby—showed up, and the three of us went to Fernald. We found Lavers Hall empty; not a soul was around, not even a staff person. We walked around to the back of the building and found all the boys and the staff on a concrete porch with chain-link sides and top. Staff people were sitting at the doors to keep the boys in. The big surprise was every boy was naked! It turned out that the boys hated to wear clothes when it was hot, and this was a hot night. We then found that one boy named Michael was dressed, so we took Michael for a walk and played games with him. Before we left, we told them we would be coming every Tuesday at five and requested that they have a few more dressed next time. By the middle of the summer, the boys would insist they get dressed as soon as they got up so they would be ready for us. Meanwhile, David and I talked with a psychiatric nurse that went to our church to try and get some ideas on things to do with the Lavers Hall boys. She was our lifesaver! She told us to pick a topic and spend four to five visits on one topic and always try and quiet them down with music at the end.

We picked trains as our first topic. The first night, we (there were four of us the second night) took them out (they were dressed) and played train games with them and showed them some pictures of trains. When we got back to their building, we played some train songs and ended by telling them a train story. When we turned them over to the staff and left the building, a strange thing happened. We sat under a big tree outside their building and spent a few minutes talking about what had happened that night. When I got home, I wrote a report of our night and sent one to the Fernald Hospital and to members of our group. The next Tuesday, we brought some wooden trains to add to the pictures and games, had more train songs, and ended with another story. We spent about fifteen minutes talking under the tree, and that night, there were eight of us. The third night, we brought an electric train, and a couple of us stayed back and set up the train while the rest took them out and played games. When we got back, they ran the train plus music and a story. We had requested permission to take them to see a real train the fourth night but didn't get it in time. Instead, we started a series on animals. It was now standard that we would have music and a story plus what went with the topic. With animals, we had pictures the first night, toy animals the second night, small live animals the third night, and the last night, we took them to a zoo (we now had permission to take them off campus).

The next topic was music. We started with a few simple instruments and pictures, and then we got some help from the jump start program going on that summer at our church. They not only loaned us a bunch of instruments, but their leader also came with us. We had our kids marching around playing the instruments as well as all the other stuff we had been doing. The next night, we had a campfire and cooked hot dogs and roasted marshmallows and told stories and sang songs around the fire. The final night, we had a little band set up with drums, guitar, etc. It was partly faked, but they thought it was real.

Every night, the number of participants increased, and the sessions under the tree increased. By the end of the summer, we had over thirty members there, and we spent about an hour and a half under the tree. I got a call in the middle of the summer, asking if we would mind if they invited other youth groups to come and observe. You better believe our group was feeling very proud of their efforts.

One boy in our group fell so in love with an autistic boy he asked his parents if they would adopt him. His parents said no. When school resumed, the nights were getting too dark and cold, so we switched our program to Sunday morning before church and to playing more games that kept the kids warm. We had one problem with our early morning; it meant the youth came to church in non-church clothes. Some of the church elders complained about their clothes. I guess you can't always please everyone.

We had all of the Laser Hall boys we had worked with during the summer over for a Halloween party. That was the first time most of our church members saw our boys. Right after that, I got a call that there was another outbreak of hepatitis. During the period from November to January, there was a series of articles in the newspapers about how awful Lavers Hall was, and it was closed for good. After Christmas, they asked us to come to the new building where most of our boys had been put. We did. It was much nicer, but it just didn't fit our program. One reason was the snow and cold.

I am sure if you asked any of the youth that took part in our Lavers Hall program today, they would say something like it was the most meaningful and best thing their youth group ever did, and probably, tears of joy would roll down their faces. Tears run down mine when I think of that summer.

The Peace Movement

We had a new minister, Harold Fray, at my church in the early '60s who turned out to be very liberal. He started talking about the peace (antiwar) movement whose aim was to get us out of Vietnam. I remember my first thoughts were how can anything we do affect peace? I was a deacon at the time, and we had lots of discussions about the war, how to get peace, burning draft cards, and taking someone in sanctuary. One night, we went into Cambridge to a friend's meeting to meet the solider they held in sanctuary. After that, I kept getting calls from our members expressing their feelings against sanctuary. When talk of the death march and mass march in DC came up, I decided to try to take the youth group to participate. I got some of their parents and some other adults to sign up to go with us. A member of our church had just moved up from Virginia and arranged for us to sleep on the floor of her old church right near DC. I had some friends living in Salem, New Jersey, that offered to make supper for all of us on the way down. For several weeks before the trip, we went to meetings to make name posters of soldiers killed in Vietnam. These were to wear in the death march.

The death march started Thursday about 9:00AM and went nonstop until Friday afternoon. It turned out that Massachusetts's time for the death march was about 3:30 AM Friday. We started off late Thursday afternoon. We got to Salem at about 10:00 PM for dinner with my friends, the Robisons, and then ended up at the capital at about 3:00 AM Friday morning. We were given name posters that hung around our necks, and we were ready to march. You may wonder how I was able to do this. The secret was I had a youth group that took turns pushing me. The reason I was so successful with the youth was because they helped me and I helped them. It was weird walking through strange places at 4:00 AM. There were people posted along the route to guide us. After we went through Arlington Cemetery, we crossed a bridge back to DC. There was a patrol of soldiers manning a machine gun, surrounded by sandbags at the crest of the bridge. It was a shock to realize we had to have troops out guarding our capital. Next, we went by the White House where we were instructed to call out the name of the soldier we carried. Their instructions were simple: Wake up, Nixon! Finally, just as the sun was coming up, we ended back at the capital. The capital really looks great at that time of morning. After the death march, we went to the church where we slept on the floor for a few hours. Friday afternoon, we went to the Smithsonian Museum. It was pouring rain, so we stayed in the U.S. history building that housed the giant pendulum clock. Toward the end of the afternoon, when the death march was over, we went to a peace service at the Washington National Cathedral. It was standing room only. It seemed like every great folk singer (I had ever heard) was part of the service, including my favorite, Pete Seeger. On the way to the service, we went by some troops of soldiers in riot gear. It gave us the feeling violence was going to break out any minute. After the service, we went to the Potter's House, a coffeehouse run by The Church of Our Savior, then back to sleep on the church floor.

The next morning was a cold clear day, and off we went to another march. The mass march started at the capital and ended at the Lincoln Memorial; however, there were so many people we got no more than halfway. By the time the march and the program were over, it was almost 5:00 PM, and boy, were we cold and hungry. We somehow found our cars and started back to Newton. It was the most incredible weekend of my life. It was also the most tiring one.

Another highlight of the peace movement for me was the Sunday morning after Nixon had first bombed Cambodia. I think it was in April. When it was time for Harold Fray's sermon, he got up to preach and said he was so destroyed by Nixon's action he couldn't preach. He took his robe off and sat on the chancel steps and cried. All of the more liberal members joined Harold and cried along with him. The decision was made to put a coffin on the church's front lawn covered with a U.S. flag and have a vigil around it with posters from 7:00 AM to 7:00 PM every day until Nixon left Cambodia alone. Our church faced a main road, so our protest was seen by many. The Veterans of Foreign Wars saw it and set up a countervigil across the street from us. Then they tried to steal our flag, hit a deacon who tried to stop them, and hurt a little girl that was near the coffin. We kept the vigil going seven to seven though June and then at seven to nine in the morning and four to seven at night. It ended because of actions finally taken by Nixon, but I don't remember what they were.

The February right before this happened, I had gone with some friends for a weekend at a Howard Johnson's motel with an inside pool. We swam most of the weekend when we were not eating or sleeping. I scraped my ankle in the pool, but it seemed all healed up, so I didn't worry about it. One day in March, I was on my way home from work when I started to have chills. Within a few hours, my temperature was 104. I was in the hospital for a few days, but when I came home, I had a big hole in my ankle. My ankle never did heal and was the cause of me losing my foot in 2004. I wasn't in church on the morning the protest started; I was home with my foot up. I did take part in the vigils; I brought a chair to put my foot on.

On Christmas following the mass march, we had a special service before the main service. We had a coffin covered in black, all participants dressed in black, and a reading of the names of soldiers from Massachusetts killed in Vietnam. It pointed out that Jesus was Prince of Peace, and it was about time we all worked for peace.

Our church supported a Vietnamese couple with four children moving to the USA. They had two sons in middle school, whom I tutored in math, and two younger girls I tutored when they got a little older. Today, both of their boys are lawyers, and their boy who was born in the U.S. is a computer scientist. Both of their girls have completed college. I have maintained contact with that family even though I moved to Florida. In fact, a few months ago, I was surprised by a visit from their oldest boy, Au, who is now forty. We had a wonderful visit, and I look forward to many more. Our church went on with the help of a few other churches to support many more families. I had a few of the children in my youth group and was pleased at how much they added to our group. It made me realize how what we do comes back to benefit us.

I kind of laughed at myself for thinking in the beginning what good can we do! We did a lot, learned a lot, had unforgettable experiences, and made friends for life.

Retreats

I accepted the job of running our high school youth group because I knew the youth through coaching basketball and all the parties and recreation that grew from it. I had very few youth meetings before the youth started asking when we were going on a retreat. I contacted my friends, the Wells, who helped me so much with Beginnings[6] and from whom I learned how to run a retreat. The pattern of our retreats was always the same:

1. Select a place to go where the group could meet in private.
2. Select a theme.
3. Plan some activities to do after Friday's dinner (all meal cooking and cleaning up was done by the youth).
4. Plan some activities to do Saturday morning.
5. After lunch, plan some outside physical activities for the afternoon.
6. After dinner on Saturday, have a talent show, talk a little, and go to bed.
7. Sunday after breakfast, we would have a short religious service planned and run by the youth.
8. Have a feedback session.

By this time, you are wondering what in the world is feedback? Of the eight steps above, this step ties the whole weekend together. The supplies I would bring were enough sheets of poster board cut into quarters for each youth and each leader to have one. Also, a lot of labels about 3.5" by 1.5", enough for each person to have one for each person on the retreat. The leader selects a person to start; that person passes their poster board piece to the person on their right. The person receiving it writes a comment or two about

---

6.   See Part II, Beginnings.

the person whose board it is and sticks it on the board and shares their comments with the whole group. This process continues until each person's board has been to each person in the group. It usually takes hours to complete. Each person would take their board home and have a great memory to last a lifetime.

One of the places we often went was Craigsville, whose beach was once rated best in the world. My youth had the choice go to the beach. There was no contest; feedback got all the votes. After feedback, we would pack up, clean up, and go home. I would bring home the highest, happiest, closest, supportive bunch of kids in the world. The effect on our youth would keep the group running great for a few months, and then we would plan another retreat.

GTE International

I was in my fourteenth year of working at Sylvania / GTE when my life took a major change. At that time, I had been a department head for several years. I was making more money than I ever thought I would make. I was putting most of the money into savings for my retirement and very content with my life, I thought!

I went to one of my church's outreach board meetings one night that dramatically changed my life. One of the members of the board started telling the committee about a citywide meeting that was coming up to discuss what could be done by the churches to help the youth of Newton. I decided to go. The result of that meeting, which had people there from most of the churches in Newton, was the forming of four subcommittees. The four committees were to do the following:

1. Start a hotline for the Newton youth.
2. Start a crisis center for youth in trouble whose families need some time to cool off.
3. Start a house for youth who need a long-term place to stay.
4. Start a drop-in center for youth.

I signed up for the drop-in-center committee.

For several weeks, I didn't hear anything about the next move, and then I got a call from Dick Wiseman, who was chairman of the drop-in-center committee. I went to a meeting that formed The Newton Youth Foundation and when all was said and done, I was one of the directors of the foundation.

Part II of this book covers in detail the forming and running of Beginnings, the drop-in center that emerged from the foundation. The rest of this part will continue with how the rest of my life continued in addition to the effect of Beginnings.

I decided I was tired of working on military projects. I wanted to go back to the commercial world. GTE, at that time, had developed a metal label about eight inches by thirty inches, and these labels were on all rolling stock in North America. GTE had a car track division that designed and implemented systems to scan and use the data on the labels. I applied and got a transfer to the car track division. At that time, there was a reorganization of the laboratory I was working in at government systems. I was offered the largest department of the new lab if I would stay, much to my surprise. Why in the world would they want me that much? In spite of the honor offered me, I moved to the car track division.

It was a very small division. I was the only programmer working there, so I went from running a department of maybe eighty to a hundred people to simply running me! The first job I worked on was a system for weighing coal cars as they came out of a coal mine. It would scan the car information, correlate it with the weight information, and assemble bills to go to the buyer of the coal and remit payment of bills to the railroad car owners and track owners. It was fun and a good change from mostly management, but alas, it didn't last long. Word came one afternoon that the Car Track Division had been sold to a company in Long Island, and to stay with it, I would have to move to New York.

I had heard that an international switching project was starting up at the GTE laboratory right near where I lived. I gave the manager a call that afternoon, went to see him the next day, and I had a new job as software manager for the development of an international telephone switch. The project was really just starting. There were four of us on the payroll: the manager of the project, his secretary, a retired colonel who was his administrative assistant, and me, the software manager. My job in the beginning was to read a mountain of specifications for the system. We would build and design the software architecture for it. It turned out that I had several months to expand and improve the architecture we used in the DDM (December Demonstration Model) switch. What I designed at that time grew to become the "generic architecture" that was used on almost all software development at GTE government systems for at least twenty-five years as well as in other parts of the corporation. A couple of years later, I had about forty people working for me on the switch. It was the best project I had been on since I left school.

As I said before, this was an international project. We had people working on it from GTE-owned companies in Antwerp, Belgium, and from Milan, Italy, from our research labs in England, plus people from France, China, Australia, Israel, Ceylon, and Spain. My eyes were open for the first time to the fact that people from other countries were great and a lot of fun to be with. One of the reasons the project was fun and moved along so well was because of the variety of people who were part of it and how well we got along. Since most of the staff had come from other countries, we planned lots of social things like international potluck dinners. I got to travel to Europe a few times and visit the homes of people in other countries and even got to visit Israel. I began to learn about other's cultures and enjoyed them all the more.

It wasn't that I realized there was a lot more to the world than the USA until I actually went to Europe. Before that, I realized, to me, it seemed like something in a book. We had a lot of problems with visas to get staff into the USA. It seemed to me the whole world should be like one big village and everyone could go where they want. One night at a party, there were five of us talking. Each person spoke a different language; enough of us spoke two, though not me, so we made a chain and carried on a conversation. That was the point when I understood why we were forced to take languages in school.

It's always when you are having a real great time that the axe falls. GTE International Corporation was being shut down! Wow, what a blow! After almost six years, all of our work was for nothing. We were in a race with Automatic Electric, a GTE plant in Chicago which builds all of the telephone equipment for our domestic telephone companies. We started after them and yet were now well ahead of them. Guess who won the race? Automatic Electric won by default. The reason the International Corporation was closed was because some of its staff was caught in a payola scandal with some companies in Europe.

I was offered a manager's job in Chicago but turned it down. There was no way I wanted to move to Chicago and drop my Beginnings and church activities in Newton. After being in one job for nineteen years, I started looking for a job. I had one interview that didn't interest me much. Then I got a call from the assistant general manager of the GTE Government Systems Corporation I had been in for so many years. He wanted me to move back and take charge of designing and building a system to support the management of large software projects with hundreds of programmers working on them. I went over and talked with him and realized he didn't know what he wanted. He was expecting me to apply the great development and design techniques he had heard we had been using on the switching project to his dream development system. I took the job and went to work and applied our techniques.

Here, I was working on a project for the general manager that would eventually cost the company more than twenty million dollars. It was a big difference from hiding in a cubicle in my wheelchair, writing programs. Things went well, and a few years later, my project won the Lesley K. Warner award,

the highest technical award given in GTE. My project was the first software project to win this award; in the past, it was given for patents of things that helped the manufacturing arm of the company. Warner winners were invited for a weekend at corporate headquarters to meet and have their picture taken with the president, to go on a tour of headquarters that was in Stanford, Connecticut, and to attend a banquet at which the awards were given out. My project was given a $10,000 award. I remember when I was told about Warner awards when I first started working, thinking I will never have to worry about winning one, that that's far beyond my capabilities. I always thought I was inferior, but somehow, even the wheelchair did not stop me from coming out on top.

Options[7]

Out of the blue, I got a call from Barry Corbet, who wanted to know if he could interview me for a book he was writing. He was

---

[7.] Barbet Corbet, *OPTIONS — Spinal Cord Injury and the Future* (Denver: A.B. Hirschfield Press,1986), writing a book on the lives of people with spinal cord injuries. He got my name from Bruce Marquis, one of my basketball players on my first team. Bruce was then executive director for the National Spinal Cord Injury Foundation. (Bruce told me I was his inspiration for going into this branch of work.) I was shocked to think anyone would want to publish anything about me. At the time the interview took place, I had two teenagers waiting for me to get through so we could do the shopping for tomorrow's retreat which was a camping trip in Vermont. I guess I shouldn't have been surprised as being selected, with a friend like Bruce in the right position.

STEP

The project I started for Frank Gica, the assistant general manager, was named Phoenix. Frank was general manager by the time. Version I of the system was running and the system we built became known as STEP, Structured Techniques for Engineering Projects. The first version was a time-shared system that ran on a Digital Equipment Corporation G-40 mainframe. The second version was a multicomputer system that was composed of several Digital Equipment Corporation's VAXs that held the database of a project, and each user had a Macintosh computer. I managed the expansion and supported the use of STEP until I retired in 1990.

In the early eighties, I was told they were coming to take my picture for a government brochure addressing handicapped people in management. It turned out I was selected as GTE's handicapped manager. When they came to take my picture, they brought more equipment than there was on a movie sound stage, and they took over an hour setting it up, taking pictures, and tearing it down.

When the brochure finally came out, they had all the people in it come to DC for a weekend, which would include meeting President Reagan in the Rose Garden. The weekend they picked turned out to be when the Persian Gulf crisis occurred, so instead of Reagan in the Rose Garden, it was Bush in the Indian Treaty Room. We had a long wait for Bush. They lined us up so they could take our picture with Bush. I was in the front row when Bush showed up; he was a little late. He went around shaking hands for photos. When he came to me, I shook his hand and said, "How do you do? My name is Fred Rosene." His response was in a nasty tone of voice. "I can read your name tag!" My father was a lifelong Republican; I was turned into an ardent Democrat by John F. Kennedy. I think I gave my father the best present ever when I gave him my picture with Bush. It was also a great relief to get that picture out of my house.

Trike

Ellen Danielson called me one Sunday to tell me to check out an ad in the paper about bikes for handicapped people. I looked up the ad, but my first feeling was it wasn't for me. When I lived on Sargent Street (grades three to eleven), there was a girl with severe cerebral palsy who had a special bike she would ride around the neighborhood. When I would see her riding, I would think, *How sad. She has to have cerebral palsy and needs such a weird bike and could still only go up and down the street.* When I saw the ad about the bike, I thought there was no way I want people feeling sorry for me as I ride a strange bike up and down the street. Ellen and her son-in-law (Tom) talked me into going to see the bike. It was a three-wheeled bike that was called a Trike. It had twenty-four speeds so you could shift way down on hills; it had pedals where the steering bar normally would be, which became breaks when you backpedaled. The brakes were just like the coaster brakes that were on bikes before hand brakes were invented. It also had a hand brake for emergencies when the coaster brakes failed. If you were going up a hill and let go of the pedals, the brakes would work as you backed up. Therefore, if you got too tired, you could just let go and you would come to a stop. It had an adjustable seat and footrests so it could be adjusted to fit anyone. It costs $2300, but it turned out to be the best investment I have ever made. I could put it in and out of the back of my van so I could take it anywhere to ride.

My first ride was with Ellen and Tom. We drove down to the Charles River and rode the bike trail into the Hatch Shell and back out, a trip of about eleven miles. It was so easy, I couldn't believe it. When I was young, I never rode my bike that far. I got a book of bike trails along the north and south coast of Massachusetts. It gave directions to a starting place and then directions for a scenic ride that brought you back to where you started. At first, we tried trails that were twelve to fifteen miles long. Then we got up to twenty and twenty-five miles, and one day we rode thirty-four miles. The good part was I could keep up with friends on regular bikes. The Trike gave me a new freedom; I planned and took the youth group on weekend bike rides on Cape Cod and Newport, Rode Island. I always wanted to go to the fireworks and pop concert held every July 4, but it was impossible for me to park close enough. The Trike made it easy. We would pack a picnic supper and ride in along the Charles and have great seats for the program and then ride home. When I retired to Florida, I would ride about ten miles a day[8], and I joined the Boca Raton Bike Club and went on several rides with them.

Biking was great because it was one sport I could do with nonhandicapped people, and it was also a good way to get

---

8.   Part III describes my favorite morning ride.

exercise. I would guess I have put over ten thousand miles on my Trike.

Clown Ministry

During the seventies while I was busy working on STEP, I still was running the youth group. I happened to see the movie *The Parable*, which depicts Jesus as a clown. I got to feeling that having the youth group doing something with clowns might be interesting. I talked enough of the youth into doing it, and we planned a short clown skit and performed it on a Sunday night at the end of a hour of hymn sing. It went over well enough that we were asked to do some more.

We contacted a church that was doing clown services, and they invited us over to show us how they did them. That church built a lot of interest in our youth and off we went. I talked with our minister about doing a clown service as the Sunday service. We set up the plan that we would meet with the minister in his study about 9:30 Sunday morning to say a prayer. The clowns would then be silent until the service was over. I remember meeting with the group on a Saturday morning we had visited the church. They had signs for each part of the service—call to worship, confession, etc. I had a couple of boys in the group who were real good artists; in fact, one of them has made a career out of his art. They made a great set of signs with pictures along with the parts of the service. For example, the poster that introduced the sermon had a head made up of elongated letters spelling "sermon" with a clerical collar and black robes. They really did a great job.

We designed skits that would be done in mime accompanied with music. We would either pick the music first and then work out a skit that told the story that went with the music or pick the Bible verse and find the right song to go with it. For example, we wanted to do a skit based on the Good Samaritan parable. First we picked the background song "Where is Love?" from Oliver. The skit started with a clown coming out playing with a balloon, and next, a clown came out and deliberately broke his balloon. This was followed by four groups of clowns. One was too busy, one was a minister trying to teach the Bible, one was businessmen trying to interest the clown in their product, and one was politicians trying to win the clown's vote. It ended with a clown who gave him a new balloon.

We came up with ways to introduce hymns in a clown sort of way. We had four small posters with the letters H, Y, M, and N on the front and the four number of the hymn on the back. The clowns would first try to get hymn spelled right and then turn them over and tried to get the number right. We decided to pass two plates in the offering—the first one filled with candy and the second for money. The youth made their own costumes and I supplied the makeup. They came to church at 8:00 AM to dress and put makeup on and then met for the prayer with the minister.

Next, they went out and greeted and seated parishioners. They had large dusters and combs and toothbrushes to dust the pew or dust their shoes (wash their feet). The service was such a great success. We had to promise to do one the next year.

People were warned when the clown service was coming, and some went to other churches, yet we had the largest attendance of any service of the year except Christmas and Easter. Unbelievably, the clown services were started in the seventies and are still going on today. In fact, the service they did last winter (2010) was repeated at the Andover Newton Theology Seminary and taped so the seminary could start teaching their future Christian educators about it.

Word from God

In the late seventies, I got a call from a girl, Joan, who I had met in the indoor sports club years ago but had not heard from for about fifteen years. She was married, had a son, had a house, and wanted me to come over to dinner to see her house and meet her family. I went over and met her husband and her seven-year-old son. Her house was in Revere, a city north of Boston; I lived in a town that was west of Boston. The quick way to get there was to drive into Boston on Storrow Drive, switch to the expressway going north, and then go over the Mystic River Bridge. The bridge was a very long, two-level bridge that went over the Charles River, part of Boston Harbor and the Mystic River. It took about twenty minutes to get there going over the bridge but more than an hour without it.

The next evening when I got home, Joan was parked outside my house. I invited her in for a cup of coffee. She told me that she and her husband were breaking up and I thought, *Oh, oh, I better be careful.* One thing led to another and she ended up spending the night. From then on, I would go to Revere almost every day after work. We would have dinner, and then I would read her son a bedtime story and tuck him in. I would usually leave at about 10:30. This went on for many months, and then the inevitable happened—she maneuvered me into a proposal. At first, I thought getting married was a good thing, but I began having doubts. I had worked hard to become independent and wasn't sure I wanted to give it up. As I lay in bed one night, I asked God to please guide me and tell me what to do. The next morning, my radio alarm woke me up with the news that the Mystic River Bridge had fallen down! The message was clear; we didn't get married.

Good-bye Newton

Ellen and John Danielson, who I mentioned before had been good friends of mine since college, suddenly got divorced. Two of their three daughters had died in the last few years. The different way each dealt with the tragedy drove them apart. Ellen continued living for a while in their big house in Needham, a town that bordered Newton, after the divorce and then decided to sell it. I suggested that we should both sell our houses and share a house. That was exactly what happened. I sold the house I had lived in for twenty-two years, and we bought a real nice house in Needham. We lived there for about five years. She got upset because too many kids kept coming over to see me. She finally moved, and I stayed put until I retired.

Brian, a boy who lived around the corner from us and cut our grass and helped me take our trash to the dump and fix things around the house, was often over at my house or biking with me and started telling me his troubles. He lived with his father and a stepmother who drank all the time and provided little supervision. Furthermore, the stepmother didn't like any of her husband's kids. One day, Brian brought over his real mother to meet me. She lived about twenty-five miles away and had a young son by her second marriage. She asked me if I would become her son's guardian. It was kind of a shock. I asked why don't you take him and would his father allow it. Anyway, I ended up his guardian. For a while, things went well until he went to high school. He started fighting going to school by not getting up in the morning. One of his teachers even came over and tried to get him up. Anyway, it got worse, and he ended up on probation. That was good because he had to be tested each month for drugs. My neighbor suggested a private school that he had sent his kids to when they got in trouble. We checked it out, and it looked perfect for him so I enrolled him. He still didn't do very well and was on probation again. The police told me I had a few days to get him back in school or they would put him in jail. A a doctor I knew connected me with a school that seemed great. It was secure as far as the students were concerned, and it would help him quit smoking pot. He was there for about a week when I got a call that he was kicked out of the school. It seemed he contacted a friend and smuggled some pot in and got his whole dorm high. Finally, I got him in a much stricter place primarily for kids on drugs. He stayed there until they felt he was ready to leave.

He wouldn't go back to school, so I helped him start a landscape business. His business started with houses close to mine, and then he got a truck and spread out. His customers liked his work, and he worked hard and seemed to be doing well. When he was eighteen and just after I retired, I decided to go to Florida for the winter. I owned a house that was not currently rented, so I decided to use it. Right before Christmas, I got a call from the Needham Police that he was suspected of selling drugs from my house and could they have permission to search the house. I said yes and, a few days later, told him I was selling the house. He cleaned it up, and within a couple months, we had a buyer. I drove back in April to get it cleaned up and get what I wanted to bring to Florida and dispose of the rest. He found a house with a garage that he could rent half of and a garage where he could keep his landscape equipment. I gave him a lot of my furniture and household things, and he moved to the new house. When the day to pass papers came, I had to have all of the stuff out. Brian wasn't there. He was in the hospital with his girl who was having an abortion. A couple of the people I used to work with at GTE called up and asked if I needed help. Thank God they called; I got all of the things he wanted out on the front lawn and what I wanted packed in my van.

Drugs and alcohol destroyed the landscaping business I had set up for him, and he has had a very sad life, staying at friends' houses and living off others while his health went downhill. Every few years, he has called and asked for money. I always refused because I knew what it would be used for.

Sometimes, you just can't make a difference no matter what you do.

Retirement

I retired thinking I had had a good life, done well, and had made a difference most of the time. I went down to Florida because I had relatives and a house there without knowing what I would do. Little did I know one small request would again turn into a great new phase of my life that is covered in Part III.

PART II

Hooked

My life and ideas changed drastically in 1960, when the minister of the church, Dr. Eusden, retired and was replaced by a young liberal man named Arthur Rouner. I was shocked to find out our new minister was going to vote for Kennedy. How could that be! Anyone knew that "good people" only voted for Republicans. Alas, how wrong I was! Arthur turned me into a Christian (i.e., made me understand what being a Christian really meant); JFK turned me into a Democrat (i.e., showed me what Democrats really stood for). Arthur followed Dr. Eusden, who had been at Eliot for thirty-three years. After two years of struggling to get past being compared with his predecessor, he left. I was devastated; no one could replace him. Little did I know what was coming next.

Our next minister, Harold Fray, was about ten years older than Arthur. Not too long after Harold came, he asked me to attend a peace meeting with him. I didn't know how to politely say, "You've got to be kidding!" So I went. I remember being bored to death and thinking what a waste of time it was. How could we have any effect on world peace? Boy, was I wrong! That began many years of active participation in war protests, civil rights protests, draft-card burning, and even a slight brush with providing sanctuary to draft dodgers.[9] The forties had turned me

---

9. See Part I for details of my peace adventures.

into a social worker, the fifties into a coach on wheels, and the sixties into a liberal who knew I could make a difference.

My involvement with a drop-in program called The Beginnings began because I went to a meeting of the outreach committee of the church. It was January of 1969; I wasn't an elected member, but there had been a request for anyone who wanted to be a member to come, so I went. I had never gone to an outreach meeting until that night, and I never went to another one. Nonetheless, that one meeting was the start of an incredible adventure! A woman I didn't know very well, Marie Gazakhian, reported to the committee about a group called YAC (Youth Action Committee) which was being formed by people from several Newton churches to address the needs of youth in the community. I think she must have rung my social worker bell because I went to a YAC meeting a few days later. I remember a crowded room, maybe thirty to forty people. The meeting was opened for suggestions, and when all was said and done, it was decided to split into four exploratory groups to look into starting a hotline[10], a multiservice center[11], long term housing for youth and a drop-in center. I signed up to be part of the drop-in center group.

Suum Cuique

The chairman of the drop-in center called me and asked me to come to a meeting at his house. The meeting consisted of the following people:

Dick Weisman, chairman of the committee. He worked for the Metal Bellows Manufacturing Company. He later became a social worker.

Janis Weisman, Dick's wife. They had three small kids. Janis worked part-time in the social service field.

---

[10] A hotline was set up which ran for several years and helped a lot of youth in crisis.

[11] The multiservice center started by this group is still in existence. In 1989, I turned to the center to get help for my ward.

Stander Wright. He had a long beard, long hair, and he wore dirty, loose-fitting clothes and soft leather boots. In other words, the classic hippie, but he had a lot of neat dreams about what a drop-in center should be like.

Karen Wright, Stander's wife. She was a social worker employed at the Newton Community Service Center. She was neatly dressed. You would never have guessed she was Stander's wife. It turned out Stander had tried to get the service center to help them start his drop-in center but got turned down.

Axel Kaufman. He was a member of the Freeport Foundation which was a home for youth with family problems that had been started a few years before in Newton.

Daniel Paracini. He was the assistant rector of the Grace Episcopal Church located across the park from Eliot Congregational Church.

Wigmore Pearson. He was an ex-Peace Corp member and a member of Eliot Church who was now a lawyer and involved in politics in Newton.

Youth. They were several hippie-looking youth from the alternate high school, Murray Road, which had been started in Newton the year before. One of the youth I knew from some past involvement with fair housing in Newton.

From that night on, things began to happen. Stander's proposal for a program called Marketplace was accepted. His idea was to create a place where youth could make and sell things such as leather goods, pottery, wood items, clothes, etc. It also would be a place where theater, music events, lectures, etc., could occur and where recreational and educational programs could take place. It was also a place where youth could come to just hang out. It sounded great on paper, albeit a dream seemingly impossible to achieve. I'm the first to admit that I didn't think the proposal was possible. As I look back now, I realize we did a lot of the impossible! We decided to rent a storefront that would serve as a place for youth to make and sell their wares and as a place for youth to congregate. A foundation, The Newton Youth Foundation, was set up to oversee it. The next thing I knew, I was one of the directors of The Newton Youth Foundation. Dick was president and Wigg was treasurer.

There was a series of meetings, and somehow some money was raised. A storefront was rented on the western edge of Newton, near Murray Road, the alternate high school, and almost across the street from the Newton dump. It turned out Stander was an all-time champion dump picker! We spent the next five years trying to figure out what to do with some of the treasures he rescued from the dump. Stander was hired as director, and the program was named Suum Cuique (Latin for "to each his own"). I had attended the YAC meeting in September of '69; Suum Cuique opened right after Christmas of the same year. I was impressed with the youth that came to the meetings and pushed for the program. They were intelligent, capable, talented kids. I was puzzled by Stander. He had good ideas, but it was hard to envision him bringing them to fruition. I was turned off by Karen. She pushed hard for the program, but she had an abrasive personality. I often wondered why she hadn't talked the service center into starting the program. Dick and Janis were hardworking, committed people who somehow always found what we needed in terms of people, money, and space. Wigg, I knew from Eliot, and he was well known in the community, and he seemed perfect as our lawyer.

I was not at the grand opening of Suum Cuique, as I was visiting my sister in Florida. When I got back, the first thing I did was go check out Suum Cuique. The store had three stairs in the front but only one in the back. I made my grand entrance by tipping over backwards trying to get up the back step. Oh well, so much for the sophisticated director! The store was small; there were a few things around for sale but no customers, no salespeople. All I could hear was some music coming up from the cellar. I wasn't too impressed; if someone came in to buy something, I was sure they would leave quickly. Stander came up and told me in glowing terms what a great success it was. I didn't know it then, but Stander always saw the silver lining. Some of the youth came up and said it was going great. I felt uncomfortable there; as soon as I could, I found a reason to leave.

Shortly after that, I scraped my foot swimming at a HoJo's pool. I ended up in the hospital for several weeks and was unable to do much but my job at GTE for the next five months. I was sure I had been dropped from the roles of The Newton Youth Foundation but no such luck.

Suum Cuique lasted until spring. The craft goods were sold out in the first two weeks. The youth were having a great time hanging out in the cellar smoking pot. Stander just wasn't there enough to control things (I guess he was at the dump), but then he wasn't paid much. Dick found another staff person who would work for very little. The name of this savior was Fred Taylor. Without Fred, the program would not have lasted until spring and certainly would not have been in existence after that. He really was our savior. He got a couple of artistic friends involved who lived in his commune. There was instant rapport with the youth and Fred. Unfortunately, there was not enough money coming in from sales to pay for the store. It was forgotten, and its name changed to The Beginnings, destined to be simply a drop-in center.

Hippies

I didn't talk to Dick until June. That's when I found out that our money ran out in May, but somehow, he worked out a reprieve by obtaining permission to use the nursery school space in the cellar of the Second Church in West Newton for the summer. That gave us three months to get our act together and find a permanent place. Dick asked me to stop by once in a while to support the staff. I will never forget the first time I did. Beginnings consisted of four craft rooms, each about twenty by twenty feet, use of bathrooms at the end of the hall, and a lounge room upstairs. The four craft rooms looked out on the church parking lot, and there was a door in one room that went to the parking lot. The woodworking room was so full of dump treasures I could hardly go into it, but lost in the middle of it was a woodworking bench, a jigsaw, a table saw, and a variety of hand tools. The leather room contained a couple of work tables and piles of cloth, leather scraps, and a table with a hand printing press and ten to twelve cases of type and some silk-screening equipment. There were also boxes piled along the walls full of more treasures from the dump. The pottery room had two potter's wheels, large and small kilns, bags of clay, cabinets of pots and bowls, and wall-to-wall clay. A trail of clay led from this room to the bathrooms, whose washbowls and floors were covered with clay. The fourth room was kind of a multipurpose room; it was the one with the exit to the parking lot. It had a couple of tables and several chairs, several boxes of stuff piled along the walls, a large loom that Stander was making (six by eight by four feet), and a smaller loom, but it was otherwise fairly empty. This room was the hangout room and contained a record player. After all, it wouldn't be a drop-in center without music.

Whenever I stopped by, there were anywhere from ten to thirty kids there from five to nineteen years old. Actually, forty to fifty youth came each day, and over 150 different youth spent time at Beginnings that summer. Let me tell you about a few of them.

Kathy (the mother). She was a Murray Road student who attended most of the meetings that got Beginnings started. She was slightly overweight and, like all hippies, tried to make herself look as bad as possible. She was an outgoing, warm person that was full of ideas and wasn't afraid to speak out. She was in the middle of anything that went on that summer and made sure everything and everyone was okay. She had two sisters and a brother who also participated.

Bill (the user). He was a junior in high school who lived across the street from the church. He was the son of a high school classmate of mine. Bill and his three sisters and brother spent the summer at Beginnings. Bill was a handsome, popular young man who, in some ways, was a leader that summer. Unfortunately, he also led the way in pot smoking. Bill was one of our failures. He went on to use a variety of drugs during the next year and ended up institutionalized. He still is and always will be! He simply burned his mind up until there was nothing left. His sisters and brother are doing fine; they are married and raising families. His brother, Jon, was my insurance agent until I moved to Florida.

Richie (the protector). He didn't fit the hippie image. He was a big, strong young man who looked something like Sylvester Stallone. The first time I saw Richie, he had a cane and a cast on his foot. I never did find out what he did to his foot, but he used the cane all summer long. Richie always came with Abby, a very pretty, polite redhead. I never could figure out why she went with Richie. Richie was our self-appointed protector. If anybody got out of line, he would handle it. He let everyone know this every day, so obviously, no one did. A year later, in the middle of a crisis with a problem youth, Richie decided he would protect one of the staff. In the process of trying to protect this staff member, he ended up breaking the staff member's nose. Richie was always on a soapbox—either extolling the virtues of Beginnings or letting someone know he didn't like what they were doing or describing great feats he was about to accomplish.

The lounge room upstairs was a quiet place where kids could go to rest from the busy pace downstairs. Folk dances, dramatics sessions, and parties were held in this room.

I stopped by for a few minutes and spent the evening. I was hooked; I spent several evenings a week at Beginnings for the rest of that summer. The conversations with the kids about their feelings, their ideas for Beginnings, and their view of the world were fascinating. When I came by, I never knew what I would find. One day the yard was covered with tie-dyed T-shirts, another day everyone was into making leather vests and hats. Of course, no matter what else was going on, there was always clay, everywhere clay. I finally broke down and tried to throw a pot. It was fun but not as easy as it looked. It took me thirty minutes to realize it wasn't for me and the rest of the night to get cleaned up. All this stuff was going on because of Fred and Stander and Fred's commune friends. They were creative, committed people. The youth loved them. When we had a dance, I was usually one of the chaperones. It was amazing. Everyone danced, there was no drinking or drugs (that I noticed), food magically appeared, everyone seemed to have a great time. Naturally, there were no problems; Richie was there!

The following description is taken from an evaluation written by the staff.

Kids came to Beginnings this summer because it was a place where they could do, create and learn, in ways they'd never had a chance to before. No formal classes were given, and instead, people learned from each other and taught each other, in an atmosphere of excited and open sharing. As staff members, we were responsible for keeping track of all the goings on, but we weren't really teachers more than anyone was. We knew a little more about how to do this, or where that was kept, but mostly, we were there to be as present to the kids as we could in whatever different ways possible. Teaching someone to throw a pot, talking to someone with a problem, learning something new from a kid who had been dying to find someone to teach it to, singing songs, leading a dramatics group, or just being a friend.

When we got into August, I could sense a sadness fall over the staff and the youth. More and more of the conversation was directed towards what a great place Beginnings was and what was going to happen when the summer was over. This progressed to anger at the board of directors for not finding a new place or holding on to the one we had.

The reality was Beginnings, as it was that summer, would die with the end of summer, but a new different Beginnings would rise to take its place. Many of that summer's participants would not be part of it; in fact, many would not feel at home at the new Beginnings. Nonetheless, many more kids than any of us had ever dreamed of would carry Beginnings to new, albeit different, heights.

In parallel with the creation and running of Suum Cuique and Beginnings, three congregational churches in Newton were working toward becoming the United Parish of Newton. Eliot Church (my church) in Newton Corner, about three miles from Second Church, First Church in Newton Center, and Second

Church where Beginnings was housed for the summer were planning to become the United Parish. As I look back, I realize if there had been no plan for a United Parish there would have been no Beginnings after that summer. By the summer of 1970, the churches had agreed to a trial union. Since Second Church was the biggest, their building would be used for Sunday services. Their members were sure that their building would be the United Parish once the trial was over. First Church was the smallest and getting smaller. They knew their building had to be sold no matter how the trial came out. Eliot had a lot of young, active, very liberal members and was the only one of the three that was growing. Eliot members did not want to give up their building. In fact, that fall, a Friday-night family education and worship program was to start at Eliot.

I got the idea of using part of Eliot's basement for Beginnings. I brought it up to the church council, and after a lot of negotiating and site visits to Second Church, it was worked out. The Newton Youth Foundation would rent (at a low price) most of the basement of Eliot under the condition that the space would be used by the church on Friday nights from five to nine. I remember suggesting that the Beginnings youth would welcome being part of the Friday-night program. The church liked this because there were not many high schools kids in the church at that time. Also, they felt that a quality youth program that paid rent would provide another reason to keep the building. It was a good thing no one, including me, knew or even dreamed about the storm that was about to hit. You have to understand that although Eliot was liberal and active, very little of its outreach ever happened in its building. The church had never had to really get its hands dirty or suffer damage to its building or put up with restrictions on how it used its space. The closest they had come was when Nixon went into Cambodia in the spring of 1970. There was a vigil in the front yard of the church with a flag-draped coffin, posters, and prayers. This vigil went on every day until midsummer, when the U.S. pulled out of Cambodia.

This protest was extremely upsetting to the more conservative part of the church, particularly when the VFW started a counterproposal across the street and tried to steal our flag, but that was nothing compared to how upset they would get about Beginnings.

The summer was over, but hopes were high, as somehow, a miracle had been worked and Beginnings would not die. The feelings and expectations of the youth can best be described by repeating a short paper the youth wrote to help convince Eliot to rent them space. The following statement was signed by eighty-nine youths ranging in age from four and half to nineteen.

Beginnings: fun . . . being myself . . . eternal . . . people . . . sharing . . . making friends . . . creating . . . life . . . music . . . rapping . . . help . . . understanding . . ."I can't say anything about Beginnings" . . . meaningful . . . getting into things . . . frantic . . . excitement . . . peaceful . . . calm . . . "I come to Beginnings to talk to people and to make things" . . . togetherness . . . contentment . . . a second home . . . happiness . . . "a place to be whatever you want to be" . . . "For me, Beginnings has been one of the most important experiences of my life—everyone should have the chance to learn how to discover with their hands, as well as their minds" . . .

We have come to the Beginnings this summer, and we've learned something here about ourselves and about other people. We feel that it is important for the program to continue. We have grown to care about Beginnings.

The summer of '70 had been a great success!

Hoods

Description of Eliot

Eliot church is located on the corner of Centre and Church streets in a part of Newton called Newton Corner. To the north and east of the church are parks—parks with benches and trees and flowers and walks. In real estate, there is a saying that the three most important things about a property are location, location, and location. In the case of a youth center, the three most important things are location, staff, and staff. Second Congregation Church, although near West Newton Square, was not near an area where kids hung out. Beginnings' clientele at Second Church came from three places: the surrounding neighborhood which was, for the most part, upper middle class or higher, Suum Cuique, and other students from Murrary Road, the alternative high school attended by most of the Suum Cuique youth. The setting of Eliot Church was quite different. The park directly north of the church on Centre Street faced the Newton Corner Business District—that is Hubbards Drugs, Wallace's Pizza Shop, Hunneywell Market, Elks Hall, and a high-rise building over the turnpike which was a Howard Johnson's Motor Lodge and Restaurant. The wall along the Centre Street edge of this park had been a youth hangout for years, and the park beside and behind the church had lots of privacy for drinking and the Lord knows what else. Newton Corner was surrounded by a lot of lower middle-class housing and some lower-class housing close to being a slum. However, to the east and south of Eliot was a neighborhood of large houses and very rich families. In fact, a mile to the south of Newton Corner was one of the richest neighborhoods in Newton.

Facilities

Once we knew we could use the space in the church, we brought the youth down from the summer Beginnings program to get their approval and to let them begin planning how the space would be used. Their eyes popped out when they saw the amount of space; it was ten times or more than we had had for the summer. The diagram that follows shows the space labeled with the church names.

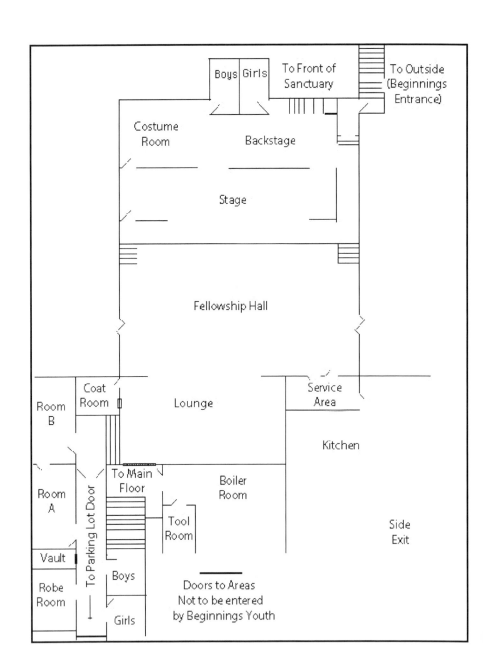

The boiler room, the upstairs, and the east end of the hallway and the three rooms off of it were out of bounds. The Beginnings entrance was the one at the front (northwest) corner of the church that came directly into the Beginnings' space and went directly out to the wall! Fellowship hall, the lounge, the boiler room, and the kitchen were at the lowest level (about fourteen-foot ceilings). The stage area and the hallway area were up about three feet, and the hallway was inclined going up as it went toward the back. Under the stage area was storage for chairs, tables, and old organ pipes.

First Impressions

I was at work when the move from Second Church occurred. I have to admit though, my mind was not on work that day. I hurried home, grabbed a quick bite, and headed for the new Beginnings. The only practical way for me to get down to Beginnings was down eight steps from the parking lot behind the church to the end of the hallway. When I got there, I had to wait for someone to come along capable of helping me in. I was lucky and got help almost at once. I remember thinking how great it would be if there was an elevator or a ramp. Little did I know those stairs may have made the difference of success and failure for Beginnings! As I came down the hallway, the first room I entered was room A. It contained the loom and mountains of stuff piled around the walls and in the center. Hidden behind the stuff were two six or seventh grade kids I didn't recognize. It turned out they lived near the church and had come in to see what was going on. Neither they nor I had any idea that we would be spending the next six years here.

I talked with them for a few minutes, the usual "Hello, I'm Fred. What are your names and what do you think of the place?" I then went into room B. Half of room B contained all the pottery equipment; the other half was like room A, full of stuff. A few youth from the summer Beginnings were working on pots; clay was already everywhere. I knew it would soon become a problem, and it did the first time one of the bathroom sinks got plugged. The lounge area contained some couches and chairs, and a few youth were sitting around talking. The hall had a coop about the size of two telephone booths made of scrap wood and chicken wire off to one side. Loud music was blasting forth from this coop, which turned out to be the music booth. It was kept locked so that kids who brought in records had some chance of getting them back. Only one or two so-called responsible youths and Stander had the keys, and hence, it was their job to play requests. The stage was piled with more Beginnings stuff and a ping-pong table. I knew the costume room was in perfect order because I had brought all the printing and graphic arts stuff down ahead of time and set it up.

I found Fred (not me) and Stander in the kitchen making tea and relaxing after a long, hard moving day. They were bubbling over with enthusiasm and talking about different ways of making use of the space. I remember jumping into this wonderful dream session and being joined by other youth whom had even bigger and better dreams. It wasn't until I got home that night that it hit me that the amount of stuff we had accumulated was incredible. It seemed like much more than we had at Second. Later, I found out that a lot more had been stored in the cellar of the Grace Church across the park because there was no room for it at Second Church. To this day, I don't know where it all came from. I guess Stander must have won the all-time dump-picking championship sometime in his life. Anyway, we spent a glorious evening weaving great plans with the various youth (from the summer) that dropped in and making specific plans for what would happen tomorrow, the official opening day of the new Beginnings. It was that night that I first thought about finding some way to spend more time at Beginnings.

The next day, the dam broke, so to speak. Beginnings opened at 2:00 PM and was soon filled with grade school kids from the Underwood School across the park. By three, junior high kids from Bigelow a few blocks away started arriving, and soon after that, the high school contingent started coming in. In the evening, we started getting an older crew (post-high school), which was the last thing we had expected and a real shock. We were in over our heads, and the water was still rising, but before I continue with the story, let me tell you about the staff.

Staff

When we opened that fall, the staff consisted of Stander, Fred, Jill, and me, although at that point, I didn't consider myself staff. Within the first few of weeks of opening, Stuart and Gail and Dick were added.

Stander Wright, director. He was best described as our resident guru. Stander was below average in height, had long dark hair, and a long slightly trimmed beard. As I have already said, he fit the hippie image well. He felt Beginnings was his creation, and The Newton Youth Foundation and the rest of us were helping him make his dream come true. The rest of us felt that he was hired to help the NYF realize its goals. This difference would eventually create problems.

Stander looked at the world through different glasses than the rest of us. He would always see the good in things, events, and kids, and he had trouble recognizing that some bad might exist. I remember one of the first meetings we had with the church committee that was formed to interface with us. The complete staff of Beginnings and several members of the church were sitting in a circle in the parlor. One by one, complaints they had were brought up, obviously expecting solutions. The first complaint was that one of the youth had taken a can of white spray paint and sprayed an archway on the side of the church (brick wall) by our entrance. Stander's reply was, "Did you notice how artistically it was done?" There was dead silence. If I could have climbed under my chair, I would have. At least the message came through loud and clear. "Don't expect any solutions."

Stander had great trouble in the director role; he didn't like being the heavy. Unfortunately, as complaints of needing a heavier hand were voiced, he would react by overreacting, thus causing more problems. In spite of this, he was great with kids, and he had a knack for making them dream and widen their horizons, and then he helped them to begin to make their dreams come true. I later heard the name "horizontal thinking" applied to this technique. It was one of the most important things I learned from Stander; I'll get back to this later. The robe room became Stander's office and the supply room. It was the only place kept locked other than the music booth; however, in this case, the staff had the keys not the youth. I remember going in to get something. The room was full of materials, but no one was in there. I had to move some stuff to get what I wanted. When I went to leave, I heard a noise, and Stander appeared from one of the cupboards at the far end of the room. He explained to me that when he needed to be alone, he climbed into the cupboard.

As the year went on, I developed ambivalence about Stander. On the one hand, I was impressed with a lot of the things he did, and on the other hand, I found it difficult to live with and interpret to the youth and the church many things he did or didn't do.

Fred Taylor, assistant director. Fred was tall and thin and had reddish-blond curly hair of about shoulder length, but you wouldn't know it because it always stuck out in all directions. He was one of the most all-around, talented people I have ever met. He sang and played a guitar. He seemed to be an expert at any type of art or craft. Fred interfaced well with people of all ages. He was intelligent, sensitive, well-read, and outgoing. All in all, it was a joy to work with Fred.

In many ways, Fred was more of a director that Stander. He would see what needed to be done and do it or speak in a nice way to get Stander to do it. If we hadn't had Fred to run interference between the church and Stander, we would have been out in the street before Halloween. Fred lived in a commune up the street from the church. It was in a large, old, run-down house that was full of worn-out rugs and broken furniture. The people who lived there were warm, friendly, intelligent, capable folk. As I said before, two others from the commune helped us out for the summer. One was a teacher and had returned to work, the other, Jill, continued to help until midwinter. I have lost track of Fred over the years, but I do know he went back to school and earned his divinity degree. I imagine some church somewhere is very lucky to have him for their minister.

Jill. She was our resident pot thrower and artisan. Although Jill was talented in lots of crafts, she spent most of her time overseeing the pottery operation. She was a born teacher and had many kids making quality items. When she left, the pottery activity was never the same. She decided to return to her home around the first of the year, and alas, she left a big hole in our program. I never had contact with her or heard any news about her since that time.

Stuart Wells. Stu was a chicken farmer who decided to become a minister. He, his wife, Gail, and four kids (ages ten to seventeen), arrived in Newton the summer Beginnings was at Second. I coordinated the summer worship services at Eliot at that time. Each week, someone different would take charge of the service. By the standards of that time, they were contemporary services. Stu and family arrived in Newton Corner on a Saturday while the coffin vigil was still in progress. As they came off the Massachusetts Turnpike and drove by the church, they decided that that was the church for them.

The next morning, our service started with coffee on the front steps. We had card tables set up with red checkered tablecloths, and as people arrived, they were greeted and served coffee and donuts. I happened to greet Stu et al. To make a long story short, Stu talked Andover Newton Seminary into sponsoring him as a Beginnings staff member as part of his work-study requirements. I know Stu looks back on that year at Beginnings with fond memories and amazement, for it was an incredible experience, and we often reminisce about it.

Stu was a big, stocky man over six feet tall who was very good at anything connected with building a house or fixing things. He was not the least bit intimidated by kids. In other words, he was the ideal addition to our staff at that time. Since Fred was thinking about the ministry, they immediately hit it off. So did Stu and I; in fact, we have been close friends ever since, and his

oldest son, John, worked for me at GTE from the time he got out
of college until I retired.

Gail Wells. An added benefit of having Stu on the staff was that we
often had his wife. Gail had just completed her BA in education
and was a teacher at a junior high school in Waltham, a town
adjacent to Newton.

Gail got her kids and some of the youth to run a snack bar out of
the kitchen on Friday and Saturday nights. It was kind of a family
affair, as their kids often came to Beginnings. Beginnings that first
year was a very frightening place to many adults; Gail's teaching
and temperament both helped her function well at Beginnings.
Once Stu completed his divinity degree, Gail went to Andover
Newton and earned hers. Today, they have an interim ministry in
Washington State.

Dick Rosenberg. I am not quite sure when Dick started coming by
Beginnings; I don't think I ever did know how he got involved.
I just know he was there. He only came on the weekends. He
would slip in and do his thing. That was playing the piano and
playing ping-pong and rapping with the youth. He wasn't paid;
he just came. Volunteers came in two flavors—those that helped
and those that needed help.

The latter kind we didn't need. If a volunteer came in and asked,
"What shall I do?" my inclination was to say, "Go home!" If a
staff person had to spend time making volunteers useful, the net
gain was usually not worth it. Dick was one of the good kind of
volunteers; he would come in and do his thing and leave. He had
a following of youth who spent a lot of time with him, and both
he and they seemed to benefit. I never spent much time talking
or getting to know the good volunteers, as we were both too
busy with the youth. Dick came in for most of that first year. To
the surprise of us all, we found out after Dick left that he was a
Catholic priest.

Other staff came and went as the year progressed. I'll cover them
as they fit in the chronology.

Michael

One of the two kids that were in room A the night of the day we moved in was Michael Solomita. He was twelve going on forty, had dark hair, glasses, and looked very studious. He had three younger brothers and seven older brothers and sisters. Michael wanted, in the worst way, to be popular, as many of his siblings were, but he always screwed it up. He took a lot of ridicule from his peers, and he reacted to this by putting them down. He would bring someone new to Beginnings and go to great lengths to tell me what a useless person this was and then watch the person become more popular than him.

Michael stayed away from sports, probably because he was not well coordinated. He liked craft-type stuff but didn't want to be laughed at. He would try to gain stature by what he possessed rather than who he was. His brothers and sisters were popular, and that kind of brought him along, but he never really made it. It turned out I had a shadow for the next three-plus years, and I also had a great source of information. Michael would tell me about kids that hadn't come in yet; he would tell me what to watch out for, and he would warn me if something was going on behind my back. His descriptions usually turned out to be much more negative than the real case, thank God.

Much to my surprise, I became the subject of school compositions and plays and was mentioned numerous times in the yearbooks of the next few years. One such composition was written by Michael, describing his thoughts when he first met me[12]. He got a B+. He stayed close to staff, primarily me, because that was safe, and it gave him a feeling of superiority that he sorely needed. His big moment came a few years later when we put on *West Side Story*. He was cast as Bernardo, the leader of the PRs. He finally got to be what he always wanted to be—a brave, tough leader.

[12.] See Appendix A.

Confrontation and Problems

Stu's Journa

The numbers of kids involved was rewarding but devastating. We didn't have enough staff, supplies, or equipment to deal with it. In the afternoon, we set up craft classes for the younger kids and tried to get older kids to help out, but the result was as inevitable as holding back the tide with a sandcastle. How can you teach twenty kids to make something out of leather when you have three sets of tools and no table? I remember those first few weeks as incredibly wild. So far, the high school-aged kids were mostly the summer kids from Murray Road and their friends. The younger kids came from the local grade school, and fortunately, most of them were not allowed out at night. The junior high was a mix from the area and the summer contingent. The clash we expected between the Newton Corner kids and the summer kids hadn't happened yet.

Stuart Wells wrote a detailed account of the period from November 6 to January 7. Here is some of his journal entries with some of my recollections interspersed.

November 6, 1970

The grand opening was held today. It was a tremendous success despite the many problems we had to overcome. Too much was left to the last minute, but somehow, we managed to get everything done.

Decided to keep this journal so I might as well record some reflections of the last week. At the present time, there are no age limits at either end.[13] I have reservations on the effect of the wide range on the effectiveness of the program. I have been surprised at the cooperation between age groups. I witnessed a 10 yr. old

---

13. We had to restrict Beginnings to Junior High and High school youth. Stander fought this for a while, but we had no choice.

girl who had just thrown her first pot teaching an eighteen year old boy how to work the potter's wheel. There is a real need for some area for quiet as a retreat from the noise.

T. was trying to get information on drug abuse by students of high school age. He wanted to use this as an English project. The answers he had received reflected bravado and, I expect, a lack of knowledge about drugs. There were comments like "I shoot pot and smoke acid," "There's no fuckin' problem with the kids, just the asses who try to stop us," "Drug problem? Just for the law." I sat and talked with him and answered his questions honestly. Several others attempted to help by giving honest answers, and a bunch of us sat and rapped a while about drugs. T2 said his Dad was working "all out" towards the legalization of pot and that all the students at a nearby college used all sorts of stuff.

I have heard for years that "you can't trust anyone over thirty" but have never been subjected to that distrust before because I have always been working in an established group, and there have always been kids that I knew well to vouch for me. I have been aware of a degree of distrust bordering on hostility from many of those who are coming to Beginnings. There are several large families that are well-represented in the program. Without exception, I find that the younger 10-14 year-olds accept me much more readily than their older brothers and sisters who might be 16-18 years old.

D. (16 Yrs) is especially hostile. He comes from a real unhappy situation. One rumor was that he is selling drugs to finance a new start when he ran away from home. Stander had him doing the lights for the grand opening. He is excellent at this type of thing and he kept coming regularly. I'm afraid that his interest was in the marketplace[14] and not in the program, but time will see. Drugs are going to be one of the real problems for the program, as already there are rumors of one attempt by

[14.] Suum Cuique

an outsider to peddle drugs. The kids sent whomever it was packing.

November 12

"I'm getting tired of this shit!" K. had just gone into the kitchen. There was cocoa spread all over the floor. Each day, the situation has been getting worse. Kids mess up the room and then leave. The regulars (and the staff) spent all their time cleaning up. About a dozen boys were racing around the room slamming doors and just raising hell. Like termites, they had infested the underside of the stage. I was in the shop at the back of the stage when I heard a deafening roar. There was total silence. Gradually, sounds started to come alive again, and I realized that the roar I had heard was Stander calling the troops to attention. About fifteen minutes later, there was a general meeting of all those present. We went around to each room, gathering all the flock. They drifted into the main room, sitting down in little clusters of two, three, or more. They spread out on the chairs that were set up for a meeting later that night. The way they sat was really where we were at now. There was no community, no awareness of each other, nothing. Just a number of kids working off their frustrations and hostilities after being cooped up all day. There were just forty odd young people encapsulated in their own separate selves and their own conclaves. I confess it was a demoralizing sight.

Stander surveyed the group assembled. He asked if they knew the purpose of the meeting. After that, they talked about the noise and the destruction. In a quiet voice, he started to explain why what had been happening was hurting the program. No histrionics, just a quiet statement of facts. He asked each of them to think about the problem and talk about it. He insisted that each person respect the others' right to speak and recognized one after another until most had had their say. There were no recriminations, just an insistence that the group set their own guidelines. People started to get up one or two at a time. I was upset until I realized that they were starting to clean up. When

I left, several were still gathered around Stander talking about their problems.

November 20

The Confrontation

Then came the confrontation. About fifty hoods arrived to check us out. (When the term "hoods" or "freaks[15]" are used, it is in the same sense that the kids use them to describe each other. They do not describe any individual kid with accuracy but are useful to describe the group involved.) Despite the noise of the record played and the general confusion, the silence was deafening. Suddenly, the Beginnings kids or freaks were a group united against the hoods. Would this set off a reaction? Did the hoods intend to call attention to themselves by violence? There was no way to know.

I am digressing from the journal at this point to fill in some details that followed the silence. Slowly, things started to happen; kids went back to what they were doing. The hoods were sitting across the front of the stage. None of them moved, none of them talked, and none of the freaks spoke to them. I remember going over and attempting to strike up a conversation with them. I think they were as scared as I was. After a while, barriers seemed to ease a little, and they ventured off the stage. I was in the kitchen along with some hoods and freaks when an argument broke out. After a little shouting, a knife appeared. More yelling and swearing. Then the kid with the knife took off out the back door and across the park after another kid. Some of the hoods went after him. It all happened so fast there was no time to react. Very soon, the hood who was in the lead after the kid with the knife, Kevin, came back. He said something like, "We stopped it. Everything is okay." Kevin, in the years to come, became a leader of Beginnings. You will hear lots more about him.

---

15. Stu's word for hippies.

Back to the Journal

November 30

We have had a second encounter. It helped define the problems we are dealing with and no serious damage occurred. Church members are upset and I don't blame them. With so many rooms and so few staff, it seemed to be impossible for us to handle the situation. After the confrontation, about fifteen of the kids representing both groups sat down to talk over their differences. The differences are considerable. The hoods are very pro-war; many of their older brothers are fighting in Vietnam. Their music is The Supremes (and nothing else). They are abusive to their friends and apt to be quite rough toward one another.[16] Alcohol is their vehicle for escape. The freaks are antiwar, somewhat more considerate of each other, go for Dylan and the Stones, and their method of escape is apt to be pot and other drugs. They are interested in arts and crafts while the hoods seem to be interested in throwing pots only to break them.[17] It may be that the expectations of the two groups are so dissimilar that we may be forced to choose one group or the other. I don't know how we could do that. We closed down on Friday and Saturday to avoid another confrontation and to give us some time to work on the problem. We have been meeting with groups of kids to talk over the problems. We will try to involve the leaders of the hoods in the discussions. At least, we may find out what each group wants from Beginnings.

December 5

We are having some success getting to know the individuals within the group of hoods, as a few of them come in during the week to see what Beginnings is all about. The problem of the two distinct groups is still the overwhelming fact we face on weekends. Friday night, we were bolstered by the addition of

---

[16.] However, if a friend is threatened, they are all solidly behind him or her.

[17.] To my surprise, this turned out to be wrong in most cases.

ix teachers from the Underwood Elementary School, who came
n response to our need. They brought refreshments—soda and
potato chips—to share with everyone at the dance we held. They
also brought a new spirit into the situation. They managed to get
people dancing, and the hostilities of the previous weeks were
not evident.

Saturday night, some of the kids put on a two-act play, complete
with costumes and scenery. It was successful, except most of
the hoods were background noise, not audience. After the play,
we arranged to have a rock band perform for a dance. For some
reason, it took them an hour to set up. The tension in the hall
became unbearable. The same people were there, and we tried to
do the same type of things as the previous night. Nothing worked
and the two groups were separate and distinct.

December 18

Friday night was terrible and we decided to close down. Saturday,
the staff agreed to adopt four rules: No drinking, no drugs,
no fighting or abuse of people, and no willful destruction of
property. Actually, these rules had been in effect, but we decided
they should be posted and a means established to deal with
the violations. If any rule is broken, we would stop things long
enough to notify everyone. The third violation meant closing for
the night. The kids had to police the place for themselves now.

December 24

Christmas Eve, I refused to try to keep the place open by myself.
The rest of the staff was away. I did not think that many would be
there, and I wanted to spend the evening with my family. After
I walked through the snowstorm to Eliot for a church service,
I went over to the drug store across the street. Met five hoods
who wanted to know why we were closed. While I was there, two
of them went over to the phone booth and sat with the receiver
to their ear. The owner came over and grabbed the phone, said,
"Just as I thought, you didn't put money in." He pulled both out
and kicked all five out into the storm.

January 7

We held a meeting to see what could be done to meet the financia
crisis that besets us. Ten thousand dollars in debt; unable tc
effectively run the very minimum program; run by a staff tha
gets less than fifty cents per hour, a staff physically, emotionally
and spiritually exhausted. We came together as a staff meeting tc
try and decide what to do. We had announced that we would be
closed. We had the doors locked. We had a sign saying we were
closed until later that afternoon. A pallor of doom pervaded the
room. The final blow had been that the state grant was a mere
$2500 instead of $60,000 that had been requested. All illusions
shattered, it looked like Beginnings would close.

Despite the locked doors, despite the sign, despite the feeling of
hopelessness, they came. Pounding on the door, demanding to
be let in. They came and a new resurgence of hope came with
them. The very people that the program exists to serve came to
serve the program. Not a large number as numbers go, perhaps
not over twenty-five. J. came with a jar filled with money.
Having typed out fifty-five statements about Beginnings, she
and M. stood outside one of the local grocery stores and collected
money. She brought in $100—enough for one day and enough
for hope.

S. was there. She lay down in the snow outside the window,
peering through and pleading that we open the door so that she
could come in and add silent witness to our cause.

C. was there. A few nights before, he had admitted that he was
a drug-dependent person and had pledged to himself—through
the help of one of our staff—not to use drugs at all this year. In his
own continuing need, he still wanted to give of himself.

One after another, they came and, in a most orderly fashion,
offered advice and expressed their willingness to help. A new
children's crusade is starting, a crusade to save a place to be. If
there is only time enough, if we can find the right adults to help,
perhaps it still possible that the dream might be kept alive.

Three months' time and some kids are speaking to us for the first time. Three months and now you find a girl stationing herself outside the door, warning kids not to bring in liquor and to "behave 'cause we got two offenses already and one more and we close up." My mind goes back to Christmas Eve. Is there really no room in the inn? Kids are thrown out of the store when they just want to get warm. There is much more to be gained here. Must Beginnings also kick them out?

Hoods are People

Michael who was always near was next to me when the confrontation described in Stu's journal started. Michael's remark as the hoods came in was, "Oh my God, it's Malcolm!" Michael had been filling me in on Malcolm for days. Malcolm was a ninth-grade boy who had a reputation of destroying whatever he touched. Last winter, the Newton Community Center where Stander's wife worked had opened a drop-in center a block up the street from Eliot. Malcolm, according to Michael, single-handedly closed it before it had been open a week. He had ripped radiators off the wall, trashed everything, thrown pool balls through windows, etc.

Malcolm had an older brother a few years out of high school, who, according to Michael, would come and beat up anyone who gave Malcolm a hard time.[18] Needless to say, at that point, one thing we didn't need was Malcolm, but as things turned out, we had Malcolm until he graduated from high school. Malcolm turned out to be a very positive force in Beginnings.

When I was growing up in Newton Corner, there was a kid named Bill Byrne who I thought of as kind of an idol. He was three to five years older than I and a leader among his peers. He went on to be a social worker and director of the Newton Community Center where Stander's wife was now working. Bill Byrne died of a brain tumor as his wife was giving birth to their

18. I never met or even saw Malcolm's brother.

sixth child (fifth son). Kevin was his next to oldest son. The Byrne brothers—Bill, Kevin, Tom and Jimmy, and Johnny—when they were old enough, took an active role in Beginnings and had a lo do with its success. Somehow, I became a pseudofather in some ways to Kevin, Tommy, and Jimmy. You will hear more abou the brothers Byrne as this story unfolds, but let me tell you some about them now.

Bill, the oldest, was in the Marines going through basic training at the time Beginnings opened in Newton Corner. He came back around Christmas because of a medical discharge. Bill had left home at fourteen, shortly after his father died, because of problems with his mother's new boyfriend. Somehow, Bill supported himself and got through high school. His goal was to become a policeman. During those early Beginnings years, he was a police cadet on the Newton force and also worked as a railroad security guard. In the years to come, he helped me in so many ways it's impossible to describe them all; suffice it to say, he helped me handle many difficult situations. Today, Bill is a detective with the Newton Police Force.

Kevin was the next oldest. He loved sports as did all his brothers. He was a leader, he was a comic, and he was really great individual. Kevin was in the middle of the knife incident the night of the encounter, and in the years to come, he became a big help in controlling the program. Kevin married Lorraine, a girl he met at Beginnings. He went to college at nights while working at Raytheon and has had a long successful career as an \engineer at Raytheon.

Tommy, the next oldest, was in ninth grade at the time we opened. His whole life was sports and girls. Tommy went to UMass and got a degree in history. Since then, he has worked as a painter and a barkeeper and at Raytheon. He is still active in sports and is still chasing girls.[19]

---

19. Since I wrote this, Tommy has married and is running his own business.

immy was in the sixth grade when Beginnings opened. Jimmy played Tony in *West Side Story*[20] and Sodapop in *The Outsiders*. He graduated from UMass, painted houses, and then did very well selling insurance. He also married a girl who came into Beginnings. He gave me a picture of he and I at the wedding; the caption still makes mw fell real nice and brings tears to my eyes. It was:

"Never reluctant to give, but hesitent to receive.
There can be no finer friend, on that you can believe."

He has recently quit the insurance business to become a social worker. He has been a Big Brother for several years and is a leader in that organization. From the very beginning, I felt the time I was spending would be worth it, and I would be a success if just one youth in future years picked up the torch. Jimmy did for a while but is now running his own painting business.

Johnny was too young for Beginnings but did come in a little in the last year it was open. Johnny also graduated from UMass.

The encounter in Stu's journal was the beginning of the end of the hippie control of Beginnings. The funny thing is that in the long run, Beginnings turned the hoods into hippies rather than the hoods changing the goals of Beginnings. Unfortunately, many of the youth who were so active in starting Beginnings dropped out one by one for a variety of reasons—the distance they had to travel, the problems and fears they had of the hoods, the inability to exert the control they had had during the summer, and just the fact that their needs and lives changed.

Church Conflict

As the first year at Eliot progressed, the church had lots of reasons to be angry, frightened, and puzzled about the Beginnings' program. In this section, I have summarized this situation.

---

20. Our dramatics program is covered later.

Wear and Tear. Let's face it—the building was taking a beating
There was more kids in the fellowship hall in one week that
there had been people in the hall since the church had been buil
in 1958. The hall had always been kept immaculate. Ernest, the
sexton, had kept the floors clean and waxed so you could see
your reflection in them. There were twelve big lights that hung
down about four feet from the ceiling in the hall and four more
in the lounge. The stage had a shiny, unmarred hardwood floor
and the grounds had always been kept clean and neat. After a
few months, the floors were filthy and full of cigarette burns. The
lights were prime targets for anything that could be thrown and
one by one, were biting the dust. The panels along the front of
the stage were rapidly disappearing from kids sitting on the edge
of the stage and kicking their feet. The yard was always full of
beer cans, especially on Sunday mornings, and the kitchen and
bathrooms were disaster areas.

Ernest had a desk and an easy chair in a small room off the boiler
room. He would sit in there and shake his head. The agreement
had been that Beginnings would take over responsibility for
maintenance of the space they used. This helped the church,
as Ernest was close to retirement and had been having more
and more trouble keeping the building clean. We tried, Lord
knows we tried, but it was a losing battle. We would sweep up
each night, and we would mop the floors every week or two.
We mopped the pottery area every day. We made a clay washer
out of a fifty-gallon drum and a pump and screen, which kept
most of the clay out of the hall and bathrooms. We cleaned
the bathrooms, and we tried to pick up beer cans particularly
on Saturday nights after we closed. Ever try to find beer cans
in the dark? It was not easy; in fact, it was impossible. The
Sunday-morning worshippers were always greeted by some
cans. One would have been too many.

Probably the major point of contention was the conflict with the
Friday-night program, which used the Beginnings' space. The
initial plan was to close by five so the Friday-night people could
come in and set up tables and chairs, etc. Some of the Beginnings
kids who lived further away would stay for the Friday-night

rogram. The Friday-night program started out with a potluck upper. The problem was the Beginnings kids brought no food ut made up for it by being first in line and taking a lot of food. Another problem was that as the program went on, Beginnings kids would show up and be waiting inside and out for the church program to be over. This caused two problems—the kids inside listurbed the program, and the kids outside frightened the church people and little kids when they left.

This was solved in a rather creative way—at least I thought t was because there was something in it for everyone. It was lecided thst we would close at five and not reopen on Fridays. It was also decided that the Beginnings kids would be paid to set up the table and chairs when they closed at five. We would hold a drawing to see who got to do the work and earn the money. What we really hadn't thought out was that we were providing an easy way for them to get their beer money for the weekend. Oh well, nothing's perfect. The next year, we closed all day Fridays and set up the tables and chairs Thursday night. This worked even better, as then almost no one was around on Fridays. I remember, one very cold Friday night in the middle of the winter, coming to the church at about nine o'clock. I was greeted by one of the older Beginnings youth. My comment was something like, "What in the world are you doing out here on a night like this!" He responded by opening the long winter coat he was wearing. Inside his coat, on both sides, were pockets, each one containing a cold can of beer. He must have had a least two six-packs. His comment was simply, "Drinking." I still get cold just thinking about it.

An example of the kind of things that happened was one Friday night (the first year), the church treasurer came in to get something out of or put something inside the vault. The vault was a walk-in vault that was along the hallway between the choir room and room A. For months, the kids had been trying to work out the combination to the vault, of course to no avail. They were obsessed with curiosity about what was in the vault. In comes the treasurer. He opens the vault and goes in, leaving the door wide open. Many of the youth gathered around to see what was in the vault. They leaned against the door, and, of course, it started to close. The treasurer panicked, pushed the door open, hitting a kid, closed the vault, and ran. Needless to say, the kid who wa hit, some weeks later, got even by inflicting some compensatory damage to the treasurer's car.

I remember one Sunday morning sitting in church. The sermor was just about to begin; everything got very quiet. All of a sudden Beatles music comes blasting up from downstairs. The minister left the pulpit with robes flying and me right behind. He and I went charging downstairs. What we found was two Beginnings kids mopping the floor. They decided to surprise me by cleaning the place up and, without thinking, turned the radio on. Some days, you just can't win.

Needless to say, whatever happened at the church, Beginnings was at fault. If something was missing or broken or misplaced, Beginnings did it. I remember getting to be almost paranoid about what would happen next. As I look back, I don't see how we got through the first year. We had a lot to learn, the Church had a lot to learn, and the youth had a lot to learn. Somehow we all got an education.

Weekend Nights

In the fall of that first year, Friday and Saturday nights were a nightmare. We would usually have a hundred or more youth, most of them either drunk or high. Our rules, of course, were no drugs and no alcohol; however, enforcing these rules was not a simple thing. We didn't have enough staff to be everywhere. We had a rule that if we had three-rule infractions we would close down for the night. The problem was this meant over one hundred mad, drunk youth would suddenly be let loose on the neighborhood. You can imagine the results. A lot of the kids would drink first and then come to Beginnings to sober up. I'm not talking about just high school-aged kids or junior high age but grade school age!

.et me introduce you to Charlie. He was in the fourth grade when
ve opened. He had a brother in the eighth grade, a sister in the
ixth, and a sister in the tenth. He also had a younger brother
nd sister. Charlie was a permanent fixture at Beginnings; he
vas there afternoons and evenings whenever we were open. He
vould come in drunk every weekend night and, once and a while,
t other times. Charlie was a major problem to us when he was
ober; he was a tornado when he was drunk. About eight months
after we opened, Charlie's father showed up and bawled us out
or letting Charlie come in when he was drunk and for not letting
iim know. First, we let him in because we were afraid of what he
would do outside. Second, we found it hard to believe that his
parents couldn't tell their sons and daughters were coming home
drunk. Third, we had a hard time understanding how parents
could let a fourth grader out until nine on school nights and
eleven on weekends. However, the main reason was the minute
we started calling parents and telling on their kids, the show was
over. We had to walk a very thin line. On the one hand, we had
maintained the respect of the youth and, on the other, keep them
from killing themselves and others.

One Friday night, Charlie showed up drunk as usual but also
crying and yelling, "I burned my dick! I burned my dick!" It seems
Charlie had been drinking with Eddy in his barn, where they had
a table and a candle and two six packs. Once they downed their
beer, Eddy dared Charlie to stick his penis into the candle. He
did and, hence, the entrance. We were left to deal with a crying
Charlie while Eddy stood around laughing.

I remember people expressing fear of coming in to help, but
some brave souls did come to try and help. As mentioned in the
journal, the principal of the elementary school across the park,
three teachers, a teacher's aide, and her husband showed up. The
aide's husband always carried a hammer; he wasn't taking any
chances.

They came with guitars and tried to get the youth singing. In fact,
one of the teachers, Lisa Newstat, started a gospel-singing group

a few years later called The Angel Band, which became quite
popular. They had heard about Beginnings from the children tha
had been coming in the afternoons and decided to help. One o
them taught kids to carve soapstone in the midst of the madnes
of a weekend night. We were beginning to make progress wher
one Friday night, two older boys were caught shooting dope ir
the bathroom by one of the teachers. It was brought to Stander'
attention, and they waited to see what action Stander woulc
take. Stander's response was simply far less than they expected
and as a result, they decided they couldn't back the program
anymore. It was a big loss; they had had a big impact on many
youth.

Fears and Progress

Killer?

We had several real scares that first year, but probably the one
event that scared me the most was dealing with a youth named
G—. Michael had filled me in before G—ever showed up. G—was
out of high school, real mean, and had killed one of his teachers
a few years ago. Supposedly, he had been driving along and
saw his teacher on the corner and swerved and ran her over.[21]
G—had been in jail and had just been released. One afternoon,
G—showed up. He looked mean, he pushed kids around, and
he scared the whole place, staff, and kids. The staff had been
discussing the advisability of limiting the program to high school
and under for several weeks. All were in favor of it but Stander,
who didn't like the idea of excluding anyone. After a few visits
from G—, we announced that from then on, only kids in school
or eighteen or under would be allowed in. Obviously, G—didn't
like it.

Rumors went around that G—and a few of his friends were going
to take it out on some of our younger kids. These guys were real

---

[21.] To this day, I don't know whether that story was true.

rave! The next few weeks were real scary. The anticipation was
aking its toll on the staff and the kids. We stationed Stu, our
iggest staff member, at the door whenever possible and waited.
One night, some older kids showed up. Stu met them at the door
and explained the situation. They obviously weren't too pleased.
Richie, the protector, was protecting Stu, backing him up so to
speak. One of the kids started getting real rude so Richie went to
hit him. Back came Richie's elbow, and—*crack!*—Stu had a broken
nose. At that point, the youth left. G—finally did come by, and
the word quickly went around that he was waiting outside to
grab some little kid. Somehow, we got G—to leave, but I don't
remember how. In spite of many threats, he left and nothing ever
happened. We kept waiting for him to reappear but he never did.
Then we heard he was back in jail, and all of Beginnings breathed
a sigh of relief.

Drugs

Drugs were one of our biggest concerns. Beer was hard to
smuggle in without getting caught, but drugs were another
story. At that time, I had no idea of what pot smelled like; it
wasn't long before I learned. We began to smell pot in the stage
area and bathrooms. One Friday night, we noticed a guy in a
raincoat, who would come in and sit on the stage. Every once
in a while, one of the youth would go over and talk to him,
and then they would both leave. In a little while, the youth
would reappear, and then the guy would come back and wait
for someone else to come up to him. It was obvious we had
a dealer; it was not clear what the best thing to do was. If we
called the police, he would probably be arrested and out of
business at least for a while. The problem was we didn't want a
big headline the next morning that says Drug Dealer Captured
at Beginnings.

We finally came up with a plan. The next time he came in, Stander
would go upstairs and wait at the top of the stairs that went from
the back of the stage up to the church. Then Stu would go up to

the dealer and say he would like to talk to him and ask him to come upstairs where it was quiet. Once they got him upstairs, they planned to search him, find drugs, and quietly call the police. The first part worked great. With a little encouragement—Stu was a lot bigger—he came upstairs with Stu. When someone as big as Stu has your arm, you go where Stu wants you to. Stander met them and they confronted him with dealing. Of course, he denied it, so they said, "Prove it. Let us search you." All they found was one joint. They threatened him, told him not to come back, and led him outside. All this happened without the rest of the youth in Beginnings the least bit aware of what was going down. We found out later that his car parked around the corner was full of drugs. He would make his contact in Beginnings and take them around the corner to make the deal. Fortunately for us, we never saw him again.

Ricky

Almost as soon as I met Michael, he warned me about the Barrisanos—Ricky and Bobby. According to Michael, these guys were really tough. Bobby was the oldest. He was out of high school, and once we changed the age rules, he wasn't allowed in. Ricky was younger and an alcoholic. He was a real nice kid when he was sober but a major problem when he was drunk. Right after we opened, Ricky came in and asked Stander to go to court with him, and somehow Ricky stayed out of jail. It seems that one night, when Ricky was drunk, he got into an argument with his girl's father and threw a flat iron at him. Ricky wanted Stander to be a character witness, so Stander went to court with him and somehow Ricky stayed out of jail. I'm not sure what Stander said, but Ricky seemed to think it helped, and hence, Ricky tried not to cause us any problems. His brother Bobby, in those days, was heavily into drugs. It was some of his friends we caught shooting up in the bathroom. Bobby was quite angry about the age limit, but he stayed away. Ricky didn't cause any big problems the first year, but he made up for it the next year, and amazingly, Bobby helped us handle it, but that's another story that comes later.

Unholy Duo

've already mentioned Charlie and Eddy, the unholy duo. I
;uess when you get a large group of kids together, you end up
vith a few that will do anything to get attention. Charlie was
n the fourth grade and would do anything the big kids dared
1im to do. Big kids to him were anybody in the sixth grade or
)lder. Eddy, on the other hand, loved to get others in trouble.
3ringing Charlie and Eddy together were like bringing gasoline
1nd a match together. The first time I met Eddy, he had a bonfire
;oing on the sidewalk outside the church. He was mad because I
nade him put it out. It seemed like I spent that first year trying to
<eep Charlie from hurting himself and Beginnings and trying to
<eep Eddy from hurting everyone else.

Eddy didn't like one of the hippie-type girls, so he spread a rumor
that she had made sexual advances toward him. This, to Eddy,
was the best of both worlds. He got attention as being a stud and
he hurt the girl. Eddy didn't seem to realize that everyone was
laughing at him because they knew he was lying; unfortunately,
the girl wasn't laughing because she thought everyone believed
it. It took Eddy about a month to drive her out of Beginnings in
spite of efforts by our staff members to get her to stay.

One afternoon, Charlie came running in, yelling, "Hide me, hide
me! They're after me!" "They" were members of the Elk Lodge
across the street. They were after Charlie because they caught
him stealing liquor from their bar. I remember waiting for the
Elks to show up but they never did. It puzzled me for a while
until one of the kids filled me in. Beginnings was a haven no one
would follow them in. Adults were too frightened of the place
and some kids were too. We tried to change that image, but I am
not sure we ever did.

Progress and Problems

It wasn't all bad; lots of good things happened that first year.
We managed to keep a reasonable amount of crafts going,

primarily pottery, leather, and printing. Games also became a major activity. Belt tag seemed to always be going on, bu there was also a big interest in ping-pong, chess, and Stratego Some of the youth put on a play one Friday night for the res of the youth. It wasn't received too well. Chucky Manning, a ninth grader who was kind of a leader of the ninth graders really liked the games. He was a very good-looking young man albeit very small. He was also a fierce fighter and demanded respect from everyone. Chucky liked to win and that was my edge. Chucky would come from school to Beginnings; he got there so fast I was sure he must have run most of the way He would come in and say, "Fred, I'm going to beat you at ping-pong. I'm going to beat you at chess, and then I'm going to beat you at Stratego. I would then proceed to beat him at all three. This happened day after day. Chucky eventually became a very good ping-pong player and finally was able to beat me.

The ping-pong table had been on the stage and covered with junk. One day, one of the kids decided it would be a good idea to bring it down into the hall and start using it. When they got it set up, I challenged one of them to a game. At first, they didn't think I could play because I was in a wheelchair, but when I beat them, they had a tough time handling it. How could they get beaten by someone sitting down? The truth was I was a good player, but I also had an edge because it threw off even good players' games to play me. I became the standard—beat Fred and you were good. Chucky[22] tried as hard as anyone, and he finally did succeed in spite of the fact that he had a very short reach.

One of Chucky's brothers, Mark, was really into crafts. Sometimes in the middle of one of the weekend madhouse nights, he would ask me to let him work on his latest leather project.

[22.] Chucky had a severe drinking problem but overcame it and is now an electrician.

It was always refreshing to have someone do something on weekend nights besides drink. Mark did excellent work; he made a pair of boots that were envied by everyone else. Mark really liked crafts and spent a lot of time at Beginnings making things. The other Manning brother was Glen. He liked sports and games like Chuckie. Glen was the least demanding of the Mannings, caused the least trouble, and has done well with his life.

Streetcars

One day, I came in to find a sixteen-year-old boy, Paul, setting up a tent in the hallway outside the boiler room. It wasn't just any old tent; it was a very expensive tent. He had great trouble understanding why he couldn't have a tent in the hallway. Fortunately, I got there before he started driving pegs. I had met Paul before but never had a chance to talk with him. I found out he lived in the very rich neighborhood up the street but was in a constant battle with his father although he had a lot more that any teenager had a right to expect. As I talked with him, I had the uneasy feeling that he wasn't playing with a complete set of blocks. He started telling me about the streetcar his father had given him for his birthday—an old broken-down car that he was going to fix up. It was currently sitting on a back track at the Lake Street Car Yard. He explained that he had a love affair with streetcars, and someday, wanted to drive one.

It happen sooner than I thought. A few days later, the story o
the day was that Paul had stolen a streetcar. Actually, he stol
a car and drove it into Boston, collecting fares and droppin
them off. Then he got stuck on a switch, so he got out and lef
a carful of riders. Next, he stole another car and wrecked it to
the tune of $60,000 damage. Paul ended up in the psychiatri
ward at McClean Hospital, and I never heard what happen to
him after that.

Signs of Progress

The youth had a hard time with Stander and his office. They
wondered why he needed an office and what he did in there
they never knew he was hiding in the closet. The staff had a lo
of the same feelings but didn't say much. For some reason, it was
decided to move the office up to the costume room behind the
stage and to move the graphic arts stuff down to room B. When
this happened, it left the choir room full of junk but unused.
Malcolm and Chucky and their gang of friends talked me into
letting them clean it up and use it for playing games. I didn't
want to do it because I thought all they wanted was a drinking
room and told them so. After a lot of bargaining, it was decided
they could use the room on a trial basis, but if they got caught
drinking, it would be closed. I've never seen those kids work so
hard. They came in early one Saturday and started cleaning and
furnishing their room. By suppertime, it was clean and neat; it
had a big table in it and chairs surrounding it. Saturday night,
they announced they were going in the room to play cards. In
they went, and, of course, they locked the door. I checked up
on them quite often. Fortunately, I had a key so they couldn't
keep me out. The first few times, everything seemed fine, but
then the next time, I went in I got some bad vibes. Something
wasn't right.

There was nothing wrong that I could see but it just didn't feel
right. I asked them if they had smuggled beer in, as the room
had a window that made that very easy. I thought Malcolm had
something under his jacket, but I wasn't sure. They were all

ilent, and then Chucky took a beer out from under his jacket
nd said, "Hell, Fred, I can't lie to you!" Then one by one, each
ne of them pulled out beers and said essentially the same
hing. Their next question was, "You're not going to shut the
vhole place down are you?" Here it is—the classic dilemma
vhen dealing with kids. Do you punish them the same way
vhen they admit their guilt as when they are caught? I asked
hem how they got the beer in and got the answer—"Through
he window." My response was, "Get it out of here the same
vay, and get lost for the night." They never asked to use the
:ard room again.

_ater that year, after the hoods were well integrated into
3eginnings, Stander earned his keep in one of the most brilliant
noves I have ever seen. One of the girls from the summer
3eginnings had put her pocketbook down in room B, the craft
:oom full of junk. When she came to get it, she found someone had
itolen all her money—a few dollars. She reported it to Stander,
who stopped all activities to announce what had happened,
delivered a minisermon on stealing, and suggested that the guilty
parties return the money. A little later, a timid sixth grader came
to Stander and told him he had been in the room behind one of
the piles of junk and seen Malcolm and Chucky take the money.
He pleaded with Stander not to let on he had told or he would be
severely beaten up.

Now comes Stander's move. He waited until he saw Malcolm
and Chucky alone and asked them to come in the boiler room
with him. (The boiler room was almost the only place where
you could get privacy in those days.) Stander then pulled out
his wallet and said, "All I have is ten dollars, but if you're
so in need of money that you have to steal it, you need this
more than I do." Of course, they protested and denied their
guilt and refused to take it, but Stander handed them the ten
bucks and walked out. A short while after that, I went into the
men's room and found Malcolm and Chucky whispering in the
corner. They handed me a fistful of change and bills and said,
"Please return this to Carol, but don't tell anyone we gave it
to you."

While I'm talking about surprises—one day, I had Eddy Smith and a few other kids with me. We had been doing some errands and on the way back, I stopped at my house for something. The kids were excited about finally seeing where I lived. When we got back in the car, Eddy said, "You have a six-pack of Miller in your fridge. I didn't know you drink." My answer was, "What were you doing in my refrigerator?" Eddy then explained that he had hidden the beer in the backseat of the car but then took it back. His explanation was, "I don't know why, but I can't steal from you." In the youth-center business, sometimes there are rewards.

To the hoods at that time, stealing was second nature. I think they felt that if you got away with it, it was okay. They were planning to ride their bikes out to a lake about ten miles away, and to prepare for it, they were each going to steal a bike. I asked why steal one if you have one? Their answer was that if their bike broke down or they got tired, they would discard their bike and hitch a ride, and, of course, they didn't want to throw their own bikes away.

An inevitable question someone in a wheelchair gets asked is, "Can you do wheelies?" Beginnings youth were no exception. They made me demonstrate and then they wanted to try. Wheelies are tough on a chair; learning to do wheelies is even tougher, so I didn't let them. Soon after that, I brought in an old wheelchair. Within a couple weeks, more kids in Newton Corner could do wheelies than probably any other town in the country. They spent hours, nay days, practicing and practicing and then having contests going up and down the ramps. I'm sure wheelies were not on Stander's agenda when he made plans for Beginnings, but until the wheelchair totally fell apart, it was a popular activity. Sometime later, we took a group of the kids to the Boston Art Museum. In one corner, they had about ten wheelchairs for visitors who needed them. Before I knew it, ten Beginnings kids were racing down the corridor doing wheelies.

Around midyear, we picked up an excellent volunteer, Lois, and a new staff member, Henry. Henry came in looking for a job and was willing to work for almost nothing so we hired him. He

ad moved to the Newton area because he was going to marry
 local girl in the spring and needed something to do until that
 appened. When I met him, I was very skeptical about him as staff
 member, but fortunately, I was wrong; he was great. Lois was a
 member of Eliot and worked as a teacher in the Carol Center for
 he Blind. She observed Beginnings on Friday nights and decided
 she wanted to help.

Actually, she had become interested in Fred Taylor. She was very
 good with kids and an excellent addition to the program. Lois
 was into the outdoors and decided to organize a camping trip.
 She and Fred ended up taking about fifteen youths up to Maine
 for a weekend. The group was a mix of the hippies and hoods.
 The trip was a great success. There were no behavioral problems,
 everyone seemed to have a good time, and the sharp line between
 the hippies and hoods was getting very fuzzy.

Softball

That spring, a few of the twelfth-grade boys approached me about
starting a softball team. The city had two men's leagues—fast and
slow pitch. They wanted to put a team in the slow pitch league
made up of the older Beginnings kids and some of the kids that
were too old for Beginnings. Some of the older kids also came
to talk to me about it. They pointed out that they had stayed
away and hadn't caused problems, so now it was my turn to do
something for them. They had tried to put a team in the league
and were told there was a long waiting list, and it would take
three to five years before there would be an opening. I was on a
first-name basis with the recreation commissioner so it was easy.
One call and Beginnings had a team entered in the league. They
asked me to be their manager. This was like asking George Bush
to be a Democrat; I knew nothing about managing a softball team.
In spite of that, I became the manager. My job was to pick the
starting lineup, with some help from them, and keep score; they
did everything else. They were terrible but they had a great time.
They kept the team for more than fifteen years; they considered
their spot in the league to be one of their most prized possessions.

In the early eighties, they made the finals and invited me to come to the game. I was really impressed at how good they had become, but what really impressed me was how they had worked for so long to get there. I heard, years later, that they had won the league. It is weird how one phone call can mean so much for so long to a group of kids.

Winds of Change

It was spring of '71, and Beginnings was still in business. The change from hippie to hoods was almost complete. A few of the youth from the preceding summer still kept coming, but the majority of the kids were now from the so-called hoods group. I had switched to part-time at GTE in order to have more time to assist with Beginnings. I worked twenty-four hours (Mondays, Tuesdays, Thursday mornings, and Fridays) at GTE and spent about fifty hours at Beginnings. Fred Taylor had told us he was leaving in June to resume his studies; this left us with one paid staff, Stander plus Stuart from Andover Newton Theological School, and myself. However, even with only one paid staff, we were running out of money. The initial rush on contributions had slacked off, but our rent, salaries, and supplies still required money. In fact, I had been paying most of Stander and Fred's salaries, meager as they were. Then the church put its foot down.

In a nutshell, the church had had enough of Stander. They realized he had a lot of talents; however, they also realized one of them was not directing a program like Beginnings. I remember several tense Newton Youth Foundation board meetings over this issue. The board, at that time, consisted of Dick, the president, Allen, our lawyer, myself, two youths from the hippie Beginnings, and one or two other adults whose names I can't remember. The final result was that we decided to hire a new director. Stander was urged to keep helping with the program, but we hardly ever saw him again. Stander's wife worked for the Newton Community Center, and as you might expect, that link disappeared with Stander. Somehow, we worked out some financial arrangements and, after several interviews, hired a new director.

will refer to the new director as "Daffy Duck" because that is
what the kids called him, and I don't remember his name. Daffy
Duck started out well. He closed the program for the summer to
regroup, clean up, and plan for the next year. I felt kind of sorry
we had to close for the summer because the preceding summer
program had been so great, but we all needed a rest. Daffy Duck
led the cleanup and repair of our facilities, and two or three
afternoons a week, we would take some of the kids that always
hung around swimming. I had a sailboat (Sunfish), which was
sitting gathering dust in my yard. I decided to make use of it.
moored it at Lake Waban, on the Wellesley College Campus;
this was about five miles from Eliot Church and Beginnings. I
started taking kids out one or two at a time that summer. These
kids had never sailed so it turned out to be a great experience for
them. Lake Waban was swimmable but had no public access for
swimming. There was only a private beach club for Wellesley
students and staff. The only public access was a boat ramp
(required by the state). Whoever came with me to sail had to
swim out to get the boat and paddle it in. Then they would help
me get in the boat and put my wheelchair back in the car, and
away we would go. Once we got out in the middle, we could
swim as well as sail.

It proved to be a great success, sometimes too much of a success.
The kids soon learned when I was going sailing and who was
picked to go. One Sunday, I was on the lake with two kids
from Beginnings. I saw someone swimming toward us. It was
another Beginnings youth. To make a long story short, when the
fourteenth kid showed up, I jumped off and swam to shore. At
the time I jumped, the boat was a foot under water. Little did
I know how much sailing I would do the next few summers
with Beginnings kids and how much fun I would have with
them. We ended the summer with a trip to Paragon Park, an
amusement park on the ocean south of Boston. It had been a
great summer. I was feeling pretty positive about the future and
looking forward to the year coming up when Daffy Duck quit
because he had a better offer, and alas, Stu became the interim
minister at a church about fifteen miles away and, thus, moved
away.

I looked around and realized the only one left was me! Sure, we still had a board (i.e., Dick, Allen, and me) but no staff. Somehow I was talked into taking the director's job. Since I was paying the salary anyway, it was not what you could consider a lucrative position. I didn't think we had much chance of keeping the program running, but we did. In fact, we were going to have a great year.

Good Times

Making It Work

In spite of the sudden change of staff, we somehow we were ready to go. I got another student from Andover Newton, who worked out very well. I also had a few volunteers who helped and sometimes hindered. We had the facilities in pretty good shape although we had been cut back in space. Classroom B and the choir room were taken from us, but the space we had left was ample and enough to take care of. Also, I had one very important thing that we did not have the preceding year. I had the support of the entire community of hoods in the area. The kids that had taken over from the hippies felt very protective of the program and would do whatever it took to keep it open. Don't get me wrong. That does not mean kids would not screw up; it just meant that I heard about things fast and had the support needed to take effective corrective action. What little money we raised went to the rent; it was left to me to handle the rest.

One thing I had learned, it was essential to include the youth in making the decisions that affected the program, and we sure had a lot of those. The second thing I had learned was who their leaders were. You had to get the right kids involved in the decisions or forget it. I started by having several youth write rules for the program. Kids can be tough on kids. In some cases, they were much harder on themselves than I would have been, and in some cases, they wrote rules that I could never have enforced. Next, we had a meeting to discuss the rule suggestions, and somehow, ve came up with an excellent set of workable rules[23] and, even more important, a way to enforce them. We created a system of fines. What was most important to these kids was their spending money, which they had very little. Plus, you must realize they had to pay a premium to someone to get them beer for the weekend. At first, I thought fines would be impossible to administer, but with the aid of the youth, we came up with a great system. The infractions were very specific. For example, the youth were not supposed to use the back door that would require them to come through a part of the church, which was not our space. If caught, twenty-five cents.

t worked this way. I always carried a little book. If I fined someone, the amount and date of the offense went into the book. If they didn't pay within a week or if they accumulated too many fines, they were not allowed in until their fines were paid. It worked like a charm. I once had to put Malcolm out for a week. Deep down, I didn't believe it was possible, but he stayed outside every day and caused no problems. We had come a long, long way. In fact, he was so good I let him back in a day early. They didn't want to be fined, but they loved to see someone else fined. I was often told to check out a certain area or damage so I could fine someone. A byproduct of this solution was that it was a way to make money for supplies. I have to admit, I got pretty tired of counting change each night.

The next issue I had to solve was when Beginnings would be open. The kids wanted it open every day from two to eleven and, later, on weekend nights. We finally settled for Monday to Thursday, from 2:00 PM to 9:00 PM; Saturday, from 1:00 PM to 11:00 PM; and later added Sunday, from 1:00 PM to 5:00 PM. Friday was not overlooked; it was the best way to solve the problems with the Friday-night church group. It also avoided being open on the major drinking night. Another important issue was cleaning up each night. We had a lot of floors to sweep, stuff to put away, and a kitchen to keep clean. Sweeping and putting things away was no problem, but the kitchen and bathrooms were impossible.

---

23. See Appendix B.

After all, what self-respecting kid would clean a toilet? There were two bathrooms at the back of the stage which were the only ones the kids were supposed to use. It was their job to keep them clean. There were two other bathrooms in the space where the kids were not supposed to go. The kid's bathrooms quickly became disaster areas. When they complained, I offered them cleaning equipment. They stopped complaining. Instead, they would try and sneak out to the off-limits bathrooms. Solution — a twenty-five-cent fine. It worked well.

The kitchen was another problem. It was full of a collection of pots and pans and dishes, etc., which over the years had been left by church members. All this stuff was on the counters because the multitude of cupboards and drawers were full of church dishes and utensils. It was very big and nearly impossible to keep clean. There was no place to put things away. Plus, we were one of many groups who used it. The kitchen continued to be a problem with the church; we never really solved it.

The other tough problem was cleaning up outside. I think kids everywhere are brought up to believe all the world is a trash barrel. Our kids were no exception. Our problem was aggravated by the fact that a lot of the trash on Saturday nights was beer bottles. We tried, but I don't think we ever pleased the church on this issue. There was just no way, with the staff I had, that we could watch the parks outside as well as the inside.

One Saturday night, the kids asked me if I would take them to the Midnite Market, about a mile from Beginnings, so they could get subs. The last thing I wanted after a long day was to take a bunch of kids for subs and then have to make sure they all got home, but I did it. It became a ritual, a very effective ritual — a fun ritual. Every Saturday night, once the place was cleaned up inside and out, I would take them to the Midnite Market. I had a station wagon, so it was easy to take eight to ten kids, which was usually the number left. Then I dropped them off at their homes. It worked out well, as it avoided sending out a bunch of half-drunk kids on to the street at eleven at night. It also made a way to be sure they went home. It also gave me some leverage in getting the outside cleaned up and ready for Sunday even though there were always some beer cans and trash outside to greet the parishioners on Sunday morning. The preceding year, Saturday nights had been when we had the most kids at Beginnings, but during the next few years, it turned out to be the quietest night. The kids on drugs knew they weren't welcome, the drug dealers were not around, and the Beginnings kids kept their beer and their drinking away from Beginnings. Also, I had to deal with very few drunk youth. They did this not because I asked them to, but because they didn't want to lose Beginnings.

Divinity School Students

Andover Newton students, in the first couple of years, were a big help to Beginnings. Probably without them, Beginnings would not have survived the first year. Unfortunately, divinity students also caused one of the worst problems we (I) had to deal with. A harbinger of things to come occurred because of our music system.

We had to have music; kids without music were like trolleys without tracks—they went nowhere. Our music solution for the first year and a half had been the cage. It held the speakers, the amplifier, the turntable, and the records. As we gradually went from hippies to hoods, the music changed and its variety decreased, but it still stayed loud. The kids would not risk bringing their records to Beginnings, which even further limited our music selection. One day, a few of the kids came to me with a proposal. Why not get a tape recorder, and then we could record kids' records and play the tapes. That way, we would not have to keep the fragile records around, and they wouldn't get stolen. My response was, "Great idea, but where do we get a tape deck?" Back in the seventies, they were quite expensive.

A couple of days later, the same kids came in with an expensive tape deck and explained that they were donating it to Beginnings. Now as much as I hate looking a gift horse in the mouth, it just seemed too good to be true. My first question was, "Where did you get it?" The immediate reply was, "It isn't hot!" After a long conversation, the truth came out. A couple of the kids had broken into a house a few years ago and stolen the tape deck. They assured me that it was no longer hot, and we had nothing to worry about. Of course, my reaction was, "No way will I let you bring a stolen tape deck in here." Of course this was accompanied by a sermon on, "Thou shall not steal." They wouldn't take no for an answer and kept after me to keep it.

It happened that one of our divinity students, Tom, was due in that afternoon. They countered, "I bet Tom would think it's okay." I jumped at the opening they gave me. I offered to leave it in Tom's hands. When he came in, they would explain the situation to him. I would listen but say nothing. The deal was that if Tom said okay, we would keep it; if he said no, I wouldn't hear any more about it. After all, I felt any self-respecting minister-to-be wouldn't consider accepting stolen property, especially not in a youth center. We waited. Tom arrived. They explained the whole situation to Tom, except the part about what rested on his decision. Tom's reply was, "If Fred won't let you keep it, I'll buy it from you!" The tape recorder was there for one day and then disappeared. I never was told what happened, but I expect Tom enjoyed his music.

Answering Dreams

Stander had been big on getting kids to dream and then working at getting them to find ways to make them come true. In many ways during the next few years, I tried to do the same things. A lot of the activities that we had the first year fell out of favor. The pottery room was gone, the looms went with Stander, the leather tools were almost never used, and the graphic arts equipment was never used. I knew I had to keep the kids busy, so again, I turned to them as I always did whenever I felt it was time for something new. We had brainstorming sessions (maybe a better term would be dreaming sessions) and ended up with lots of ideas that were not too outrageous. The ideas included things like making models, a TV room, a pool table, a jukebox, floor hockey, basketball, and silk screening. I don't know how the silk screening got in there, but it did. They also wanted to get bumper ars from an amusement park and electrify the ceiling, but for ome strange reason, we never did. I always tried to include them when obtaining new things. What follows are some of the things we did over the next couple of years.

The models came first. I had taught crafts at the Y and at a Y camp and had some connections at the local model store, Al Rogan's. They agreed to bring in models they were working on at home, and I went over to Rogan's store and got a good deal on some models and supplies, and we were in business. For several months, models was the activity of choice.

The floor hockey sounded like a great substitute to belt tag, so I let them bring in hockey sticks and a tennis ball. It turned out the sticks were too tough on the building, so I had to invest in some soft, light plastic sticks and plastic pucks that wouldn't bounce and a couple of nets. Hockey became an activity that was always present during the next few years.

They wanted a TV room, so I made a deal with them. If they would clean out the area behind the stage, I would see if I could get a TV. My part was no problem. I worked for GTE who owned Sylvania. I had a little talk with the VP I worked for, and soon, I had a donated TV. Later on, we added black lights and posters to the TV room; it was really something. I remember one day, the movie *West Side Story* was on TV. All week long, they talked about this upcoming movie. They all jammed into the TV room to watch it. I had never seen it so full, and I was amazed at their excitement over the movie. I watched it too; I had never seen it before. Little did I know that *West Side Story* would add a whole new dimension to Beginnings as well as a major new funding source in the years to come.

They wanted to play basketball. This was also not a problem, as I had coached basketball for about fifteen years before I got involved in Beginnings and had lots of connections in the basketball leagues in the city. I had a talk with the recreation commissioner and got a team put in the senior-high city league. They didn't have a junior high league, so I approached the Newton Church League that played at the Y down the street and talked them into letting u put a team in their league. After all, we met in a church.

As you might imagine, I was running out of time to do all this How could I be at Beginnings and coach at the same time. I go Bill Byrne, the older brother of some of the kids, to coach the senior high team, and I got Stuart[24] from Andover Newton to coach the junior high team.

It really hurt not coaching because there is nothing I would have rather done than coach the teams. As things ended up, I coached both teams.

We needed uniforms and shirts with numbers on them. We bought T-shirts and added numbers to them, and we were ready when the leagues started in January, except we had no place to practice. There was a Catholic convent about a mile up the street that ran a girls' school and had two real nice gyms, but I had no prior contacts with the school. Somehow, I got connected with them and was invited to have dinner with the nuns. I was kind of nervous having dinner with them, as I was afraid of saying the wrong thing, but I actually had a good time and a good dinner to boot. I must have said the right things, as I got them to let us use the gym a couple of hours each week. My contact was Sister Damion; she was built like a tank and made it known exactly what she expected. Fortunately, we never had a problem.

Stu had never coached basketball but he tried. The kids had a good time, won a few games, and lost a lot. I took over when he moved away. The senior high was a different story. The coach and the players just did not get along. Maybe it was because two of the players were Bill Byrne's brothers, maybe because Bill had a quick temper and little patience, but for whatever reason, it was a disaster. There were six teams in the league. They had played five of them and lost each game badly when Bill came to me and quit. He had had it. I made a deal with him; he helped at Beginnings, and I did the coaching. The next game was with the team that

---

[24.]   This was before Stu moved away.

was in first place. They had easily beaten all the teams that had beaten us. They expected a pushover. In spite of our losses, we had an excellent team. They had just been too busy fighting each other and their coach to beat anyone else. Not only did we beat the first place team, but we also went on to beat all six teams in the second round and ended up in the play-offs.

We made it to the finals in the play-offs and had to play a two out of three series with the team we had already beaten twice. We each won one game. The final game was down to about twenty seconds left; we were ahead by one point and had to take the ball out of bounds on the side of the court, near our own basket. Some of our best players had fouled out, so I was down to four good ball handlers and Hoops. Hoops was big and a good shooter hence the nickname, but he was not a good ball handler. I had a brainstorm; I would have Hoops take the ball out. Whoever got it would then stand a good chance of being able to dribble the clock out. I called time-out, explained the strategy, and away we went. Hoops took the ball out all right; he threw it across the court, into the crowd at the other side of the court. Thus, the clock didn't start and the other team had the ball with time to score. They scored and that's all she wrote. The team was disappointed, but they had done well.

More Dreams

Sometime that winter, one of the kids found someone who would donate a jukebox to us. The downside was the playing arm was broken off, and we had no idea where we could get parts to fix it. I had never looked inside of a jukebox, I didn't have the slightest idea how one worked, say nothing of how to fix one, and yet, I said, "Sure, we'll take it." It seems like I spent the rest of the winter with my head inside that jukebox. I found a place to get the part we needed and proceeded with the help of Beginnings kids to take out the old part out and put in the new. It looked fine, but it scratched the records and sounded awful. It turns out there are more adjustments in a jukebox than Heinz has pickles. I tried all sorts of adjustments, but I would wind up with the box able to play one side of a record or the other side but not both and often not either one. Finally, I went down to an arcade equipment company I found about fifteen miles from Beginnings. I talked them into giving me a copy of the adjustment instructions. They wanted me to bring the jukebox to them, but we didn't have the money. When I followed the instructions, I found I had everything correct except I had missed one adjustment. Once I set that, we had a working jukebox. The arcade company sold forty-five records along with labels that fit into jukeboxes. It was great. We retired the music cage, sent all the records home, and had great music with no fuss.

Now that I was an expert at electronics, I didn't blink an eye when we were offered a pinball machine—not working, of course, and without directions or schematics. The arcade company sold pinball machines and parts, so I, at least, knew where to go for parts. With the help of a few of the kids, we traced all the circuits and found out what was wrong and fixed or replaced relay contacts until we got it to work. Another dream had come true.

The kids wanted to silk-screen. We had some of the equipment, but I had no idea how to use it. Kevin said he did, and again, a dream began to take place. Kevin cleaned up the equipment, determined what supplies we needed, found a place to buy what we needed, and before I knew it, all sorts of neat stuff were being turned out. Remember Malcolm? Well, Malcolm was doing fine but surprised everyone with his silk screening. Of course, his subjects were beer signs and beer mugs, but for the first time, Malcolm was doing something creative. He eventually switched to cartoons such as the Road Runner. It just proved again that you never know what may happen.

Next, I began to get pressured for a pool table. I explained to the kids that good pool tables were expensive, and even if we found one, moving a pool table was a major undertaking. They reminded me of last year when I had gone to an auction of old school equipment and bid and bought an old motorized printing press. I had always dreamed of owning a press. It weighted over 1500 pounds, but with the help of my pseudoson, Charlie, we got it down into the basement and into our craft room. Anyway, ne day, Jimmy Byrne, who seemed to want a pool table more han anyone, came in with a *Want Ad* magazine with a pool table or sale. It was in a house in a town about ten miles north of Beginnings. The kids insisted we at least go and check it out. It vas in the cellar of a large house. It was a full-sized (eight feet), late bed table with beautifully carved legs and sides. It came vith about a dozen cues, a cue rack, a scoring cable, a rack, and a bridge. Its felt was worn but not cut or torn. It was great, but vhere were we to get $300 plus whatever it would take to get t moved? I also realized that if you move a table, you have to ake it apart, and that might mean new felt when we put it back ogether.

remember going to the board and asking them for some money—money they didn't have. My edge was the program was going great, we had very few problems with the church, and it vas, in many ways, a version of Stander's dreams. Somehow, we got the $300.

Several Beginnings kids came with me to get it. We took it apart, which was like solving a Chinese puzzle box. We loaded what we could in my station wagon and then came back for more. We thought taking it apart was tough; that was easy compared to putting it together. Somehow, we got it back together without having to buy new felt. Before we knew it, we had a pool table, a really nice pool table. Unfortunately, it was set up right where the Friday-night group put their serving tables for their potluck dinners! Oh well, you can't think of everything, and besides, it was the only place to put it. Of course, no one could move the table, but everyone at the Friday-night group complained. We solved the problem by getting a piece of plywood to cover it, and voila, it became a serving table.

Everything seemed to be going our way. We were given an old but working Coke machine, which proved to be a great moneymaker. I put Malcolm in charge of the Coke machine. He had to fill it and collect the empties that didn't get returned to the cases next to the machine. I began to find capped Coke bottles with no Coke in them in the supply room. Malcolm would carefully remove the cap, drink the Coke, and put the cap back. He kept telling me we were getting cheated by the Coke company. The Coke machine was such a success I went to a vending machine across the street from where I worked and talked them into giving us an old candy machine. We made a lot of money off the Friday-night group with those machines as well as from our own members. The only problem was the coin changers in both machines kept breaking, so I had to learn how to fix and adjust them.

In one year, I had become a jukebox expert, a pinball-machine wizard, a coin-changer ace, as well as a pool-table mechanic. At the time, I was too busy to realize how great things were going. As I look back, I realize how much had happened and how thankful we all should have been.

I was always looking for new activities to keep the youth busy. The minute they got bored, I knew I would start having problems. Often, I would go to bed and not be able to sleep because my mind was so busy thinking up new things to do. One night, the idea came to me to have a treasure hunt. I made a Beginnings flag and buried it in a tin by the shore of Edmond's pond in a place a couple miles from Beginnings called Cabot Woods. Each Tuesday, I posted a clue. If and when a clue was solved, they got more information toward where the flag was buried. Each week, a new clue provided more information. I remember one clue had them call a phone number between eleven and twelve and sing "America" to get the information. It was my number, and eleven to twelve was the only time I was home and not sleeping. I had several families call and sing "America" to me. It may have been the first time these families had ever done something together. After solving the clue and singing the song[25] and receiving the information "try the fifth in the park," two families met each other in Farlow Park, the park behind Beginnings, with shovels. They each tried to hide their shovels and pretend they were just out for a walk. They didn't realize they were in the wrong park. The prize was $20. It took six or eight weeks, but finally, someone found the flag. Guess who? Charlie and one of his friends.

[25.]   See appendix C for clue.

The flag hunt caught the attention of the *Newton Times*, a small weekly newspaper that was renting office space at Eliot. Actually, they rented room B we used to use. Next, we had a citywide treasure hunt with a clue appearing in the paper each week.

Parents

We were in the third year of the program, and we had had very little contact with parents. I guess when you get right down to it, we were scared to death to deal with parents. We had the trust of the youth because the parents were not involved, and we were not too pleased with the freedom most of the youth had during evenings and weekends. The parents seem to want to get rid of their kids.

Nevertheless, we decided to have a parent's night. Of course, we told the youth ahead of time and got their help in planning some refreshments. Invitations were sent out, and we crossed our fingers and waited. The turnout was much better than expected, and for the most part, the parents were very positive. My biggest surprise was meeting Malcolm's mother. First, I was surprised she came because I had been led to believe she had little interest in Malcolm. She turned out to be a very warm, polite, educated woman who was a joy to talk to and was very concerned about her son. I wish I could remember more of that night, but all I can remember is that it was a positive, interesting, enjoyable affair, and the parents did not tar and feather us and run us out of town on a rail.

The first year I took over, I had planned to keep open for the summer. I even hired a teacher from the local junior high school to help me out. This teacher had applied for a summer job. I asked the kids about him, and they said he was pretty good. They explained later that all they were saying was he was a good teacher. Needless to say, he and the kids did not hit it off. I ended up closing for the summer a week after the teacher started working, not only to solve the teacher problem but also to get a much-needed vacation. I kept the teacher busy cleaning, fixing, and reorganizing; and as in past years, I took the kids swimming and sailing whenever possible.

Slot-Car Track

The second summer I was director, I really put my foot in it. The kids wanted me to see if I could get the city to let us use the go-kart track that was in a corner of Newton called Oakhill. The track had been closed for a long time, but I agreed to try. I made an appointment to see the mayor, and one afternoon, I went off to city hall with a couple of Beginnings kids to help me in. City hall had lots of steps and the mayor's office was on the second floor. Of course, there was no elevator. I had never been in the mayor's office before and had no idea what to expect. I was ushered in, and there sat the mayor, who was short and slightly overweight, behind the biggest desk I have ever seen and smoking the biggest cigar I have ever seen. It was like a scene out of the movies or a Norman Rockwell painting. I couldn't believe it.

We had a talk about the go-kart track and Beginnings, and he said he would look into it. I never heard from him again on that issue, but in the years to come, I had a lot of contact with him. In fact, one day, he called me up and bawled me out for not supporting his reelection, but that's another story.

Anyway, the kids then talked me into the idea of getting a slot-car track. They had it all worked out, and I was a pushover because I loved things like slot-car tracks. This was just at the end of the slot-car craze. There was a model shop in Newtonville that had a big professional track they wanted to sell; the kids insisted we go look at it. I was disappointed when we found the track had been dismantled and was stored in a garage behind the store. The owner assured me it was easy to take care of and that everything worked. He also said it was easy to set up.

We measured our stage and determined it would fit on the stage, and so we became proud owners of a slot-car track. Again, my station wagon became the truck, and piece by piece, we moved t to Beginnings. We had been right; it would fit on the stage, but las, we hadn't counted on the fact that it blocked access to the TV oom and the bathrooms and, of course, the complete stage area o me. We finally gave up and set it along one side of the hall. You nust keep in mind that this was the middle of the summer, and nost church people and the church staff were away. Thus, I made he decision to set it up in the hall without consulting anyone. I knew if I could have asked anyone, they would have said "no vay" loud enough to be heard throughout the city.

t turned out to be fairly easy to set up the track. It was an eight-lane, igure-eight track with one end stretched out to provide a long straight way and a crossover such that one set of tracks went over he other. It had eight bar stools in front of eight control stations. It vas really something. There was one small problem that kept me ousy for the next year. Each track was a groove with a strip of wire nesh about a quarter of an inch wide down each side. In order for a track to work, both of these mesh strips had to make a continuous electrical loop. Where the sections of the track structure butted up against each other, these mesh strips were folded down between the sections and soldered to make contact. I was and still am the world's worst solderer. I worked with a few of the kids, setting it up and getting it running before we opened in the fall. It seemed to me after that I was soldering all year long.

To the youth, it was a big hit. It was incredible to have their own track and not have to pay to race. I found a place to buy slot-car kits, and a lot of kids were kept busy making and fixing their cars. To me it was a godsend. It kept the kids busy and contented. They even cut down their Saturday night drinking so they had more time to race. To the Friday-night group, it was an outrage. We had taken over more of the space they used and hadn't even asked. Somehow, we got to keep it. I bought three big canvas drop cloths to cover it on Fridays to lessen the danger of the little church kids from messing it up. In fact, we covered it up every night to keep the dust off it.

I know I haven't been too clear on the time line during which all this happened, probably because I am not too clear myself. I think

the junior high basketball started the first year when Stander wa
director. I think I started the softball team the summer Stander left
All of the other things happened during the three years following
Stander's exit. The slot-car track was bought the summer before
the third year.

So far, I have been telling you about the good stuff I can remember
during this period. However, there were a few very serious
incidents that occurred.

King of Beginnings

Remember Ricky, the boy Stander went to court with and the
boy who had a drinking problem? For the next few years, we
did not have too much trouble with Ricky. If he got too high,
his older brother or father seem to show up and take care of
things before they got out of hand. One Saturday afternoon,
about 2:00, Ricky showed up drunk out of his mind. He started
ranting and raving that the little kids (junior and senior high)
were allowed into Beginnings and he wasn't.[26] I tried to talk him
down and get him to leave, but he just got worse and worse.
All of a sudden, his older brother, Bobby, showed up and told
Ricky to leave. He didn't and a wrestling match broke out. When
Bobby had control of Ricky, he told me to call the cops, which
I immediately did. The police must have been nearby, as they
came in almost before I had hung up the phone. Once they had
taken Ricky out and found out from me and others what had
gone on, the lieutenant told me he was Ricky's uncle and that
he would take care of it, and we would not be bothered again.
He also asked me not to file charges. I told him I would have to
discuss it with my board of directors. That is always a great way
to avoid an answer.

About six that night, I was in the kitchen with three or four youths
and Bill Byrne, the police cadet, making my supper—a frozen

[26.] By this time Ricky was too old to come into Beginnings.

dinner and a cup of tea. Everyone else had gone home to eat. All of a sudden, the kitchen door slammed open and in walked Ricky ranting and raving like before. He picked up a flat iron that was lying on a table and threw it across the room and then went back out in the hall. I followed him, but out of the corner of my eye, I saw Bill heading out the back kitchen door so I was sure he would call the police. I told the youth to stay put, which they didn't, and went out into the hall. Ricky was on the stage by this time, saying he was king of Beginnings, and from now on, he would decide what happened here. At this point, I heard footsteps coming in; it was Mark Manning coming back after dinner. Ricky grabbed him and started ranting that these little kids were the problem. I kept talking to Ricky and kept explaining that the little kids like Mark didn't make the rules, I did. I kept suggesting he let Mark go, but he held on tight. I was not scared for myself, but I was scared to death he would hurt Mark. I kept talking, keeping his attention from Mark, and eventually, the police showed up and arrested Ricky.

As a result, Rick ended up spending a long weekend at the Billerica House of Correction. Obviously, I was a little worried what would happen when he got out. One night, about a week later, I was leaving Beginnings. A couple of youths helped me up the stairs and then whispered to me that Ricky was in the park behind us. As I started to get into my car, the kids told me that Ricky had started across the parking lot toward me. I told the kids to get going, it was okay. Of course, they stayed. I tried to be nonchalant and started to get into my car. I actually was scared to death. He threw his arms about my neck and said, "Thank you. I never want to go there again. I think I have learned my lesson." We hugged each other, and I said I hoped so because I didn't like having to see him go there.

Ricky married a girl from Beginnings and has done very well. He has a great family, started his own business, and has stayed away from the booze. He never was a problem to me again at Beginnings, and he continued to be a star on the softball team.

Death Threat

Another frequent problem was Tony Caira. He had been in Vietnam and came home hooked on drugs. He was too old for Beginnings when we started, but he seemed never to be able to accept it. He often hung around the church, and every once in a while, he would come in, and I would have to ask him to leave. He always did after a few complaints about the little kids, but felt uneasy when I knew he was around. He wrote some stuff on the sidewalk outside the church and told the minister that anyone who read it would be saved.

One Saturday night, when Beginnings was very quiet, there were a few kids in the TV room, a couple playing pool, and a few on the stage, when I got a rude awakening. I looked up and saw Tony sitting on a couch on the stage, drinking a beer. I went up on the stage and told him he was not welcome and asked him to leave. This time, he said, "I am not going. I am sick of being put out for the little kids." I explained, probably in a shaking voice, that either he left or I would call the police. At this point, he stood up, picked up a folded metal chair, and held it over my head. He said, "You are not going to call the police; I will kill you first."

I realized I had two choices—say, "Welcome, Tony. Would you like another beer?" or head for the phone. I repeated my statement about calling the police, but he didn't budge. I turned and went down the ramp from the stage and headed toward the pay phone at the other end of the hall. Tony followed with the chair in hand over my head, followed by a couple Beginnings kids and Bill Byrne, the police cadet. They couldn't do much for fear Tony would carry out his threat. When I got to the pay phone, I reached in my pocket, and as luck would have it, I had no change. I didn't think it was the appropriate time to ask Tony if he had change for a dollar. Next, I turned and went up the ramp to the craft room and into the Newton Times office. The parade of Beginnings youth and Bill Byrne followed. I went in the Times office and picked up their phone; Tony grabbed it and ripped it out of the wall. There were other phones there, but it seemed

utile to have him rip those out too. I turned and went back into
he hall and headed for the kitchen door. The parade followed,
nd Tony taunted me about giving up and going in to make some
ea. When I got to the kitchen door, I reached up and pulled the
ire alarm! The look on Tony's face was priceless (I never have
 camera at the right time). He dropped the chair and took off.
The fire station was two blocks away so I got almost an instant
esponse. Once things quieted down and the firemen and police
iad left, I became an instant hero at Beginnings.[27] In truth, about
wo weeks before, Jane Merrill, one of the church staff, had told
ne to remember that in case of an emergency I could always pull
he fire alarm. I remember thinking at the time that I probably
vouldn't have thought of that, but I knew I would never have to
lo it. I had things so well under control. It's amazing how little
ve know sometimes.

The youth foundation filed charges against Tony, and in a few
weeks, I had to go to court. In those days, the Newton District
Court was not accessible, thus I was faced with about twelve
steps to get into court. When I got there, no one was around to
help me in. While I was waiting for help, Tony came along and
asked if he could help me up the stairs. I said yes with a smile,
out I was not feeling too comfortable. Once we got in the court,
his parole officer gave me a long pitch on how much better
Tony was doing and wanted me to drop the charges. I assumed
that the parole officer and judge were in agreement on this. I
went into court, and when asked by the judge, I dropped the
charges. The judge, Monte Basbas, then read the riot act to me
for what seemed like hours but was only about ten minutes. He
essentially said it was because of people like me that we had no
law and order. I never had though much of Monte; now I knew
I was right.

Peter Skalar

One day, a young man in his twenties walked in and introduced
himself as Peter Skalar. He was renting a room across the street

---

27. Something like Mayor Guiliani.

from one of our members and came in to see what the program was all about. Peter had just moved into the area and was working at the Harvard Coop, Harvard University's bookshop, and wa also an accomplished musician. He had graduated from the Berkley School of Music. He could play anything on the piano, mean anything. No one ever stumped him. He began dropping in regularly and playing Name that Tune with the kids. He related very well with youth.

He had been coming in for a couple months when *West Side Story* was on the TV. He saw the interest of the kids and asked me if he could put on *West Side Story* with our kids. In spite of the memory of how fascinated they were with *West Side Story* when it was on TV, I thought he was out of his tree. You have to understand that our clientele were the kids who had dropped through the cracks at high school. If they went out for dramatics, they would have been asked to leave the first day. I held back a smirk and a "You have to be kidding!" and said, "If you're willing to try great, but don't expect too much."

Peter had tryouts and then rehearsals and rehearsals and rehearsals. I never sat in on the rehearsals. I had enough to keep me busy, and I didn't want to embarrass the youth. Groups of boys and girls would come in and go off with Peter to a room in the back of the church or the crafts room and practice where no one could hear them. I could tell a lot of enthusiasm was building but was concerned that the downfall would be too great. They painted scenery on the drop cloths we used to cover the slot-car track; they brought props from home and used the track's stools as props for the scenes at Doc's Cafe. They were really getting into it. I helped some youth make programs on our press and got a volunteer who helped them silk-screen some posters.

It finally came time for the dress rehearsal. No one was allowed in but me, the cast, stage crew, and, of course, the director, Peter. I remember sitting in the hall all alone in the dark, waiting for it to begin and wondering how I could convince the kids that I liked it. I got the surprise of my life; it was more than incredibly good—it was sensational. The singing and dancing and acting were great, nd Peter on the piano made the whole thing come alive. In many ways, the kids were playing themselves and, at the same time, displaying singing and dancing talents I never dreamed they had. By the end of the dress rehearsal, I was speechless. I don't think I have ever enjoyed an evening more. Our first performance was the next night, Friday. This was in June after the Friday-night program had stopped for the summer. We had about two thirds of the seats full. The youth did great;

they brought the house down. I called Gail and Stu and insisted they come on Saturday. We had a sellout and lots of people standing. A lot of the people who came Friday came back Saturday. The kids were better than ever; it was simply unreal. When it was over, Stu came over and said four words I will never forget: "I don't believe it!"

The next year, dramatics were in; we put on three shows. First, we put on a musical version of *The Outsiders*, a book that all the kids at that time read in junior high. Peter wrote the words and music to our version. We called it *The Other Side of the Tracks* so we wouldn't get into copyright trouble. Next, we put on *Gypsy* and, finally, in June, *Guys and Dolls*. All were big hits and very well done. The kids decided some time that year to sell the slot-car track so we could fit in more people. Drama was almost too much of a good thing; everything else took a backseat to it.

To me, the important part was everything was done by the Beginnings youth—no talent was imported, they made the programs and the scenery, and they brought in props. We had progressed so far from where we started out five years ago i was unreal. This is the kind of thing I would have expected the hippies to do, not the hoods. We had really, in many ways, turned the hoods into hippies. We applied for a state grant for our drama program and received one for more money than we had ever had In fact, the next year, we hired Peter full time.

Some Comments

Looking back at the five years since it all started, I found it hard to believe it wasn't a dream. We had our ups and our downs, but we always seemed to come out on top. At the start of this book I mentioned that the eight stairs I had to go up and down were both a pain in the neck and a blessing. It was often a pain to find someone to help me; many a time, I had to wait outside in rain, snow, and cold. It was restricting to not be able to rush outside if something was amiss. On the other hand, one of the secrets of my success and my relation with the youth was that it was a two-way street. I helped them and they helped me. In the long run, that made all the difference.

Betrayal

It was six years ago that I first attended the YAC meeting and got involved in forming The Newton Youth Foundation and starting what turned into "The Beginnings." It seemed like a long time ago and yet just yesterday. A lot had happened and many people had been involved and many youths have been part of it. As all things in life, nothing stays the same. The youth that was initially involved had moved on, and most of the adults had found different interests or new windmills to joust. In fact, Dick nd Janis Wiseman and I were all that were still active from the nitial group that formed The Newton Youth Foundation. I had een director of Beginnings for five years, and Dick had been resident of the foundation since it was formed. It seemed that we ad fought our toughest battles and solved our worst problems nd were now ready to sail smoothly into a great future. Alas, not ll was as it seemed.

had been working at GTE twenty-four hours a week for over ive years in order to be able to help create and run Beginnings. When I cut back to twenty-four hours a week, I transferred to he commercial division of GTE. I gave up managing the largest lepartment in GTE Government Systems Division to work in a mall group in which I was the software developer—the only oftware developer. One afternoon, during the first year I directed Beginnings, I got a call that the commercial division had been old to a firm in Long Island and that we would have to move to New York or find new jobs. I made one call to the director of the nternational switching group that had just been formed in GTE International and I had a new job. It was ideal for me at that time. I had a lot of experience in stored program telephone switching. In fact, I had designed and written the software for GTE's first program-controlled telephone switch. The GTE International group consisted of the director, his administrative assistant, and me, the software manager. The director, a man I had worked with before, was happy to have me even for just twenty-four hours a week. By the time we were getting ready for the sixth year of Beginnings, my job situation had changed slightly. I now managed about thirty-five people, who we had assembled from all over the world. We were in the middle of a major software development and in a race with our Chicago plant to get there first. I had to do a lot of travelling to Chicago and Europe. Moreover, it was such a fascinating experience working with people from other countries, and the project was so much fun I wanted to go back to working full time and did that summer.

I talked with Dick a lot that summer about how to keep the program going. We decided to hire an assistant director who, if he or she worked out, would become the director starting the next year. This plan would cut back my involvement slowly and give the youth time to adjust to new staff. After Daffy Duck and the teacher, we were a little gun-shy. Herb Davis, the current minister of Eliot Church, came to us with the suggestion we hire Kurt Abbott. Kurt was a graduate divinity student at Andover Newton and had expressed interest in the job to Herb. Kurt was one of two students that filled the church's sexton job the year before. Herb did some teaching at Andover Newton so we had good reason to accept his recommendation.

I have to admit I was a little uneasy with Kurt although I had no firm reason to be. He came to me once during the preceding year and started telling me things to do to improve Beginnings; I always have an alarm go off inside me when someone starts changing something before taking time to understand it. Normally, we would have done reference checking, but since Herb was such a strong reference and we knew it would please Herb and hence the church if we hired Kurt, we did no further checking. Not checking references was my first big mistake.

At this time, I was back at GTE full time, so Kurt was in charge during the days, and I would take over evenings and weekends. My first real concern came in the aftermath of the church's fall fair. Eliot always had a big fair early in the fall. It upset Beginnings schedule but that was okay; we all had fun at the fair. We had the youth plan and set up a couple of game booths. We had a Name that Tune and a Dunking booth. During the fair, the Beginnings kids ran the booths and everything went well. When we were picking up and moving our stuff inside, we had a slight problem. We were almost done when two of our kids starting fooling around a little more than they should. Nothing was broken or damaged; it just meant a little more mess to clean up. I quickly forgot about it; unfortunately, Kurt did not.

We were used to having our weekly staff meetings on Sundays between church and when we opened. The next day at our staff meeting, Kurt brought up the incident at the fair when we were cleaning up and said we should do something about it. My comments were that the youth were well behaved all day and he incident was minor. The staff at this time consisted of Kurt, 'eter, Mary, a woman that handled crafts, and I. Kurt thought ve should open, tell the kids why we were closing, and then ask hem to leave. I was against it, but Kurt talked the other two into his approach. I guess I should have objected more forcefully, but t that time, I was trying hard to tread softly as far as Kurt was oncerned. When we opened, of course it was my job to explain his all to the kids. Right before we opened, Kurt told me to be sure to stick to what we had decided and not back down.

We opened and the kids filed in, and we had them sit along the ront of the stage while I told them what had and was about to happen. Of course, I got complaints that it wasn't fair and that most of them were not involved. I stuck to it even though I didn't agree with it and said they would have to leave. At that point, Kurt jumped up and said, "Wait a minute, let's review this," and gets the other staff to come over to where I was and suggested we stay open. This, of course, was what I had wanted all along, but to the kids, Kurt was their savior, stopping their mean director from closing. I was upstaged grand style. My first inclination was to tell all the youth exactly what had happened, but if Kurt didn't earn the respect of the youth, he would be a failure. Then I would be stuck with no way to keep the place open during the week, so I bit my lip and said nothing.

There were a couple other minor things that occurred. Kurt came to me and told me one of the boys was very sick, and his parents wouldn't take him to the doctor. I arranged a free doctor's visit for him, and he turned out to be fine. Another time, Kurt told me that the girl that had played Gypsy in the play last year had a serious circulation disease and wouldn't live long. I believe she is still alive today.

Kurt had brought in Mary; she was someone he knew. She was very good with the kids and a creative arts-and-crafts person. My only concerned was she never disagreed with Kurt no matter what. She just did not seem to have a mind of her own. I was used to a staff that always discussed and argued over things and usually reached a consensus on what to do.

There was a high school girl, Jeanie, who seemed like a real tough girl that could take care of herself. She was in charge of our stage crew. Kurt told me she had major problems with her parents and that he was counseling her. He was concerned she would run away or kill herself. During our next performance, Jeannie collapsed backstage, and we had to call an ambulance to take her out. Kurt's counseling had succeeded in making her a basket case.

Kurt decided he wanted to have an all-night sensitivity group with some of the youth. He was supposed to have been trained for this, so I didn't worry about it, but I should have. I noticed that there seemed to be a strong bond developing with him and the kids after the experience; which I thought was a good thing, but I realized later, it was a dependence more than a bond.

One Saturday afternoon, early in the fall, I left Beginnings with a couple youth to pick up some art supplies that were being donated to us. When we got back, we came in the back door, as that was the only way I could get in. Kurt had everyone sitting on the stage in a meeting of some kind. He looked around and saw me then turned to the kids and said, "That's all for today. We're closed for rest of the afternoon." Next, he ushered them all out the front door and followed them. The two boys with me and I proceeded to store away the stuff we had picked up and started discussing what might have happened.

We waited for Kurt to come back in; he didn't. We sat and talked and waited and talked and waited. About an hour later, I sent one of the kids out to find out what was going on. Kurt had taken the kids out and then upstairs and continued his meeting in the church parlor. I felt that he had done that so I couldn't be part of it; he really wanted to be in charge. I realized he was so insecure he was afraid to hold a meeting in my presence. He finally came down, and I let him know I didn't appreciate being shut out.

Near the end of October, I got sick and ended up with pneumonia and spent a week in the hospital. I had never had pneumonia, and I have never had it again, but I was really sick and then very weak

fter I was home. During this period, Kurt had complete charge
f Beginnings, as all I did was go to work at GTE and sleep.

he first night I came back to Beginnings was the Wednesday
efore Thanksgiving. The kids, with the staff's help, were cooking
a turkey dinner. The dinner went well; the food was incredible,
and everyone seemed to be having a great time. After dinner, I
vas sitting in the lounge kind of observing while Kurt and Mary
vent out to the kitchen to supervise the clean up. There was an
ipbeat feeling, as the kids had just started a vacation, and the
irst dramatic production of the year was coming up in a few
veeks.

only noticed two boys who had obviously had some beer before
hey came in and were a little tipsy. Peter wanted the piano moved
o the side of the hall for some reason. He asked the two drunken
kids to move it. When I saw this, I held my breath. They tried to
do it right but moved it a little too fast, and when they tried to
change direction, it fell over. Peter was upset, as some damage
was done to it, and it was the only music we had for our play. I
thought he really didn't use his head on that one.

I went up to the craft room for some reason and got in a conversation
with a couple of the youth. When I came back out to the hall,
Kurt had all the youth in a meeting and was going on about this
awful thing the two boys had done. He was making them out
real villains while I knew the blame was really on Peter. Peter
was staging a great show at acting upset because now we had no
piano. When I saw what was going on, I was furious. I thought
Kurt should have spoken to me before calling the meeting; after
all, I was director, and I had seen what had happened and he
hadn't. I sat and listened for a while without saying anything,
again biting my lip to stop from sounding off at Kurt. Kurt had
led the group to the point where the two boys were going to have
to pay for the piano before they could come into Beginnings,
and then he turned to me and said, "Fred, don't you think that is
right?" Somehow, I became a politician and managed to answer
without saying anything or even hinting at what I thought or
letting on how mad I was.

After the kids had left and I was about to leave, I finally got to talk to Kurt alone. I pointed out to him that when I was not there he was in charge, but when I was there, I expect him to consult with me before holding such a meeting. I also pointed out to him that I had seen the whole thing, and at the very least, he should have checked the details out with me. I felt he was way off base and hadn't handled it well and let him know it. He gave me no response. I was not a happy camper as far as Kurt was concerned, but I didn't seem to have any better alternative to keep Beginnings open. I hoped he would become more secure as the year went on so he would be able to take over the next year. I also began to notice that often when I came in, the kids seemed a little cool toward me.

During the next few weeks, I got on Peter's case about him keeping the kids too late for rehearsals. We were supposed to close at ten, and he was keeping them until eleven. He kept saying he had to, to have a good production, and I kept answering, "Okay, then we won't have such a good production." I was concerned their parents would start complaining. Also, I was the one who had to wait until rehearsals were over and then give a lot of the cast a ride home. That meant it was almost twelve by the time I got to bed, and I had to get up early for work. I still wasn't back to full strength so that was a considerable hardship. Peter, however, could sleep all morning.

Finally, the first night of the play arrived.[28] When I came into Beginnings, all the staff and Dick Wiseman were in the craft room. As soon I entered, all the staff got up and left looking very guilty. Dick started talking about how well he thought Kurt was doing and what I thought of being made executive director and making Kurt director now instead of waiting until the end of the year. My first question was, "What's an executive director supposed to do?" He didn't have a good answer. Then I asked him if the staff knew he was asking me about this plan. He said no. There was no question in my mind that they did and that Kurt had gone to him and complained about me and wanted to be director then. I

[28.]   I don't remember what the play was we were putting on.

was shocked that Dick would lie to me and hurt that he would talk about something like this with the staff before talking to me. should have confronted Dick right then about my concerns, but was too shocked to think straight and respond. Later, I began to wonder exactly what Kurt had told him. I never did find out.

was leaving after that weekend for Florida for a couple of weeks, so I told him I didn't think much about the idea and would like to talk more about it when I got back. I also suggested he draw up a job description of the executive director.

When I got back and went to the next staff meeting, Dick was there. He gave me an executive director's job description and announced at the meeting that Kurt was director and I was executive director. If I hadn't been so shocked, I would have quit on the spot.

While I was in Florida, I drew up plans for reviewing our staff performance so far that year. I decided I wanted to go through with that review before I quit. Little did I know that in six months, I would be firing Kurt. A week or so later, we had a meeting at my house at which I carried out the evaluation I had planned in Florida as well as voicing my concerns about what had happened. During the discussion, Dick Wiseman apologized to me for lying, and Peter Sklar expressed his concern over the whole episode and said he was glad it had come to light because he was feeling guilty about it. Kurt said very little. Mary said nothing except agreed with whatever Kurt said.

From that time on, I dropped into Beginnings very seldom. Kurt had a couple of new helpers that seemed like zombies to me. They showed no emotion and did exactly what Kurt said—no more, no less. It turned out that Mary and the two zombies were people Kurt was counseling. Unfortunately, Kurt's counseling made his subjects very dependent on him. Kurt stuttered, and I think this was his way to gain self-esteem.

Dick came to me several times that winter and spring with concerns over Kurt. He kept telling Dick things that turned out not to be true. My first reaction was, "Welcome to the club," for I had seen this since last summer. We both agreed Kurt was a pathological liar. Finally, right before our last musical of the year Dick came to me with definite proof that Kurt had been stealing money from Beginnings. He said I would have to fire him. I am not sure why me, not Dick, but I did it, I guess with a little bit of joy. I had Kurt stop by my house and told him what we knew and that he was through. Of course, he denied it but not very strongly He finally agreed he would leave gracefully if I wouldn't tell any of the youth why. I quickly agreed to that, as I didn't think it would help for them to know all of the sordid details.

He asked me if it was okay if he went back to Beginnings to pick up a few of his personal things. I was so relieved to have it over that I said it was fine. That was my second major mistake. Kurt went back and picked up his stuff and spun some kind of a story for the youth. The next time I went down to Beginnings, which was for the musical, no one was speaking to me. I never did hear what he said, but it must have been a lulu. It was probably just as well, as I would have lost a lot of sleep over it. I told the minister of the church, Herb Davis, what we had done, and he was very upset and felt we were wrongly accusing Kurt.

Here we were again at the end of another year and no director. I guess if you don't do it right, you get to keep doing it until you get it right. We got it wrong the next time too.

The Final Problems

The board of directors set out to find yet another director. I am a little vague about if and how we advertised the position and how many candidates we interviewed. We finally settled on a young man, Bruce, who had been running a similar program in a town about five miles from Newton Corner. I got the job of calling the program Bruce was working for to check out how he had done and why he wanted to make the change. Bruce had told us he wanted to run a bigger program. I talked to one of the staff of the church where the program was located. She answered all my questions easily and completely. When I was through with my list of questions, I asked her if she could add anything else to what she had told me. Unlike all her other answers, she hesitated for longer than I expected and then said she could not think of anything.

Meanwhile, Dick Wiseman had checked some other references, which all had positive replies. So we hired Bruce. We closed for most of the summer as we had done before and opened when school started right after Labor Day. Things seem to go okay. Bruce introduced us to a friend of his, who was interested in joining our board of directors. This was a surprise because no one had ever asked to be on our board. He came to a few meetings, and then we officially made him a member of the board.

Things went along pretty well until midwinter. I was there very little, so I really had almost no firsthand knowledge. Then a problem came up. Our new board member had been dropping into Beginnings once in a while and had made contact with one of the kids to buy pot. When we talked to him about this, he didn't deny it. In fact, he said that Bruce knew he was doing it but knew if he said anything, he would spill the beans about Bruce. Every few weeks, Bruce would take a day off to visit his girlfriend, Michelle, who lived in Maine. It turned out that Michelle was really Michael! We removed our pot-smoking board member and then set out to determine what we should do.

I wanted to make Peter Sklar temporary director for the rest of the year. Dick, for some reason, never liked Peter in spite of the great things he had done at Beginnings, so he wanted to keep Bruce at least until the end of the year. We had a couple other board members at that time, and when it came to a vote, they voted to keep Bruce. I then resigned from The Newton Youth Foundation.

The program continued the rest of that year and, I think, to early spring of the next year. Peter Sklar resigned from the staff in the spring because he felt he should have been made director. Bruce hired someone else to do the dramatics. Instead of having the

Beginnings kids do everything, they went up to the high school drama club and imported youth for the lead roles.

The next year, I was elected moderator of the church, but I tried to stay out of anything dealing with Beginnings. One day at work Channel 5 TV showed up to talk to me as moderator of the church about the protest Beginnings members were staging in front of the church. I knew very little about it, and frankly, I no longer remember what caused Beginnings to be closed, but the protest was the last gasp of the youth. Beginnings was no more.

Looking Back

Through the years, several of the Beginnings kids have kept in touch with me. A few years ago, a boy who was in the eighth grade when we moved to Eliot called me. The last time I had seen him, he was in a drug treatment center about a year before he graduated from high school. I had gone in to visit him several times and felt kind of bad because he was one of the most intelligent kids to come to Beginnings. I kept telling him he should be a programmer. Somehow, he finished high school and went to a school to learn programming. I wrote a reference for him to get his first job. He called to tell me he had just retired and now had enough money that he would never have to work again. However, he had just got another job because he liked programming.

Peter Sklar moved to New York City and started a young actors' program that got kids experience to get on Broadway. He called the program The Beginnings. I believe it was a very successful program; the advertising materials Peter sent me were very impressive. Peter wrote to the author of The Outsiders to get permission to put his musical version on Broadway. She never answered him. I bet it would have been a big hit.

Up until the time I moved to Florida, I used to run into Beginnings kids quite often, so I kind of kept tabs on many of them. I went to a wedding dinner at a hotel in Natick, a city west of Newton, and ran into one of the Beginnings kids working at the desk. He

was one youth I never thought wouldn't make it; I was glad to
see he had a job and seemed happy. A couple of weeks later, he
committed suicide. I guess you can't win them all, but that really
hurt me. I was inspired to finish this book because one of the kids
called this fall just to say "I love you."

Right before I moved to Florida, some of the kids—I guess then.
They now were adults, but I still think of them as kids—came
to me and said they wanted to organize a Beginnings reunion.
I offered to try to get the church to let us use the hall, but they
would have to contact the kids. I talked to the church and got a
date set and then it was up to them. I let Dick and Janet Wiseman
know and got word to Pete Sklar, who was now living in New
York. None of us knew the location of any of the other ex-staff
members. I expected maybe ten or twenty kids, but seventy-four
showed up! One flew up from Florida to be there. It was an
incredible evening. It was neat to see what the kids looked like
all grown up and to find out what they had been doing and how
successful most of them had been, but the most fun was talking
about the days of Beginnings.

No one had seen or heard from Malcolm since he graduated from
high school, but somehow he heard about the reunion. This tall,
slim, good-looking man walked in, and at first, I didn't know
who he was. Malcolm had moved to New Hampshire after high
school and was out of touch with all of his old friends. He built
himself a house on a lake, became a plumber, got married, and
had done very well. He said, "I had such a bad reputation around
Newton I had no choice but to leave."

I was sitting, talking to Malcolm when he put his hand out to
shake my hand and said, "I never had a chance to say this to you.
Thank You."

APPENDIX A

Michael's Letter

This story is about a friend of mine; his name is Fred Rosene. I met him about three and half years ago. I met him at a youth center I go to. It was at church supper and saw him talking with one of the staff members. He was in a wheelchair, and to me, he looked like a nice guy. A few weeks, later he was at the youth center helping out. I was introduced to him. I had never talked to a crippled person before then, and I was watching what I said, but as we talked, it got to be nothing. He told me that he was thinking of working there. He was the type of guy who gets along with everybody and he did. He had his own car, and he lived alone and has got hand controls in his car and ramps in his house. He was very busy there; I don't think I could have done it. When he was about nineteen, he was on a toboggan going down a hill, unconsciously sitting on the end of his spine. Well, after one bump, it was all over. He could not walk, but somehow, he managed. He was always very good with kids, especially of junior and senior high school age. He took his friends sailing in his boat, and then the trouble started in the youth center. The funds weren't coming in any more, and there was no money, but of course, Fred pulled us through. He was working at Bell Telephone with computers (it was really GTE), so he was making a good amount of money. He would always help me out when I needed help, whether it was with kids or money or anything. If I had a problem, I could talk it out. He was there when I needed someone to talk to. It was a weird relationship for a twelve-year-old boy and a thirty-nine-year-old

man to have. The youth center director quit, and so we hired a jerk
for the rest of the summer, and he did not do a thing. Well, there
was no one left but Fred there, so he took the director's position,
but it was a lot harder now to get along with the kids because he
had to make and enforce the rules. Whatever he did, it was the
wrong thing to do in someone's mind, but he tried the best he
could. You can't ask any more than that, and some of the stupid
asses in the youth center caused trouble, so it almost closed down
for good, but it is still open today after a lot of shit taken by this
man who is a great guy and my friend.

Michael Solomita
3/8/73

APPENDIX B

Beginnings' Rules

Calling Parents

Parents will be called for the following reasons:

Coming in before Beginnings is open.

Bringing illegal substances in or around Beginnings.

Getting kicked out for four or more days or getting kicked out and refusing to leave.

Fines

The following acts will result in loss of membership and expulsion until the membership fee of 50¢ is paid:

Playing pool with a cue without a tip.

Placing a drink on the pool table.

Running on the slot-car track.

The following acts will result in a 25¢ fine; a warning will be given only where indicated. Fines are payable within twenty-four hours or the person responsible will face expulsion until they are paid.

Bouncing a pool ball on the floor or on the table or throwing a pool ball around. If one of the staff hears a ball bounce, anyone playing will be fined if the person is not known.

Playing with pool balls on the table without cues.

Throwing any equipment or furniture for any reason.

Spilling a drink on the pool table. (This is in addition to the 50¢ fine for placing drink on the table.)

Placing or spilling a drink on the track.

Sitting on the track or placing feet on the control panel. (A warning will be given.)

Smoking in nondesignated areas of Beginnings. (Smoking is only allowed on the stage and in the TV room. (A warning will be given.)

Using the doors we are not supposed to use or going into the part of the church where we are not allowed without permission.

Anyone breaking windows, glass, or equipment will be expected to pay for the damage.

If someone continually breaks rules or steals from Beginnings, he or she will be expelled for a period of time set by the staff and selected youth representatives.

APPENDIX C

Flag Hunt Clue

FIGURE OUT THIS CLUE AND YOU WILL GET THE NEXT ONE!

YOU MAY FIND THE TREASURE!

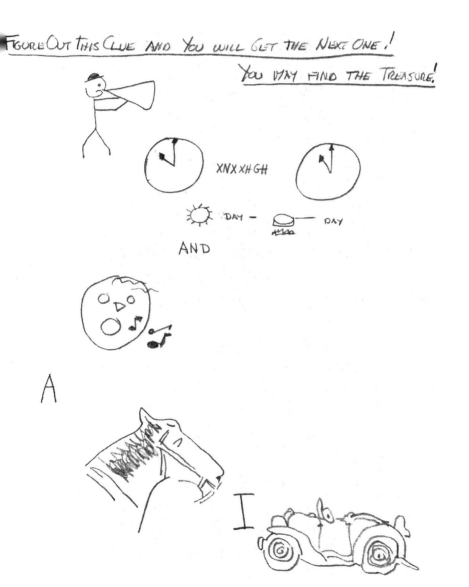

PART III

Retirement

"That's nothing I want to do" went through my mind when I first heard about the special retirement deal they were offering senior staff. It gave you your full pay for a year and then computed your retirement package based on the number of years you had worked plus the extra year. I had three months to make a decision, but as far as I was concerned, my decision was made. I would keep working. The three months were almost over (a couple of days left) when suddenly, it hit me. I had been working for thirty-four years at GTE, I was about to turn sixty, I had lived in Newton my whole life, and all my relatives had moved to Florida or elsewhere, so maybe it was time for me to make a change and live somewhere else. I took the offer! Another case where a message comes from nowhere and changes my life in a positive way! The decision was made in February, and my last day was the Friday before Labor Day weekend. I had a lot of time to wonder if I had made a mistake.

I had to train someone to run my department. For the last fifteen years, I had led the design and development and support of a system (STEP) for managing a software project from specification to design to support and to adding new features. STEP had been chosen for use across all of GTE. They picked someone to take over for me, who I felt would not fight to keep it going, and in a few years, its use would begin to fade away. That made it tough to leave, but there was no turning back.

Labor Day weekend was here! I was having a cookout for my staff to wind up my last day, Friday before Labor Day. My staff presented me with a scrapbook of all the landmarks in my career that was so nice it made me cry and wonder how I could get on without working. When everyone had left, I thought, *I have a three-day weekend ahead of me. What am I going to do to keep busy?* hadn't yet grasped the fact that it wasn't just three days—it was the rest of my life.

The first thing I did was have an operation on my left foot to try and repair an ulcer I had had on my ankle for twenty years. It seemed to be successful. I spent the next year working on a hypercard application that would both teach people how to program and teach them to use the STEP system. I just couldn't get away from my career. In the morning, I would read the paper and then work on my hypercard application. At noon, I would go to a French bakery up the street and have soup and a scone for lunch. Then I would push myself around Needham Center, stop at the market, come home, and hop on my bike and ride about ten miles. I did break up this routine by taking Brian on a month's trip to Florida. It was a great life, but come the next fall, I needed a change, so I headed to Florida. This time, for the whole winter.

A Major Change

I left my Neehham house in charge of Brian, my ward, who was now eighteen. I thought that now that he was off drugs and had a good business going he wold be alright.I stopped to visit some friends on the way down and finally got to Florida. I had a house in Deerfield Beach that I had used as a tax shelter for many years. At this time, it was empty, so I had a place to stay, but it was totally empty. I stayed at my sister's condo for a few days until I bought a bed and then moved in. All I had were my clothes, my bike, a partially done ship model, a TV, and my computer.

My daily activities started with a ten-mile bike ride and picking up a newspaper and a cup of coffee on the way back. My table was a cardboard carton to help me balance my coffee and paper.

When I had read the paper and had done the crossword, I would take a bath and get ready for the day. At first, my main concerns were getting a coffeepot, a few dishes, and pans. However, with the help of my sister, I slowly furnished my house, and except for a few problems, I enjoyed my first year very much.

Morning at Quiet Waters Park

I think my morning bike rides convinced me this was where I should live. What follows is a meager attempt at describing what one of these rides was like. However, the best way to find out is to come down and try one on for size. I used some names (Herb, Colin, Andy, Gisela, Jane, and Lillian) from Eliot Church in describing this ride because I feel like I am with them when I ride.

The light wakes me up. *It can't be time to get up already,* I say to myself as I roll over and start to go back to sleep. Alas, it just isn't meant to be. If I wait too long, it will be too hot to bike. I roll out of bed, put some shorts on, and head for the kitchen. Now let's see. It's Monday so it's not a rubbish day, so all I need is some juice and to fill my water bottle and I'm out of here. I realize as the bright sun hits my eyes that this is one morning I won't have to worry about rain. I ride off with the garage door closing behind me, feeling wonderfully free, just nature and I albeit once in a while interrupted by a car. Sometimes, there is someone fishing in the canal, but this morning, no one is around except for a few birds. A small yellow-and-black bird flies in front of me and then lands on a hibiscus tree by one of the houses. I remind myself to get a bird book so I can identify what I am seeing. Somehow, I never got one. Up ahead, a car turns into Country Club Boulevard at the same time as I do. The oleander trees really look great. In fact, everything looks great. I decide it's a great day to ride to Quiet Waters Park, my all-time favorite morning ride. Quiet Waters Park is a Palm Beach County Park about two miles from my house. It's particularly nice early in the morning, when it really lives up to its name. To get there, I ride through Deer Creek, the subdivision I live in, through a small mall and then through a development called Deer Run. I first go north on Country Club

Boulevard for about 1.5 miles. As I pass the golf course, I see an overweight golfer struggling to get out of his golf cart so that he can make a shot. If someone could figure out how to swing a club while sitting in the cart, it would allow the golfers to avoid all the exercise! The only hill, if one can call it that, is a bridge over a brook. I stop on the bridge to look for alligators and birds and then continue on my way. I stop and talk with one of the walkers and his little poodle, Heidi. I'm on a first name basis with many of the dogs. I know Florida is not supposed to be a good place for dogs, but someone forgot to tell this to a lot of people. There is even an Egyptian tomb and St. Bernard dogs here.

When I leave Deer Creek, I am in one of the quietest shopping malls in the world. Half the stores are empty, and most of the others are not open this early. The mall has three ponds in it, so even here, the scenery is not too bad. I pass one of them, turn by a McDonald's, and cross Hillsboro Boulevard. I enter Deer Run, a residential area of small but well-kept houses. I make a couple turns and end up at the entrance to Quiet Waters Park.

Now the best part of the ride begins. I enter the park from the east and go north, riding along the shore of a lake. This lake is used for water skiing; a cable encircles the lake and pulls up to eight people at one time. The road is lined with coconut palms, most of which sport several coconuts ready to drop. I reach the north side of the lake and head west into the area where the skiers start and where spectators can watch the spills. You can ski on boards and a variety of other implements of torture. Across from the ski buildings are a snack bar and a lemonade stand. This place reminds me of the days when I was a counselor at Camp Chickami when it was at Riverside. We used a public pool and lunch area, and when we arrived in the morning, it had the same empty feeling this area has before it opens. Behind the lemonade stand is a miniature golf course. I checked it out but it has too many steps for me. Up ahead is a playground with a giant clown statue towering above the play yard. I always find a clown.

I turn onto the bike path behind the miniature golf course and head west along the lake. On one side are several large playing ields separated by clumps of palms and picnic tables, and on the other, are pine trees with the lake sparkling behind them. Whenever I see sand and pine trees at the same time, I think of Cape Cod and egg salad sandwiches. Some of the pines look like pines up north, but some have much longer needles. I think weeping pines is a perfect name for them. As I reach the end of the skiing lake, the path forks. One fork turns south, the other continues west. I go on the west fork; the south fork is for later. After the fork, a new lake appears on my left. This is the boating and fishing lake. As I continue along the lake, the pines get a little thicker and scattered, and along the shore are picnic tables and grills. There are several hexagonal picnic pavilions (concrete pads with roofs) along the path. Each contains six picnic tables and a large grill and a water tap. In between these pavilions are volleyball courts with boundary lines and everything. I swear I hear Herb (the minister of Eliot) yelling out, "What do you mean you won't play volleyball!" as I go by.

The last pavilion, which is twice as big as the others, is rectangular with big stone fireplaces at each end. It has a sign on it that says "Reserved." I imagine it also says "For Eliot." It seems the perfect place for an Eliot picnic. I picture Colin and Andy running back from the lake with several large fish, meat sizzling on the grills, and some serious disagreements over the latest antics of politicians and some singing in the background. Of course, Gisela, Jane, and Lillian are putting out more food than anyone can eat.

Just about when the sounds of the Eliot picnic begin to fade, I arrive at the boat rental facility. Canoes, rowboats, and paddleboats are available, and an area is set aside for launching wind surfers. I see a sign that says End of Bike Path and decide it's a good place to stop and drink some water and enjoy the lake that almost surrounds me at this point. A large black duck with a red head and a white neck waddles toward me. The duck is more interested in eating grass than looking at me. I watch it for a while and then turn and head back. For some reason, I usually look to the left when I ride, so when I retrace my steps, I often see things I had missed on the way out. One thing is the cats, lots of cats. At last count, seventy-five stray cats live at Quiet Waters. The county catches and fixes them and returns them to the park. The water on the lakes is like glass, and the sun reflects off the limestone rocks and sand on the bottom. I hear a lot of birds but don't see many very close. There is one type that looks very plain until it spreads it wings, and then it becomes a rather spectacular black-and-white bird, as both wings have white insets in them. As I watch them, see a flash of red. It turns out to be a cardinal.

When I reach the point where the trail forked, I take the fork that heads south. Along here, the water is on both sides, kind o like a land bridge that divides the lakes. On the other side of the lakes, the path turns east and runs between the water-skiing lake and another lake that is to the south. This lake has a clay bottom hence, it's not quite as clear as the others. There are a lot of wild flowers along both sides of the path. Particularly, I like a kind o small, yellow, daisylike flower. Sure beats dandelions. I continue east until the path meets a path that runs north to south. This path parallels the road lined with coconut palms, which I rode on as I entered the park. I go south around the end of the clay-bottomed lake and then turn west and proceed up the south side of the clay lake. I come to a camping area. It contains tent platforms with tents whose sides can be pulled up to make them screen houses One of them is ramped so someday I may try it out. At this point, I look west and realize that the camping area is really a peninsula that sticks out in the lake. The path that I am on goes by the park headquarters and ends at the other end of the road I was on when I first entered the park. To the right is a really nice sandy beach with floats and diving platforms and another boat rental place to the left of the way out.

When I leave the park, I ride along a canal until I come to a traffic light to cross Powerline Road to Deer Run. There are more birds along this canal than anywhere in the park. White egrets, herons, a variety of ducks, and several kinds of smaller birds. One day, a family of ducks was on the path and didn't want to let me by. The rest of the ride is spent retracing my path home except that I stop to get a newspaper and coffee at the little mall and to pick up my mail at the entrance to the Hollows. All in all, the ride is about 8.5 miles, just enough to work up an appetite for breakfast before I ake my morning swim. As you can see, this is a tough life, but someone has to do it!

Two Unneeded Christmas Presents

t was getting close to Christmas and things were going well. I had a small, comfortable house, an enjoyable life, and between my relatives, reading, and my computer, I kept busy. Then the phone rang! It was the Needham police; Brian was in trouble! He was selling drugs from my house. This meant he was back using again. The police wanted permission to search the house which, of course, I gave them. I thought about it for a couple days and then called Brian and told him to get the house in good shape; I was going to sell it. Meanwhile, I was asked to take my great nephew, also named Brian, in and home school him. He was in the seventh grade and causing a lot of trouble at school. He seemed to be doing well at my house until one night, I got up in the middle of the night and found he wasn't home. It turned out he had been waiting until I was asleep and then helping himself to some of what was in my wallet and going out on the town. Right after that, my house was sold, so I made plans to drive north and took Brian with me. We hit the road in late March, and he was quite excited about seeing snow. We did see a little. He promised he would behave and help me get everything out of my house.

We had only been in Needham for a few weeks when I found out he was sipping my bourbon each night after I went to sleep. That was it; I put him on a bus for Florida two days later and sent him back to his mother. That solved that problem, but I now had no help to help me empty the house. Brian, the drug pusher, had cleaned the house up well and found half of a house to rent with a garage to hold all his landscaping tools. He rented out rooms to a couple of his friends and seemed to be self-sufficient. His landscaping business was going well, his clients liked him, and he kept getting new customers. I gave him most of my furniture and tools and just took a few special things south that would fit in my van. I also gave him my waterbed, but he couldn't take it until the day I left. The day of passing the papers, I was left alone to get the rest of the stuff he wanted, including my waterbed out of the house. Ever try to take a waterbed down? I couldn't do it. As I wondered what I was going to do, I got a call from one of my ex-employees. He and a couple of others came over to help. I left about 4:00 PM with everything for Brian out on the lawn and the house clean and empty. You might ask where Brian was. He was at the hospital with his girlfriend, who was having an abortion. Great, one Brian I had to send home, the other was involved with girl problems.

I stayed at some friend's house until Sunday because I wanted to go to one more service at Eliot. It was sad to think about all my memories for sixty years and all the friends I was leaving behind. Of course, I cried.

What Am I Doing? Am I Crazy? I Just Lost My Whole Life!

I broke the sadness by first going to Danbury, Connecticut, to see a college roommate. And then I went to Union Town, Pennsylvania, to see my first boss and his family and then to Mount Vernon, Ohio, to see the Wells family that had helped me so much with Beginnings and, finally, to Warsaw, Indiana, to see Charlie, the boy I had brought up a long time ago. It was a long trip, but this time, it was a one-way trip. I was going to a new home in Florida. While I was gone, I had a pool installed in my patio thus when I got home, I had a beautiful home waiting. The summer of Olympics was coming up, a special one at that because you could get most of it on TV for a reasonable price. I got it and it was well worth it. In fact, it was so good they never did it again because so few people watched the commercial versions. My great nephew, Jeremey, a student at University of Florida, also stayed with me that summer. That also helped me get through the summer, my first summer in Florida. My sister, two nieces, and a nephew and their kids were the only people I knew. I had one other niece in Virginia. My oldest niece, Linda, and her family are the only ones that still live near me. I am sure glad I have some relatives near.

still was feeling lost, so in the fall, I drove up to Newton for a couple of weeks to help with the church fair and see friends. I was here until the end of October, and I got to see the autumn's color one more time. At the fair, I bought a dollhouse for my littlest great niece, and when I got back, I kept busy trying to finish the dollhouse by Christmas. Little did I know that something was going to happen that would change the rest of my life! It was another one of those shots out of the dark, like when I was asked to coach basketball or when I was shown a computer or when I went down a hill on a toboggan.

My nephew's family had been living in my patio home while looking for a house. They moved to Delray Beach, about sixteen miles north of my house just before I retired. I remember wondering why they moved way up there and wishing they had stayed closer to me. Anyway, their kids were going to a school right behind where they lived, and my nephew's wife had become active in the PTA. A few days before Thanksgiving, she asked me if I would tutor math at her kid's school. I said I don't want to do that, and besides, I have to finish Molly's dollhouse. She talked me into it but insisted it would only be a couple of hours a week. She took me to the school, Plumosa Elementary, the day before the Thanksgiving break. I met the fourth grade teacher, Mrs. Laseter, who I would be helping and the principal, Mrs. Masonberry, and got a quick tour of the school. I would tutor math two hours a week, one on Tuesday and one on Thursday. While I was driving up to Plumosa my first day, I was thinking, *I am not going to do this long drive often. It's too long.*

I found Mrs. Laseter's room and went in. Of course, every child turned as I jumped up the small step into the room. Kids always look up when someone comes in their classroom, but a man in a wheelchair popping a wheelie really got their attention. Of course, she had given them a heads up that I was coming. My first task was to help a boy called Ernesto with his multiplication facts. He was a very handsome Hispanic boy and he tried hard. My second task was to help a boy named Izzie and a girl named Monica with their multiplication facts. It turned out Izzie was one of four boy in a family that lived right behind the school that I would get to

know very well, including the soon-to-arrive fifth boy. Monic
was a pretty black girl, who was really easy to teach.[29] Once
finished with them, my hour was over, and I drove home thinking
it was a lot of driving for a short time. The next time I came, I wa
asked if I would also spend a couple hours in a fifth-grade room
My first student in the fifth grade was a boy named Michael, who
had been in a gifted school for his fourth grade but had opted
to return to Plumosa. My job with Michael was to teach him
sixth-grade math since he already knew fifth-grade math. Tha
was a real fun assignment.

When I was in high school, I had worked with fourth—to
sixth-grade kids at the Y and at their day camps. I began to
remember how much fun it had been, but this was a lot different
I was now in a wheelchair and a lot older. Then I began to notice
how students would go out of their way to smile at me or speak
to me and then to want to push me. I also was very impressed
with the school. The Christmas programs were neat. Right before
Christmas vacation, the fourth graders came to school in their
jammies with their teddy bears, and they had a special breakfast
and watched a movie. I was hooked. I asked Mrs. Laseter if after
vacation I could work full time!

I began this section with saying I felt like I lost my whole life, but
just like that, I had found a new one! I must be blessed, as every
time I feel like I have lost everything, I end up with more than I
ever dreamed of having.

Michael

Michael was the fifth grader I was teaching sixth-grade math to.
I noticed very quickly when I came into Michael's class that he
had been watching for me. He was obviously looking forward to

---

[29.]   I was at the DelRay Beach Community center in 2010, waiting for
the parade to begin, when a voice called out. "Did you used to work
at Plumosa?" It was Monica, who I hadn't seen since she graduated
from Plumosa in 1993. I was pleased to find out how well she was
doing.

ny coming. He was really good at math, so I could easily teach
im the sixth-grade curriculum. Michael came over to me one
day and asked about a problem he didn't understand. It gave
bout ten numbers and asked what they had in common. I asked
im what their factors are, and he immediately lit up and said,
"Prime numbers." He was right, but what really impressed me
was I didn't know what factors or prime numbers were until I
was in ninth grade. While I continued to teach him, I brought
ome relays and stuff at radio shack and taught him how to make
a one-stage electric circuit that added binary numbers. Michael,
n turn, showed me how to run the various programs they had
n the computer lab and taught me all about the school. I really
ooked forward to the time I spent with him. I soon got to know
his parents and his younger brother, Bobby, and to this day, we
have stayed in touch and remain good friends.

Roger

n January, we had a new fifth-grade student named Roger. Roger
was having trouble and became one of my students. It was very
frustrating dealing with Roger; he would seem to catch on, and
by the next day, he had forgotten most of it. I continued working
with Roger, but it was always the same. He would unlearn as
fast as he learned. He was transferred to a special ed class, but
I still spent an hour a day with him. I made flash cards for him
and told him to use them at night whenever commercials came
on TV. That didn't work either. He asked me in March if I would
teach him long division. He said he really wanted to learn what
his classmates were doing. I told him I would love to teach him
division, but he needed to know his multipliication facts really well
to be able to divide. He was stubborn and I was a marshmallow
so he won; we started division. I started to teach him division
but I kept the divisor the same. Thus, as we went over and over
dividing by the same number, we were using the multiplication
facts of that number. It was magic! He wanted so much to divide
he started remembering the multiplication facts for the divisor I
picked first. I then switched to another divisor and another one
and so on. By May, he was dividing very well, and that meant
he was also multiplying well. I was ecstatic; all my efforts had

paid off. A few times a year, they have what they called Math Blaster—when all the classes of a grade would be brought to the cafeteria and given a page of fifty multiplication facts to do in one minute. I had watched Roger try and do this once before; he got nowhere because he would quickly get stuck on a fact. I said a little prayer as I watched Roger this time. He went zipping along without stopping; he finished ahead of time; he looked up and gave me a big smile. That was the most wonderful thanks I could get and was worth a year's work; that is why I love working in a school and have now just finished my twentieth year.

That one smile made the whole year worthwhile. By the way, he got forty-nine out of fifty right. Since then, I have used the division technique whenever I run into a student who can't seem to multiply. So far, it has always worked. Roger went on to middle school the next year. I would see him occasionally because he lived right behind Plumosa, so I kept up with how he was doing. Then he moved back to New York. I hope he has had a good life and that he still knows how to multiply! I know I will never forget him.

Mr. Harris

"That's enough! Take your work and go see Mr. Harris!" That became a frequent occurrence when someone started fooling around; he or she went to see Mr. Harris. I began to wonder who Mr. Harris was, but I was too timid to ask. One day, I was asked to go to Mr. Harris's room to get a blank science project board, and I have to admit, I was a little scared. Mr. Harris turned out to be a fifth-grade math teacher, nay a great fifth-grade math teacher. In fact, he was the best math teacher I had ever known. He didn't have any more science folders, but he didn't scold me or spank me. In fact, he was one of the friendliest people I've ever met. Mr. Harris (Clyde) and I became the best of friends. Whenever I had a break at school, I would go and help Clyde with whatever he was teaching.

Clyde had grown up in central Florida. He came from a very poor family, but he did well in school and got a football scholarship to ollege. When I met Clyde, he had been teaching at Plumosa for bout twenty-three years; he eventually retired after thirty-eight ears at Plumosa. As the years went by, I learned more and more bout Clyde's life and family. I was even invited to his family atherings.

ach year, the school district had a trip to Washington DC for he students who made safety patrol. Fifth-grade students who vorked hard, did well, and stayed out of trouble got to be on he safety patrol. The patrol had all sorts of assignments, mostly telping with getting students in and out of school each day. Clyde an Plumosa's patrol and was in charge of taking our patrol on the DC trip. The first year I was there, fifth-grade students that were 10t on the trip kept asking me to give them their long-division est. It was a small book with about twenty questions in it. I had to vatch them do it and then correct it. If they passed, they went on o the next book. If they failed, they went back to more studying. was really impressed how much they wanted to learn; I don't hink I did when I was their age. You'll hear a lot more about Clyde in the later parts of this book.

Dean

I hope he doesn't have cancer, I thought as I saw this handsome boy from another class walk by our door. He was missing half his hair. Thank God I was wrong! He had been pulling his own hair out.

His teacher thought it was because there were no males in hi
family. He lived with his mother and a girlfriend of hers. He had
a grandmother who lived nearby, but the grandfather had passed
away. His father and other grandfather lived in Oregon. He lived
with his mother during the school year and visited his father
each summer. When he finished grade school, he would live
permanently with his father and visit his mother every summer.
was asked if I would spend an hour with him each day from 1:00
to 2:00. I was to get to know him, do things with him, take him
places, etc. The idea was to kind of be his big brother. At first, he
was kind of shy and so was I, but things quickly got better. We
talked about storms because, for some reason, he was fascinated
with storms. Even though the school had a real nice library, we
went to the city library so he could lookup more about storms
We became very good friends. He had been put in tae kwon do to
help him quiet down. One Saturday, I went up to the mall to see
him perform. He was real good. As things went along, he started
staying with me after school so he could watch interschool games
and take part in some after-school activities I was helping with
I took him to a science museum one weekend, and often Mrs
Gomez, his fourth grade teacher, would bring him and her kids
down to my house to swim. When you come right down to it, we
were having a great time. Saying good-bye when he was ready to
leave for Oregon was hard, but at least I knew I would see him in
a couple months.

Dean had a real bad summer after fourth grade. Dean spent most
of his time on his grandfather's ranch when he was in Oregon
His grandfather was gored to death by one of the bulls, and Dean
was the only one on the ranch. Dean tried to help him and then
ran for help. When Dean got back to school, he refused to talk
about it even though we were good friends and spent a lot of time
together. It was hard for me when Dean left after his fifth grade;
I kind of wondered if he would ever come back. The following
Christmas, I sent Dean a Macintosh computer, and from then on,
we communicated on immediate mail [30]on AOL several times
a week until Dean went to college. He always came back a few

[30.] IM is texting using a computer instead of cell phones.

weeks every summer to see his mother, and we spent a lot of time together. He used to help me with tasks associated with getting the computers ready for the next year at Plumosa. In fact, he was helping the person in his school who had who had the same job as mine. The last time he came was the summer after he graduated from high school. While he was here, he found out his mother had a boyfriend about one year older than he was! This hurt him so much that he never came back again. In fact, he went off to college for one year, and since then, I never heard from him again. I have never stopped thinking about him, and I will always miss him.

Mrs. Gomez, his fourth-grade teacher, and I found out from his father that he had a job in another town and thus his father didn't see him very much. His father gave us his telephone number. I tried over ten times to reach him by leaving messages on his answering machine and so did Ms. Gomez, but he never returned any of our calls. It was good to hear his voice on his answering machine; at least I knew he was alive! I think about him often and pray he is all right. I will never forget him.

Mysterious Visitors

One of the main things I used to do was take small groups aside to work on math while the rest of the class was doing something else or had gone to the computer room. One day after lunch, Mrs. Laseter surprised me by asking me to teach the science lesson. It was on simple machines. Of course, I said sure. We had a teacher's science book with the details of the lesson, but I had never looked at the book. However, I had had simple machines many years ago, so I kind of knew what I was teaching. About halfway through the lesson, two very important-looking women came in the classroom. Mrs. Laseter told me to keep going, and she talked with our visitors. When the lesson was over, she introduced them to me. One was the superintendent of the Palm Beach County Schools, and the other was the associate superintendent. My first thought was Mrs. Laseter might get in trouble for letting me teach the science. Instead, it turned out that

the superintendent arranged to have one of the newspapers com
and interview me, and it ended up with a large article in the *Su*
Sentinel about me, including a big picture of me teaching. Th
associate superintendent turned out to be the mother of Clark
one of our students. Although no one ever told me and I didn'
ask, I think that Clark told his mother about me, and she told he
boss, and it was setup to have me teaching when they came in.

A Big Surprise

One day near the end of my first year at Plumosa, I was tutoring
Roger in division when his class suddenly lined up to leave
Roger said, "It's okay. You can come with us." We followed hi
class outside to where some big trees were growing near the
front of the school. There were a couple of classes up ahead of us
and suddenly, they all jumped up and yelled, "Happy Birthday
Mr. Rosene." It was then that I realized it was my birthday;
had forgotten. They had a grill going and tables set up. We had
hotdogs and hamburgers, plus a real big birthday cake. I was
blown away; it was the last thing I expected. It was another way
I got paid when I volunteered. A few days after the party, school
was over for the year. I left school feeling very satisfied with my
year but also very sad. I kept wondering if they would want me
back the next year. I wouldn't think of asking because I didn't
want to put them on the spot. I went home and wondered all
summer what would come next.

School Was About to Begin!

It was finally the week that the teachers returned. Would they
want me? What should I do if they didn't call? Should I go up to
the school and ask them if they wanted me? I just didn't know.
Each day of that preschool week, I waited but no call came. It got to
be Thursday afternoon and I had about given up when the phone
rang! It was Mrs. Laseter. She told me that Mrs. Masonberry, the
principal, had asked her to call to see if I wanted to come back. Of
course, I answered yes, but I think I dropped the phone first. Then

he asked if I could come up the next day and help Mr. Church fix his room up. Mr. Church last year had been the permanent substitute. That meant he was on the staff because each day they always needed at least one sub. They had just found out that one of the fourth-grade teachers wasn't coming back, and he was asked to fill the job. He only had one day to get his classroom ready, and they wanted me to come in and help him.

I had a hard time sleeping that night. I just wanted morning to come so I could go back to school. Needless to say, I was there bright and early to help Mr. Church. It was so great to see all the staff again, and it was open-house day, so I got to see a lot of students who came to meet their new teachers. It was a wonderful, glorious day. In the middle of the afternoon, I met one of the students from Mrs. Laceter's class last year. We had hardly started talking when his mother came around the corner and said, "Michael, I thought you wanted to go, so let's go." Michael's response made me know I was home. He said, "Not now, mother. Mr. Rosene is here!" I left school that day as happy as anyone could be. I had a tough time waiting for Monday to come.

Computer Lab Manager

I came to school on Monday wondering what I would be doing. Mrs. Laseter was assigned a student teacher, so I wouldn't be needed in her class. The first thing I did was to help the office staff generate the bus list so we could get the students home. Then I went down to the media center to check out the computer room. It was a mess. Nothing was connected, and it looked like an attic that had been used for storage for years. I found out later that most of the teachers didn't know what programs were there, say nothing of knowing how to use them. I asked the media specialist if she would like me to fix up the room so it was usable. She jumped for joy. She had been wondering how she could get it working with all the other stuff she had to do. I didn't know what I was getting into, but I worked about two weeks in getting rid of what shouldn't be there and rearranging the tables to make it easier to teach the computer classes. Also, I had to figure out how to run all the programs and how to manage the server and connect the network.

Once I had the lab ready for use, I ended up teaching all the computer classes to the students and their teachers. It turned out to be a great way to get to know the students and the teachers. Like any computer lab, there are passwords required to get behind the scenes and manage the network. After all, things always go screwed up just from regular use. I got to know the person on the district level who was responsible for our lab, Dr. Cornell, a really knowledgeable guy who kept bailing out the elementary school staff. At that time, he told me that he would be fired if he gave me the sysops passwords although he knew I could make changes to the operating system without destroying it. Partway through the year, he set up a log-in for me that could do all of the stuff the sysop did, but since it wasn't a sysop, it was okay. I was calling them so often they had to do something to avoid coming out and doing the things for me I couldn't do without the password. I also talked the school into mounting a large monitor on the wall to make it easier to teach whole classes at once. I was beginning to use some network capabilities most schools didn't use. They had to let me set it up or keep coming to Plumosa.

The teachers were impressed that they had a lot of programs they never knew they had. Some of them always used the same program for their class because it was the only one they knew how to use. The only catch was I was tied up almost full time teaching computers. I spent one hour a day helping a second-grade teacher by going over missed math problems with her students. I was also asked to help kids do their homework after school and then, once they were done, let them use the computers. Things sometimes didn't go as I had planned.

The lab network had the ability to let kids talk to each other over the network. It seemed safe enough to me, but it backfired. The students found they could send swear words and no one would know. One day, a bunch of the boys got together and sent all of the four-letter words they could think of to a girl. The girl printed the messages and took it home to show her mother. Her mother showed the principal, and the principal showed me. The fix was simple; I deactivated the message passing.

designed a course to teach some of the fifth graders a little about how computers worked and how you programmed them. I picked some of the sharpest students from the year before and had them spend their lunch hour in my class. It was fun for me because I enjoyed teaching them about computers, and they seemed to enjoy learning about it. I showed them what the major parts of computers were and what they did. I showed them some basic assembly language and had them writing programs like ordering numbers. This kept me more in touch with the kids I got to know so well last year.

Another Surprise!

In part I of this book, I mentioned the Robisons and how important they were in my life. They had a time-share in Kissimmee, and we would often get together while they were using their time-share. They talked me into going on a cruise with them. I have to admit I was a little worried as to whether a wheelchair could get around and on and off the ship. We were set to go in February so I would miss a week of school. This bothered me because I was always at school because I knew how much the teachers and students counted on me. The Friday before I was leaving on the cruise, I was told to report to the principal's office. When I got there, she talked to me for a while; it was a conversation that seemed to be going nowhere. Then all of a sudden, she asked me to follow her.

She took me out to the east end of the south wing of the school, where there was a black top basketball court. The whole school, students and teachers, were lined up on the bank on one side. On the other side of the court, there were some fifth—and fourth-grade students with a big roll of paper about four feet tall and some fourth—and fifth-grade teachers. She escorted me to the corner where the students were with the big roll of paper. Then as I wheeled up the court, they unrolled the paper, which turned out to be a painted mural of tropical islands and ocean a long as the basketball court. At the same time, the students wer singing "Anchors Aweigh," and as I wheeled down the court students and teachers came over and handed me gifts like roses sunglasses, and other things one would want on a cruise. The also gave me a note to let me know my stateroom would be ful of balloons when I boarded the ship.

All this was topped off, after the ceremony, by serving everyone ice cream and cake. In my whole life, I have never had anything that made me feel so wanted and so appreciated. I sobbed for joy while writing this section, as it made me think of the emotion had felt that day.

The cruise was great; I had balloons in my stateroom during all o the cruise to remind me of Plumosa, but I must confess, I couldn' wait to get back to school, my real home, where my heart was.

School Age Aftercare

As I mentioned, I started staying after school to help kids that were having trouble with math, and then I found Jane Murphy and the aftercare program. The SAC would keep students as late as 6:00 PM for parents that had to work. The first thing they had to do was their homework and then there was lots of neat stuff to keep them busy. I would help them with the homework time and play a few games with the kids before I went home. A couple of the students asked me if I would come to watch their basketball game against another school's SAC. Up until this point, I didn't even know they had after-school sports. They had a sports league of six schools with aftercare programs. They competed in soccer, basketball, softball, and kickball. I watched a couple of their basketball games, and then they asked me if I would coach their basketball team because their coach was leaving. Of course, I said yes; after all, I had a lot of experience coaching basketball. What I hadn't planned on was ending up coaching the other three sports. Before I knew it, I was at school from 7:30 to 4:30 every day, and all I had signed up for was two hours a week.

he coaching was fun and the kids loved the sports. We won
ome games and lost some games and had a great time. There
vas one school I'll call Bingo. When we went to it, they always
eem to change the rules we used at all the other schools. Of
ourse, the changes were to their advantage. For example, we
vere playing Bingo in a basketball game. The coach asked me
head of time, "Let's not play the three-second rule in the paint."
answered, "As long as it isn't an advantage to one of the teams."
)ne of our parents was refereeing along with the coach from the
ther team and me. When the teams came out, it turned out our
ipponents had one player that was eight to ten inches taller than
inyone on our team. It was now obvious why he didn't want the
hree-second rule. Their tall player stood in the paint[31], and he was
asy to pass to and had an easy layup every time. I immediately
tarting calling the three-second rule, and that got their coach
nad. Under the rules we played, you could not press the other
eam full court, but you could press starting at midcourt. Bingo
vould position three players at midcourt and not let us get into
he front court. Then when we lost the ball trying to pass it into
he forecourt, the Bingo coach would grab the ball and let his
eam immediately take it out. When the ball changes hands like
hat, the referee is supposed to hold the ball until both teams are
n place. The result was their team got the ball and made a basket
)efore most of our team got back to defend. We called time-out
ind told the Bingo coach it was not fair for the referee to not
1old it until the other team got back. The referee could not give
)ne team an advantage. He kept doing it. I told their coach what
ve thought of his cheating and that we would not continue such
i farce. We never played Bingo teams again in anything. A few
years later, the district banned the aftercare sports leagues. I was
1ever told why, but one thing I knew—our kids really missed it.

Technology

Each year, our school would get some lottery money to spend on
technology. I was on the committee that decided how to spend it.

[31.] The area under the basket.

One of the teachers was asked how she thought we should spend it. Her answer was, "I'm for whatever Mr. Rosene says." We had about $1500 each year, and I think all in all, we made pretty good choices. Of course, I had a lot of clout! I was sent to technology in education conferences, which helped me learn what others are doing with their money and also to get a feel for what new things were available. I was also sent to conflict management seminars, a program that was just beginning at Plumosa.

A program called CCC[32] was introduced in our county. CCC provided us with four computers for each of our second-, third-, fourth—and fifth-grade classrooms. Also, some of our lottery money was used to get ten Macintosh computers for our kindergarten and first grade. At this point, I was feeling real good about the state of our technology. A computer lab, computers in each class room, internet, and CCC—an excellent teaching program.

More Than I Ever Dreamed Of

A couple of years later, a new wing was built in our school, which had a large music lab, an incredible arts lab, a computer lab, a science lab, and a lab that soon became a second computer lab. As soon as I got the old computer lab moved from the media center to its new home and up and running, we were given fifteen Dell computers running Windows 95. The fifteen old IBM Model 26s were then moved out to the classrooms. A couple of years after the new wing was built, the lab next to the current computer lab that had been used as a classroom was turned into a second computer lab. At that time, we were given thirty-two Dell computers running Windows 98. Because I was in a wheelchair, Mrs. Masonberry was able to get a door put between the two labs so I could manage both labs without having to go outside. The last thing that was provided was a teacher workstation containing a thirty-inch monitor, a computer, a printer, a VCR player, and a DVD player for each classroom.

[32.] CCC stands for Computer Curriculum Corporation

While all this updating was going on, the school was wired for access to the district network and hence the Internet at a much faster rate. Each room had eight connectors to the network, and behind the computer lab, we had an electrical room that now had a new server as well as the DOS server we used to network the IBM 26s.

I have jumped ahead to describe all of the computer technology upgrades that happened at Plumosa. In what follows, I will describe what happened as this upgrade progressed.

CCC

Once I got the computer room cleaned up and rearranged so it was easier to teach, I thought I was done. All I would have to do was teach and keep the lab running. I started to explore what capacities the server had that we were not using. I found that each student could be assigned a log-in ID. That allowed me to get programs that required a user to play them for days or weeks or months before they were solved. The process was kind of long to get all our students set up with log-ins. One week, I asked the principal if I could come in on Saturday to work on it. It was too much to get done during the school days. Mrs. Masonberry laughed and said, "I can't believe a volunteer is asking me to work on weekends." She let the security know I was going to be there. I had to call security when I came in and when I left. I also had to have a key. Mrs. Masonberry has told this overtime story over and over. It was just something that never happens. Anyway, I got all the students in and bought two programs: Gizmos and Gadgets and Treasure Math Storm. These two programs turned out to be the most popular programs while I was at Plumosa.

Everything was going along great when Mrs. Masonberry asked me if I would take the job as CCC coordinator which was a new position created to manage CCC. I said I have too much to do without CCC, why not hire someone else? She asked me to help interview those that applied. When all was said and done, we had hired Mary. Mary was going to school at nights to get her education degree and liked the idea of doing something that would help her get a teaching job and earn some money. Mary ran the CCC program until she had to do some student teaching. I was asked again to take the job; this time, I took it because I thought it would be easier to do it than to break in someone else.

CCC is a program that combines management of courses with the taking of courses. It contained courses in math, reading, spelling, and science. A student would be given a starting level in a course that would be automatically adjusted as the student made or lost progress. When a student reached the top of a course, there was usually a more advanced course for them to start. CCC also had all sorts of different reports that gave the teacher the details of her student's progress and gave the principal summary information for the whole school. CCC was a great addition to our educational software. It was used all the time for the next five or six years.

My job in all this was to set up log-ins, courses, and course statuses for each student before school started along with assigning the same log-ins for our students to the DOS server. We had two servers: The DOS server ran the older programs; the new server ran the new programs. I also had to keep the numbers updated as students came or left. I also generated reports for all the students at the end of each grading period. The teachers were supposed to generate their own reports, but they soon found it was much easier to ask me. There was one other little thing I had to do. I had to keep all the computers going. This often required swapping out computers or crawling under tables to check and repair the wiring. This part of my job was very difficult from a wheelchair, so I found a great solution—I would borrow a couple of fifth graders whenever I needed help. This had a great byproduct; it allowed me to teach a lot of students how to wire up computers and how to troubleshoot them when they had problems. The students loved to help me, and they made sure they kept up with their work so they would be picked for my jobs.

Later on, the school started using a Scholastic Research Corporation program call SRI which measured students' reading evels. This meant that each year, I had to enroll students in the SRI atabase and manage the testing of all the students three times year. Of course, there was also the job of being on hand to help ne teachers in starting their computer classes and to be around if ny problems came up. I came in about seven every morning to et the computer labs running. Students used to show up early, nd I would let them play on the computers until they had to be 1 their classes. As you might imagine, I also had them help me et everything going.

Jow that I was on staff, I had to go to all of the meetings I had voided when I was a volunteer. In addition, I had to go to a istrict meeting of all the people like me, called ITSAs[33], from he other schools in our area. These meetings reviewed problems eople were having and also introduced new programs and ardware that we were being given.

Along with this buildup of computers and new programs was he network. It was my job to keep all the connections working, to atch in new connections when needed, and to put in work orders or anything that went wrong. As I look back, I wonder how I got ll this done and had time for in-house TV and computer clubs nd helping in aftercare. One year, I even had a night computer lass for families to give parents a chance to keep up with their :ids.

LinkWay Live

t was the time of year when we spend some time to see how we re going to spend our technology money. We had a visit from an BM salesman pitching one of their new products called LinkWay .ive. It was an early attempt to make a program like PowerPoint ong before PowerPoint was created. Its goal was to allow students o make presentations that combined pictures, text, audio, and utomation. After the salesman's visit, we were invited to go to a school near us called Citrus Cove to hear another presentation

---

3. Intergrated Technology School Assistant

on LinkWay Live. Citrus Cove was very excited about getting LinkWay Live and were hoping to get some others schools to use it too. We gave in and bought it.

With the program came an all-day seminar on how to use the program. The day came to gather in the computer lab for the seminar. I was appalled at the seminar; it was totally inadequate. Almost all of our teachers left the seminar with no idea how to use LinkWay Live. I then took the time to read the manuals and experiment with the program and soon became kind of an expert on its use. I was even asked to go to Citrus Cove to teach their users. I think I did a better job than the IBM teacher did, but it still was too difficult for most teachers. You needed a lot of experience with programming and computers plus training on how to read technical instructional manuals to use it.

I used it at Plumosa with students after school when I could spend a lot of time with them. A third-grade boy named Sammy who was in aftercare, came to the computer lab every day after school. He wanted to do something with pictures of animals. First, I had him look in our library for good pictures of exotic animals. Then we put them in LinkWay Live without captions. Then Sammy read enough about the animals to write a couple questions about each one. When Sammy was done, he had several pictures in his program. When you clicked on a picture, a question showed up. After trying to answer it, you drew the mouse across the picture and the answer showed up. There were little arrows so you could move back and forth to other pictures. I had a wonderful time teaching and helping Sammy do it and even a better time seeing how proud he was of his creation. I hope he still remembers it.

My favorite LinkWay Live project was created by two fifth-grade boys, Josh and JC. The boys would take two pictures of someone in exactly the same place, but in one picture, the person would have a bag over their head. Then they would record the person saying, "Who am I?" Their program would allow the user to pick a picture from a collection of student pictures with bags on their heads. When the user clicked the audio button, "Who am I?"

would be said by the student in the picture. The user would then enter their guess. Next, they would click a button, and the picture would fade into the one without the bag if they were correct. They had a lot of fun taking pictures and recording and adding them to their program.

Not too long after LinkWay Live came out, a program called Video Studio came out, which could do all that LinkWay Live could do plus a lot more, and it was much easier to use. We used Video Studio for many years with great results.

Someone Must Be Watching Over Me!

The principal's personal secretary suddenly became very sick and ended up in the hospital for a few weeks. When she returned home, she was in a wheelchair for several months. Once she was feeling better, I was asked if I would mind driving her to school for a few hours. Using my van with a lift was the only way she could get to school. Of course, I said I would be happy to do it. She lived about a mile from Plumosa in an area that I had never known existed. I was amazed to find that two beautiful lakes were so close to the school and that there was a ten-mile canal that led to an even bigger one. When I brought Elaine back, I asked her if there were any lots available on the lakes. Her answer was, "There is one next door to my house." It was overgrown with bushes so I couldn't see the lake, but it was there, and the lake's name was Eden.

I had been very content living in my patio home, but the more I thought about moving to Delray Beach, the more it seemed like a good idea. It also meant that I would not have to drive thirty miles every day. My niece's husband, Mike, was a builder; he agreed to build me a house. I bought a computer program and designed the house layout I wanted. Next, Mike, his partner, Bob, and I showed it to Mike's cousin who was an architect. He made some suggestions to my floor plan, and then he produced his plans and I made a couple more changes, and we had a final plan. I bought the land next to Elaine's house for $120,000, which seemed like a

lot of money, but it was one of only two lots still available on th
lake. My stepmother had just died (another coincidence) when
decided I wanted to buy the land. That meant that my inheritanc
from my father's trust fund would now be available to me at jus
the right time. Guess what? It was $135,000, enough to pay for th
land. I sold my patio home before the house was completed anc
spent three months living in the Homing Inn near school befor
I moved into my new home. The Friday before the weekend
moved in, the teachers at Plumosa had a housewarming showe
for me. They all gave me wonderful house gifts that sure came ir
handy, and many, I still use today.

This was the first time I had a home that was designed to make
life in a wheelchair a little easier. Wow, I was living within a
mile from Plumosa School with a beautiful house with abou
140-feet-long shoreline on a beautiful lake. I now knew why they
call the lake Eden; I was living in paradise. The next surprise was
that over the next ten years, the lot's value went up to about a
million dollars. If I hadn't said yes to tutoring two hours a week
if I hadn't transported Elaine, if I hadn't been spending my life
helping others, I would be back in my patio house alone with
very few friends. Instead, I was in a beautiful house on a lake
with lots of friends and enjoying every minute of my life. God
must have been watching!

Plumosa Staff

The staff at Plumosa was the most wonderful bunch of people I
have known. I showed up in a wheelchair knowing little about
what would be expected of me. When I met the principal, she
asked what had been my position at GTE; I answered, "Senior
scientist." She looked a little taken back. I wondered if she
thought I was too smart for the school. As time went by, I was
asked to do more and more things for more and more teachers,
and I loved it. The first year, I met Mrs. Gomez when she came
to ask me to spend time with Dean. We have been close friends
ever since. For the last eight years, I have been her classroom
assistant. When we were at Plumosa, I helped her a lot, but I was

lso very busy helping all of the teachers. Mrs. Masonberry had ome to Plumosa a few months before I showed up. The way he got along with and handled all the staff—I thought she had een there for many years. I even got to know retired teachers vho came back as volunteers. Margret Macklin, a retired teacher, nd I became good friends. She helped me a lot in the computer lasses, particularly when there were young kids that needed xtra help in reading. As soon as the school got a new Macintosh, was asked to do the monthly newsletters because the Mac, at hat time, had better publishing software than was on the PCs. I vas asked to judge science projects, I was sent to several seminars hat helped me do a better job, and I was asked to help when ve had a booth to show off our school. I didn't just get to know he teachers, I also got to know the substitutes, the parents, and nany of the district staff.

was told by friends that driving with me was like driving with a VIP because wherever we went, kids were always waving and elling, "Hey, Mr. Rosene." I also really enjoyed riding my bike around because wherever I went, I saw current or past students and lots of other people I knew. I really had found a new life—in act, a new world. It reminds me of way back when I thought that should try living somewhere else. In spite of all the friends I left, t was the best decision I could have made.

In-house TV

thought my life was pretty set when the topic of in-house TV ame up. The buildings were wired for in-house TV long before hey were wired for the computer network and Internet. The idea vas to be able to have a morning news program run by students and broadcast it to the whole school. Mr. Ritcy, a fourth-grade teacher, and I decided to see if we could do it. We had two small TV cameras, and we bought some switches so we could switch from one or the other on the air. The input to the TV network was in the media center, so we set up a small area to use as a studio. We asked a few students to help us, and we struggled trying to run a morning news program. It worked but not well. We kept getting interrupted while on the air, and before long, we got very discouraged.

Out of the blue, I was asked to go to a television broadcasting course that was to be held at Forrest Hills High School. The assistant principal, the media specialist, and I went. The first class blew my socks off. I never knew there was such a thing as a video mixer and was amazed at what you could do with it. At Forest Hills, they had a large television studio with several professional cameras and lots of other stuff I couldn't identify. It turned out with a video mixer, you could make someone fly, you could make them a talking head with no body, you could stick an announcer in the middle of anything, and lots more. I finished the course, but I wondered what good it would do. We didn't have a studio or any of the equipment needed to do what I had kind of learned how to do. What I didn't know was that all the newer schools were built with a TV studio and supplied with a complete package of broadcasting equipment. To make things more even, the older schools were going to be getting all the equipment they needed for the TV studio.

Suddenly, I was faced with more boxes of electronics and cameras than I could count. I felt like a kid on Christmas morning that had just been given all he wanted plus a lot more. Our new lab wing was finished about that time thus the old computer room in the media center wasn't being used. We turned it into a TV studio. It was a dream come true! A technician from district showed up to help us set it up. Actually, he set it up, and I watched and asked lots of questions. We had a couple of eight-foot tables with all the equipment on one side of the room, and we used one of our old computer desks as the anchor's news desk. We had a video mixer and two monitors to show what was coming from two of the most magnificent, professional TV cameras on wheels I had ever seen. We had a VCR/CD player and a monitor to show what was going over the air and to record what was going over the air. I practiced with the mixer hardware until I felt comfortable going on the air. I wrote a script that included an introduction, teachers out, what's for lunch, sports report, lost and found, and a place for special topics of the day. I defined each job that a student would do, and I picked our first team and started training them. The principal told me this was for the kids, and she would not appear. That was another action that showed the wisdom of Mrs. Masonberry. In fact, except for a few times when a teacher had something to announce or a prize to award, no adults appeared.

It came time for our opening morning. I was real nervous but things went very well. One of our anchors had just come to Plumosa that year; he was a natural. He later became top officer of the ROTC at Atlantic High School. To us, he could ad-lib himself out of any situation and make everything sound great. We had movies of after school sports, and our sportscaster would sometimes appear as if he was at the events even though he was in our studio. We made eight by eleven posters of each item they served in the cafeteria so we could show what was for lunch as the anchor read. It was kind of boring holding up lost and found items, so members of our team wore them, and we treated it like a fashion show. We even had appropriate music as they strutted around while the announcer described what they were wearing.

Then we had another surprise: district carpenters came and walled off the control tables into a separate room with glass panels. Then we got an intercom system to keep the control room in touch with the anchors and the media specialist who was then the floor supervisor. A few years later, the district gave each school a series of tapes called "Mr. Rick." It was designed for news programs like ours and it was great. We even had Mr. Rick come to our school and put on a program. His techniques were to get the students excited about how well they could do if they tried. It seemed to liven up the school. We trained fourth-grade students at the end of each year to be anchors, camera people, etc., in order to have them ready to take over the next year. All in all, it was a great success and a lot of fun. Students worked hard to become part of it.

Several years later, Mrs. Masonberry was assigned principal of a new school that opened a few miles from Plumosa. The new principal we got announced she would be on the news every morning, and we must start at eight unless she was late and we couldn't start until she got there. That was the end of a morning news show that the students liked and that kept their interest. Each morning, she said exactly the same thing and took long enough that there wasn't much time do anything else. The result was that the students started making fun of the words she used every day. "Now students, you must remember the Plumosa way," which was followed by giving all the school rules. Kids started ignoring what was on the program and started making fun of it. I felt very sad to see the misuse of all we had accomplished. It really hurt when you spend a lot of time designing a program, teaching the students, and learning how to handle a new field just to have it destroyed, particularly when it is done by a principal who walks in and says it will be done her way without taking the time to see what we were doing.

Fourth- and Fifth-grade Technology Clubs

Since the very first year I was at Plumosa, teachers started sending students to the media center after school for me to help them with their homework. The hook was that after they were done, they were allowed to play on the computers using whatever programs they wanted. This is how LinkWay Live was used. If someone asked, I would teach him or her how to use it. I never planned any special projects for after school. They would pick what they wanted to do. When the new lab wing was built and we ended up with two computer labs, about forty-eight new, more powerful computers with CD drives, an iMac, lots more software, and Internet access, I got to thinking I could do more. At this time, I decided it was stupid to refer to the computer rooms as the "old one" and the "new one". I named the old one "The Harry Potter Lab." I designed a Harry Potter wallpaper screen for each computer, put up some Harry Potter posters, and made a colored name sign for the door. At that time, each computer in the Harry Potter lab had a beanie baby sitting on top of it. It gave the little kids something to cuddle while using the computers, and it made the lab look really great. Right after we got the second lab, the theme of the fifth-grade banquet was Dr. Seuss's *Oh, the Places You'll Go!* After the banquet, I got all the little Dr. Seuss figures

hat were centerpieces on the tables and all the big figures and
astles that the art teacher had painted for the walls and turned
he new lab into the Dr. Seuss Lab. I put a little figure on each
omputer by attaching a craft stick on their backs and a hunk of
'lasticine to hold them upright. I put the big figures and castles
ıp on the walls. I downloaded a lot of Dr. Seuss pictures for
vallpapers on each computer. When I got done, I felt like I had
he best computer rooms in the county, both for looks and for
vhat they contained. I received a lot of positive comments about
he labs from visitors.

had run fourth—and fifth-grade computer clubs for several
ears. These clubs ran this way:

1. The first thing they had to do each meeting was to spend
   twenty minutes using the touch typing program.
2. They had to do this until they had passed unit I and II of
   the program.
3. After their typing, they could use any of the software or
   building kits we had in the lab. If they wanted to, they
   could go online or just listen to music on a computer.

had been intrigued with small computers that LEGO Dacta were
naking. The computers had bumps on them like all LEGO parts so
ou could build models around them. There was a picture-driven
orogramming package that allowed the user to write a program
ınd download it to the little computers using an ultraviolet link
hat was built into the computers. It sounds difficult but it was
ery easy. I ended up buying several of these computers and
several LEGO kits for making all sorts of things. The school and I
ılso invested in a lot of CDs because with our new computers, we
how had CD drives. I went to the Florida Technology Conference
on computers and education. I got fascinated with K-Nect kits for
ouilding large roller coasters, big ball machines, and amusement
oark rides. Of course, I had to have some so I some some kits and
other teachers bought some kits to.

As I built up more and more equipment, I was having more and
more students stay after school. I realized I had to do something

to get the students away from just listening to music or playing dumb games on the Internet. The plan I came up with was as follows:

1. The first two steps didn't change from what I was doing except I bought some black plastic covers that covered the keyboard keys. If they were going to learn touch typing they might as well learn the real thing.
2. When they passed unit I and II, they became members of the computer club.
3. I defined five levels of membership: member, roboteer adventurer, astronaut, and Webmaster.
4. A member was given a sash I devised to go around their neck, which could hold colored beads like the girls often wore in their hair. Each time they made a new level, they got a different color bead for their sash.

They earned levels by doing projects I had predefined. The one for becoming a roboteer was building a LEGO car around a LEGO computer with a black-and-white sensors and motors and programming it so it would solve a maze. The maze was made out of a four- by six-foot whiteboard and black masking tape.

To become an adventurer, they had to solve one of many adventure games I had in the lab. I even had a copy of the first adventure game that was made in the midseventies called The Colossal Cave.

To become an astronaut, they had to operate a Mars lander to explore a Mars site in order to find things hidden in it. The Mars site was a plywood box, about ten by eight feet in size; it had mountains and valleys and caves. To explore it, they sat at a computer, walled off from the site, and controlled a program we got from NASA to give kids a feeling of what manning a Mars rover was like. Our Mars rover was made out of LEGO parts and a LEGO computer, and it had a television camera to send back to the computer what it was seeing.

'o become a Webmaster, they had to make a Web site. I had taken course in Web site management at district and came back with copy of the Web program.

'es, I did have students that became Webmasters! I also allowed tudents to define alternative tasks for getting their beads, but hey had to have my approval. One great substitute task was naking a movie. We had an iMac with movie-editing software. It llowed the user to combine slides, film clips, and music. Some of he students in the morning TV club also used it to make programs o be used with our news program. Another alternative was to nake K-Nect models. We had several very large kits so we could ıave lots of kids making things.

At the end of each school year, we handed out certificates for all orts of things including clubs. I made a set of five certificates, one or each level a student could reach. They each had a background ⱶicture that represent the level and then were overprinted with he text describing what it represented and the students' name ınd signatures.

Was it a success? I'll give you some facts and you be the judge.

The fifth-grade technology club attendance went from about twenty to ıbout fifty. That seemed amazing to me since we only had about ninety ʿifth-grade students in the school. It got to be so big I split it into two fays, but that backfired, as kids came both days. I got Mr. Harris to ʿelp me, as it got too big for me to handle alone. Since all students ıad a choice of what they were doing, I didn't need to have a lot of fuplicate programs and equipment, and I usually could handle the ones :hat needed my help.

I had a fourth-grade club, which was exactly the same, except the tasks ʿor levels were easier, and only unit I of the typing program was needed :o pass. I had twenty-five students with a waiting list of four to five more. One of the most popular programs was Roller Coaster Tycoon. This was a great example of a simulation-type program where the user builds and runs an amusement park. The success was based on how

much money they made. A new fifth-grade boy came to our school i
March. He liked playing Roller Coaster Tycoon so much he asked M
Harris if he would fail him so he could come back next year and play
some more.

In 2010, Plumosa was moved to a new building and became Plumos
School of the Arts. I was at the farewell party when a young man o
about eighteen with long black hair came up to me and asked, "Aren'
you Mr. Rosene?" When I answered yes, he told me he had seen th
article about the farewell party in the newspaper, and he came, hoping
would be there. He told me how much he and his sister had enjoyed m
computer classes and clubs and just wanted me to know they felt I wa
the best teacher in the school.

Somehow, the people who were turning CongressCommunity Middl
School into a technology magnet heard about my club and asked me t
come and tell them about it. I have to admit I was very proud at wha
I had done and got great satisfaction watching our students enjoying
learning.

When it came to the end-of-year party, I combined the student
in my clubs with the students who took part in interschool sport
and other sports projects that Coach Tingley ran. We always
had it on Wednesday because that was the day McDonalds ha
twenty-nine-cent cheeseburgers. We would get one hundred
cheeseburgers, a dozen pizzas, plus many of the parents brough
ice cream and cookies and helped us serve all the food. Before the
food, we had a big game of Capture the Flag. Our parties were
always a big hit.

I look back with fond memories of those years. I loved seeing
how popular what I had set up was and loved watching those
big smiles on the kids' faces. It meant that I came to work a
seven and got home at about five, but it was worth every minute
of it. I can't describe the feeling of going home knowing I have
helped kids and made it possible for them to do things they
really enjoyed.

FCAT and Related Disasters

When I first came to Plumosa, the teachers gave tests as they thought appropriate. Also, they had small test booklets on particular goals. For example, the first year I was there, I had fifth graders coming to me with small quiz books for long division. The book would hold about twenty problems, and they wanted me to correct their work. If they did well enough, they would get credit for it, and they could move on to the next test booklet. If they got some wrong, I would show them their mistakes and have them do some more work. I was impressed how seriously the students took these tests and how hard they worked to pass them. In March, they would have an assessment test developed by the school district to help students and teachers know how they were doing. It was very simple to apply and seemed to provide all the data teachers needed to be able to modify their lessons to fit as their classes progressed.

Then along came FCAT!

In the beginning, FCAT was not too much different than the assessment tests that had been used, except the instructions for administering FCAT were a little stricter and the results were publicized a lot more. Then along came Jeb Bush, who made the FCAT into a tool to rate teachers and schools; that turned FCAT into a disaster! If the socioeconomic level of the schools was more or less constant across all schools, Jeb's idea might not have been too bad. However, the socioeconomic levels of the district schools vary widely, which means the FCAT results would vary widely for lots of reasons.

For example, school X is in an area where most of the parents have college degrees, where in most of the households one parent is home, where the parents all spoke English. School Z is in an area where most of the parents have not gone to college, where in most homes both parents work, and where in a lot of the homes parents do not speak English well. Why in the world would anyone expect both schools to do the same and why in the world would the teachers and principal of the Z school be considered weak because their school had lower grades?

Guess what? It gets even worse! All the teachers in school X would get a bonus for doing such a good job! School X has a lot more parents with time to be in the PTA and a clientele that would contribute a lot more money to fund-raising efforts than school Z. The question is does school X need the money more than school Z? No, obviously not! I have been working in schools like school Z, and I have seen how much the PTA helps a school. I have also seen how much the teachers still have to buy themselves to help their classes through the year and how much they need volunteers.

In addition to the unfairness of comparing grades without normalizing out the differences between the constituencies, the FCAT grades—A,B,C,D,F—were broadcast to the world, thus running down schools that were actually doing very well, if not better than some A schools. But this was not enough; students from F schools could get vouchers so they could go to a private or parochial school. This meant that students with the least educated parents, without a chance of getting much help or encouragement at home, were offered vouchers to a private school. These are the kind of students that are kicked out of private schools because they get no guidance from home on how to act and how to work. These are the kinds of students that really need testing and they get less. The worst part of the vouchers was that if a student went to a private or parochial school, they did not have to take FCAT tests. What this says to me is private schools are assumed to teach so much better than the public schools that they don't need to be tested! That is just not true! It also implies that when a student is given a voucher, he/she no longer needs to be tested. Let's face it. The main reason students are sent to private schools is to keep their children away from the lower-class students. That implies to me that we have a lot of bigots around. How sad! It seems to me that vouchers are being used as a means to eliminate public schools because public schools are a socialistic policy. My eeling is that public school is the primary thing that has made ur country strong and our people happy.

As I watched the effect on the schools that I volunteered at, I was hocked at what I saw and what I heard through the grapevine. The following are examples:

1. Almost no social studies were taught until April.
2. Almost no science was taught until April.
3. Word would filter down that on some math topics, there were no questions on the FCAT so that topic was not tought.
4. Some schools would teach nothing but reading and math all year long.
5. Time for Fine art would be used for tutoring as the FCAT got closer
6. Aftercare became mostly a teaching and homework time with very little recreation.
7. After school Clubs became fewer and limited to one hour in order to not interfere with aftercare courses.
8. Teachers were moving to the A-type schools so they could get bonuses
9. Teachers were forced to teach how to take tests rather than course content.

When I started volunteering twenty years ago, I was surprised at how much the children were taught, plus the extra special activities at holidays as well as the special programs that reinforced the subjects during the year. I was also very impressed with the efforts the teachers would go through to bring their subjects home to the kids. One class cooked a pioneer's meal and asked their parents to come share it. They even dressed like pioneers. The fifth grade cooked a Thanksgiving dinner as they learned about the history of Thanksgiving. A fourth-grade class made a skateboard as they studied simple machines.

I went to school in Newton, Massachusetts, in the '30s and '40s. At that time, the Newton schools were rated the best in the nation. What I saw in Palm Beach twenty years ago was far better than any schooling I had. I became a full-time volunteer and have worked hard to provide some of that extra incentive and awareness I saw when I started volunteering. Sadly, FCAT has taken much away from what all our students are receiving for primarily political reasons. I hope that someday, our leaders will realize schools should teach a lot more than just how to take reading and math tests.

The public schools have a small percentage of whites. In fact, we have a lot of African, Haitian, Asian, and Islamic students. I have found that across the board, all the races do great and get along well with each other. Most of them work hard, do very well, cause no problems, and are very nice, lovable kids who parents should be proud of. Of course, we have a few that cause problems, but the administration takes care of them very well and usually straightens them out.

Multicultural Activities

Plumosa was a multicultural school, there was no question about that, but the things we did because of it were interesting and a lot a fun. A nice young couple from South America moved into our area. They had two boys: one was starting fourth grade and one was starting kindergarten. They had only been here a short time when they were forced to move from their apartment. The school asked me if I could put them up for a few weeks. They stayed in my spare bedroom, their boys slept on the couch in my living room, I got to eat lots of Spanish food, and their belongings were in my garage. It turned out they stayed a couple of months before their apartment situation was worked out. I really enjoyed getting to know them and learning about their culture and country. I saw both boys graduate from grade school.

Around that same time, we had a new teacher come to Plumosa, Mrs. Castenater, to teach ESOL (English for Speakers of Other Languages). She went out of her way to plan and run Cinco e Mayo celebrations. They were great. She had all the Latino amilies bring all sorts of exotic Latino food; their kids dressed p in their native clothes and danced and sang to great Latino music. One year, we had a super mariachi band play. Each year, I lways look forward to Cinco de Mayo.

One year, we had a boy in our class from Palestine. His mother brought a complete Palestinian meal including dessert for our lass. I was surprised at how great her cooking was and how much I liked Palestinian cooking. At the end of each year, we have a talent show. Often, we are entertained by native dancing and singing. All in all, the many races and cultures bring a great ichness to our schools; I hope they never lose it.

The picture on the cover of my book I took one day in the computer room. I happened to look up and see four boys, each of a different race, working away side by side. Two were even sharing the same computer and chair. This picture to me was a great example of how I wish the world or, at least, how our country could be. It also shows how well integrated our school was then.

What It's All About

have dealt with thousands of students, and I could fill this book with stories of students with both good and bad results; however, here would be lot more with happy endings.

One year, a new student (Shimshon) came to Plumosa for his fifth grade. He was in Mr. Harris's class, he took part in our TV news, and he was very active in my technology club. I never saw or heard him get mad at anyone or cause any problems in class. He went out of his way to help others and was a friend to all. He wanted to get a computer and asked my help in picking one out. I helped him pick one and went over to his house and helped him set it up. He was the kind of student all schools would like to have.

After he graduated from Plumosa, he told me that he had gone to another grade school nearby and he had been kicked out after the fourth grade because he was causing so much trouble. He then told me that he promised his mother he would do well at Plumosa. I found out that the principal of his old school asked our principal, Mrs. Masonberry, if she would let him come to Plumosa. Only Mrs. Masonberry and Mr. Harris knew about his past. Our principal let him come because she always felt every student deserved a chance, and if any teacher could straighten him out, it was Mr. Harris. Another wise decision by Mrs. Masonberry.

All through middle school and high school, Shimshon kept in touch by coming over to my house to tell me how he was doing. He kept doing well in his class work, and he was a star on Boynton High's wrestling team. After that, he got accepted to Florida A&M, where he majored in architecture. During his college years, he would call me from Tallahassee to fill me in on how he was doing, and when he came home, he always stopped by my house. This April, he graduated with a degree in architecture and has a full tuition scholarship from Florida A&M for his master's. Not all kids work out that great, but it is so wonderful to see it happen. It makes life worth living although I can't help thinking where he would be if Mrs. Masonberry hadn't taken the chance on accepting him. I have always gone out of my way to try and help the kids that continually get in trouble, and you know what? It helps! Often, a child gives up. He/she thinks no one cares or will help. When I see this happening, I go out of my way to get to know that student and help the student realize someone cares and that he/she can do better!

At the end of the year, we hand out certificates of merit for all the things students have earned. One year, one of my really outstanding students named Elliot gave me a certificate to thank me for being a great teacher and a good friend. To me, that was the nicest thing a student could do to thank a teacher. I framed it along with his picture and put it on my wall. He is a student I never want to forget.

run into ex-students all the time. Just recently, I ran into Frank, boy that was in the fifth grade when I started at Plumosa; now e is in the marines. I never had much to do with Frank. He was n outstanding student and didn't need my tutoring. He did one hing that I will never forget. The fifth-grade students were all naking a project connected with marbles running down a track.)ne boy did not have a father that could help him so Frank rought him home and got his father to help him. The thing that vas so wonderful about it was Frank was black and the boy was vhite. Racial problems have almost totally disappeared from ur grade schools. Instead, everybody respects everyone; what a reat way to live.

)ften during the years I have been involved with the schools, one f the students would seem to latch onto me. Wherever I was, hey were there also; they would give me hugs whenever they ould. It usually turned out that they didn't have a father or had ust lost their father. One time, a student's parents had just been livorced, and I became his father figure. It took me a while to ealize what was going on, but I sure was glad I was there when e needed me.

)nce after a technology club meeting, I found a little boy kindergarten age) sitting outside the computer room. He was he brother of one of the girls in the club. I asked him why he was here, and I'll never forget his reply. "I have a bully." It turned ut he had two bullies. One was a second grader and one a third rader. With the help of one of the teachers, we tracked down the ullies and had a talk with them. He had no more trouble. I also ave the two bullies a lot of extra attention whenever I could, vhich seemed to help solve their problem. In fact, they became wo of the best-behaved students in my technology club.

How Not to Select a New Principal

very once in a while, the thought would come to me of how wful it would be if Eula Masonberry had to move to another school. Well, it finally happened at the end of my eleventh year at Plumosa. Eula was selected to be principal of a new grad school called Crosspointe, which was opening a few miles from Plumosa. Eula asked any staff that might like to go with her to let her know. Most of the staff wanted to go, but of course she could just take a few. I thought about it for a long time but I realized all the work and money and time I had put into the computer rooms and the special equipment and computer programs I had bought now belonged to Plumosa. Also, Clyde Harris was staying. We had become good friends, and that was also an important reason to stay. If I left, I would be letting a lot of kids down. That was the straw that broke the camel's back. I would stay.

The procedure for selecting a new principal was that a committee made up of parents, teachers, and administrators would interview applicants and eventually recommend a candidate. Rumors went around as prospects were interviewed. The only specific person I heard that had applied was a friend of Clyde's that was currently an assistant principal in Boca Elementary School. The vote was taken, and rumor had it that Clyde's friend had won. Each day after that, I was expecting all of us to be called to a meeting to meet the new principal. Finally, early one morning before school had started, that day came. As I was heading toward the media center, I saw Eula and two other women I didn't know heading for the media center. My hopes fell; Clyde's friend wasn't picked. The two unknown women must be our area superintendent and the new principal. I was right! The new principal was the assistant principal from another elementary school. She told everyone Plumosa was the only school where she wanted to be principal. She also went on at great lengths on why Plumosa was so wonderful. What a lot of bull! It seems to me that it would be nice to find out about a school firsthand before trying to impress people with what you think of them! Next, she handed out chocolate heart-shaped lollipops. To make matters worse, she gave them to the teachers that were going to Crosspointe first. When I left that meeting, I was about as low as anyone can be. We later heard that Clyde's friend got all of the first place votes and all our new principal got was a one-third place vote. Obviously, was all decided before the committee was even formed. Her usband worked at district, so it was easy to see where the pull came from.

The new principal knew nothing about how to manage a staff or, or that matter, treat people. During the first few months she was here, two PTA presidents quit, and she had to take over the PTA functions herself, as no parent would. She would go out of her way to embarrass teachers in staff meetings. She was just plain rude. I blew up at her when she moved a lot of the new computers in cartons into the middle of one of the computer labs, which made it very hard to teach when you couldn't see the whole class at once. She planned a Christmas party at the clubhouse where she lived and insisted we all come. You were confronted if you didn't sign up. In my twelve years at Plumosa, I never had to call the office for help because I had a student I couldn't handle. Her first year, we had the only really vicious student I had seen. You had to watch him carefully all the time. I had a practice that when a class came into the lab, if a student argued over a seat or tries to take someone else's seat, I would have the student stand by the door until everyone else was seated. The tallest fifth grader argued over a seat, so I had him stand by the door. Then the vicious student started fighting over a seat, so I had him stand by the closet door. I turned for just a few seconds, and when I turned back, the tall student was doubled up in pain; he had been kicked or hit very hard in his private parts. The vicious student was partway back to his door. At that moment, the principal happened to walk in. I told her what happened and asked her to take the vicious kid to the office. She took him with her, but five minutes later, he showed up at the door. That shows her idea of helping a teacher.

During the day, I would often have to go to classrooms to fix a computer problem. On a few occasions, I found teachers in their room alone crying. She was disliked by most of the teachers at Plumosa. Her crowning move in evilness was a couple years later, when Clyde Harris was retiring after thirty-eight years at Plumosa and it was also the fiftieth anniversary of Plumosa. She held a combined party for the two events in the parking lot of Ellie's Diner! There was no food or drinks unless you were in and bought your own. There were a couple tables and a few chairs under an awning for people to sit at. That was it; what disgrace. Her reason was that if it had been at Plumosa, there would have been too many black people, and she was afraid some damage would be done! I think that says it all about her values. A few weeks later, I had a party at my house for Clyde. Over seventy-five people came and had a great time. There was no damage, and of course, the principal was not invited. Three teachers that had been at Plumosa for a long time retired at the same time, and there was a big party at Old School Square. She was not invited to that party either.

In March, I realized I could not take any more and told her I was retiring at the end of the school year. I already had arranged to volunteer at Crosspointe. Some of the teachers told me I should take all the computer-room stuff I bought to Crosspointe, but left it at Plumosa because I felt it really belonged to Plumosa. Of course, I hoped it would get used.

I went back to Plumosa about four years after I left. There had been no computer clubs since I left, and all of the equipment was sitting as I had left it, gathering dust. Whenever I meet a student that was there when I left, they ask, "Why did you let us down?" I will always feel sorry I let so many down.

She took down all the Dr. Seuss decorations in the Seuss lab and all the Harry Potter and computer club posters. In fact, everything I had on the walls, including all the signs I had carefully made telling students how to act in the lab were taken down. I was told she didn't even look at what was on the walls. Her directions were simple—take it all down. She had the Mars sight thrown out without even bothering to find out what it was. The main office had just been refurnished just a year before she came, it was really nice furniture that was very appropriate for an elementary school. She refurnished the office with what looked to me like copies of Elizabethan furniture. To make it worse, she then change the décor of the rest of the office into a country store decor.

Good-bye, Plumosa

My twelfth year was over; I was leaving Plumosa. It had been a fantastic twelve years, and I had a lot of anger toward the principal pent up inside of me. The break was very simple. I went to the final staff luncheon of the year, and the principal presented me with a plaque recognizing my service. I felt a lot of disappointment, but it didn't come close to quelling my anger for how the new principal had ruined the school. I had a summer to get over it. I can't even remember what I did that summer. Usually, I had lots of projects planned to get ready for the next year; that year, I had none.

A few weeks after school ended, Bob Tingley, the physical education teacher at Plumosa, invited me to go to dinner with him at Tony Roma's. He came by my house for a drink first, and we drove to Tony's together. I was shocked to walk into a room of over forty friends. Some I left at Plumosa and some I would meet again at Crosspointe. It was a retirement party for me even though I wasn't retiring. I was just changing schools. But there was more! I was given a lighthouse, not a real one but a six-foot concrete lighthouse to put in my yard. The letter that came with it made me cry. Here it is:

Dear Fred,

All of us hope that our gift of a lighthouse will light the way for years of enrichment, happiness, and enjoyment. You have touched all of us during your eleven years of service to the children.

Just as this lighthouse will be a beam of light in your yard for years, so have you been a beam of light helping lead the way for our students into the future with your technical expertise.

As you leave the shores of Plumosa and old friends, the beam of light will lead you to new friends who will welcome your arrival on their shores.

We will all miss you.

ENJOY!!! RELAX!!! STAY IN TOUCH!!!

YOUR COLLEAGUES AND FRIENDS

It was a great good-bye but an even better hello!

Crosspointe

I started at Crosspointe a couple months later, wondering if i would be as good as Plumosa. The first thing I did was introduc myself to the woman who was the ITSA, the position I had hac at Plumosa. I spent the first couple of weeks trying to help her but I soon realized she was afraid I would get her job, so sh wouldn't let me do much. Then Bonnie Gomez, whom I workec with at Plumosa, said to me, "Why aren't you coming up t my room?" The next day, I went up to her room and have beer going to her room ever since. I was essentially a classroom aide I helped students that were having problems. I would take smal groups and teach them how to use some science kits. I woulc help with the math teaching. I was just kind of the teacher' "Man Friday."

One of good things about working in one classroom was you go to know the class very well. After a few years, things changed Mrs. Gomez was made the science teacher for third, fourth and fifth grades, not a homeroom teacher. I liked science so thought this move would be good, but it meant we taught eacl item seventeen times. That got a little boring. One day, wher a fifth-grade class was in the science lab, I noticed a student hadn't seen before, so I went over to his table to speak to him. told him who I was and then he said, "Hi, my name is Jean bu my mother calls me Elie. You can call me Elie." At that time, could never have dreamt the effect Elie would have on my life That story will come later.

met a fifth-grade student, Donald, at lunch and started telling im about the things I had done in my computer clubs at 'lumosa. He wanted to try some of the games, particularly the :oller Coaster Tycoon. He inspired me to start a computer games lub. I had to beg the ITSA to give me the password I would need o install things. I talked to the aftercare manager, Jane Murphy, nto buying some programs with aftercare funds. Actually, that vas easy. I had helped Jane for many years, and she knew her ftercare students would benefit from what I was doing. The ;ames I got were of two types—adventure or simulation games. n an adventure game, the user had to work out what the mystery vas, how to solve it, and then solve. An adventure game called :olossal Cave was the first computer game of any kind that took a lot of playing and thinking to solve. I first played it in 1977. iimulation games put the player in the shoes of someone else. The avorite by far was Roller Coaster Tycoon in which the user had o design, build, and run an amusement park with the purpose)f making money. I had a Roller Coaster Tycoon contest. Each)layer was given a certain amount of time measured in weeks. [heir amusement parks were judged on how creative they were, iow clean and well kept the grounds were, how well run they vere, and how much money they made. The kids really got into he contest. I also started a chess club that was good but never too)opular.

[here were two mothers that ran the PTA; they seemed to be here every day, all day. It turned out that Donald was the oldest ;on of one of them. Between the two, Joanne and Karen, they had ive sons, and they were there every day for the next eight years (2003-2010) until all their sons moved on. They organized and :an an incredible PTA, and I really wonder how we will get along vithout them next year. They also ran Boy Scouts and Cub Scouts :roops that got a lot of our students involved in Scouts. We were)lessed with the best in PTAs; next year will be tough for the ;chool to adjust to something less. I knew all of their sons well, ind we all became good friends. Donald and Carl, their oldest ;ons, are both Eagle Scouts.

Senior Volunteer of the Year

I had only been at Crosspointe a few years when I was told that my name was being put in for Senior Volunteer of the Year. Up until that time, I had never heard of volunteer awards. The way it went was each school in the district was asked to submit three nominations—one for Youth Volunteer of the Year, Adult Volunteer of the Year, and Senior Volunteer of the Year. I knew they were going to put my name in, and I think they did it more than once. Anyway, a few years later, it turned out I was Senior Volunteer of the County. I was told that each member of the reviewing team read the selections and picked me. Next, the winners from the southeast area counties—Dade, Broward, Palm Beach, Indian River, and St. Lucie—were sent to another panel of judges, and again, they told me everyone chose me.

When I saw the paper that had been submitted about me, I have to admit I was impressed at all I had done. However, I felt the real reason I won was because of the testimonials that had been included. I have included them here to give my readers a feel of what it is like to be praised by your peers for you work. It is not something that occurs often; I never dreamed of it happening to me.

Testimonials

I have worked with Fred for many years. His heart is with the students. In years past, he has helped with children that needed special one on one tutoring in math. He has always come through. I can't think of a more deserving person for this award.

Jill Brown

Mr. Rosene is a dedicated volunteer who gives many hours of his time to help students. He cares deeply about their academic success. He used to volunteer his time for a computer club after school hours also.

M. Carter-Dimon

I had the pleasure of meeting Mr. Fred Rosene when he was newly retired and looking to fill in a few hours of his weeks by volunteering in an elementary school class room. He came from a very successful career in the business industry and was looking to give something back to the leaders of tomorrow. That was 15 years ago and the few hours a week has turned into 6 hours (or more) a day, five days a week. During this time he has given endless quantities of love, understanding, encouragement, and money to these children. He has been a blessing to all he has touched during this time and we have all grown to be better people by knowing him.

Bonnie Gomez

Whenever you see Mr. Rosene at school you most always see one or more students by his side. For as long as I have known him, he has always been there for any child who needed help with their school work or just needed a friend to talk to. Mr. Rosene is a volunteer teaching science and math, leads the chess and computer clubs, and even teaches magic tricks to students.

Two years ago, my son had the opportunity to have Mr. Rosene as a volunteer in his fourth grade class. Mr. Rosene was there every day to help students especially in the area of math and science. This was a big help for my son who really enjoyed working with Mr. Rosene. The following year Mr. Rosene volunteered in the science program. Again my son had the opportunity to work with him and again with the help of Mr. Rosene he made great gains in science.

Today, even though my son is no longer at this school, he and Mr. Rosene have a bond that will endure a lifetime. This bond is also shared by many other students who have had the opportunity to work with Mr. Rosene. He is a kind, caring, and dedicated man. I truly appreciate all he has done for the students of Crosspointe Elementary School.

Thank You, Mr. Rosene. You are awesome!!
Patty Druckenbrod

I have known Fred Rosene for over ten years. He first volunteered at Plumosa Elementary where I once worked and now at Crosspointe Elementary. He is an exceptional individual. He has become a permanent fixture at our school. Both the students and the staff worry when he does not come to school. He sometimes works longer hours than the actual staff. Not only has he worked with the students having difficulty in the academics, he also mentors the students. He constantly encourages them to excel. Along with classroom tutoring, Mr. Rosene has worked with the students in the Chess Club, Video Club, and Technology Club.

Our school is a Title I school. The majority of our students come from low socio-economic families. As a safety Patrol sponsor, I am always on the look out for sponsorships to help defray the cost of our annual Washington D.C. trip. Each year, Mr. Rosene blesses our school with over $5000. This much needed money makes it possible for some of our students to go on the trip. His one request was not to make it known to the students. We are so fortunate to have such a devoted and selfless individual working with our students.

M. Cambronne

The area winners (5) were invited to go to St. Petersburg for th
award ceremony. Mrs. Masonberry, who had retired, and lots o
teachers that had retired or could get away went with me. Hav
you ever been given a standing ovation? It's really weird. I ha
to work to hold back my tears of joy and smile at the same time
After I got back, the county held a breakfast at the Kravis Cente
to honor its volunteers. I again was honored with an even greate
standing ovation. It was more than I ever expected but one of th
neatest things that had happened to me. It was all for doing wha
I loved and making a difference.

Elie

Elie came to Plumosa for fifth grade. He was a very friendly
outgoing type of boy. Although I didn't know it at the time, he
was from a poor family. A student I had stayed in touch with
from Plumosa was using my computer, and he bid on eBay for a
PSP 2, one of the new game systems that had just come out. The
problem was he hadn't asked my permission. I took the PSP 2
from him and decided to give it to a student at school. I asked a
few students if they had a game system and they all answered
yes. I asked Elie if he had one and finally got a no so I gave the
PSP 2 to him. I have never been hugged so long and so hard. I fel
I had made a good choice.

The first day of spring break, I took him to Steak 'n Shake for
lunch. All the way there, he kept saying, "I can't believe my
teacher is taking me to lunch." At Steak 'n Shake, he ordered more
food than I had ever seen anyone eat at one setting. Then he go
take-home boxes to take a lot of it home. What I didn't know at
that time was he was taking food home to his sister and mother
It turned out they had very little food at home. Elie pleaded with
me to drive by my house on the way home, so I did, and then we
passed the UCC Church of the Palms on the way to his house. Elie
said, "That's my church." I was very surprised at that comment, as
I had gone to the Church of the Palms several times since I moved
to Boynton Beach about ten years ago. It was a lily white, country

lub congregation and seemed unfriendly to me. Elie was Haitian; e just didn't fit the image of the Church of Palms I remembered. he next Sunday, I went to the Church of the Palms—how it ad changed. A Haitian church had joined with them; they had new minister who preached a great sermon, and they seemed lot more friendly than I remembered. I had gone to a United Church of Christ all of my life. I knew at once that I had found ny church down here; it was so like my church up north. I met lie's mother and sister and saw that Elie was very involved in the unday school. After that, I became Elie's family ride to church. kept going and kept meeting new members, and I found that I eally enjoyed the church. I joined the church and the Sunday I was resented to the congregation as a new member, I was asked if I vould be moderator. In a congregational church, the moderator is he top lay officer of the church. The moderator chairs the church ouncil and the congregational meetings. When I was asked, I ealized when I transferred to the Church of the Palms that I had illed out a form telling what I had done at my old church. I made he mistake of putting down that I had been moderator.

commented that I didn't know much about the church, but hey pointed out I had been a moderator, and that was what was mportant. I served as moderator for three years, which is the ongest period the bylaws allowed. When I was moderator of Eliot, my church up north, it was easy. Things just rolled along imoothly, and no major problems came up. In the Church of the Palms, we seem to have one big problem after the other. Yet, I lo not regret accepting the position of moderator. It was a great hree years; we were able to handle the problems, and I now know everyone in the church. Church of the Palms turned out to be a friendly group of Christians who I very much enjoy being with. Thank you, Elie.

got more and more involved with Elie's family. His mother lost her job and they were being evicted. The church helped find a place for them to stay, but it was in the worst part of Lake Worth. To keep Elie out of trouble, I had Elie spending weekends and vacations with me.

Then his mother temporarily lost her work papers for some reason, and I was suddenly supporting a second family. About a year later, Elie's mother got her work papers back, but because of the recession, she still hasn't been able to get a job.

A few weeks after I started going to Church of the Palms (2006) I got a real bad infection in my left ankle and ended up in the hospital.

My ankle started bothering me in 1970 when I went swimming with some friends at a Howard Johnson's indoor pool. I scrapped my ankle but it healed up in a week;or so I thought! A few months later, I started running a high temperature (104 degrees) and ended up in the hospital. I had an ulcer on my ankle that never seemed to heal up. When I retired, the first thing I did was to have my ankle operated on to relieve the pressure of the bone on my skin. Eureka, after twenty years, it was finally healed;or so I thought! About six or seven years into my retirement, the ulcer came back. I returned to taking care of the ulcer again; every morning I would put an Ace bandage on my leg and hoping it would get better. It didn't! I had sixty hyperbaric treatments and lots of infusion treatments, but they did no good.

n 2006, it kicked up again; that was enough! I had infusion reatments for a week and went back in the hospital to have my oot removed. You would think that when you are always in a wheelchair you wouldn't miss a foot. Not so—my balance was hrown off, and for a while, I had a hard time to get in and out f my car or the recliner I used to sit in a lot. I fell a few times. I ad to call 911 only once, but somehow, I got through it. One of he aides, Lilly, at the rehab center, came home with me to help ne get adjusted. It took about a month and a half before I felt omfortable again. She moved in with a daughter in kindergarten nd a young sister in middle school. I suddenly had a family I lidn't expect. About six months later, Lilly moved out. Just in ime for me to have Elie with me on weekends and vacations.

have been supporting Elie's family and helping Lilly while she goes to school to be a nurse. I went over one day to the field day t Plumosa to help Coach Tingley. I had no sooner got there when fifth-grade boy came over and hugged me. It was a boy named ean that went to the Church of the Palms, and he had wanted to neet me since he was in kindergarten at Plumosa. He and Elie vere good friends, so he started coming over on weekends. He alled me and said, "Will you please come get me? My father is nere and I'm scared." That happened several times, and then all of sudden, his father deserted his family. You guessed it; I became ean's *pseudofather*. It didn't end there. There was a student named Abraham at Crosspointe that I tutored in math for three years. He knew Jean and Elie, and he started coming over on weekends. Then Abraham's father died. I ended up calling them my three ;ons.

A year or so after Elie started spending time at my house, my rheumatoid arthritis started kicking up. I was taking something hat was supposed to help, but it didn't do much good. I finally got to the point where I was afraid I would fall getting in or out of bed or in or out of the bathtub. I asked Elie if he could live with ne, and he answered, "Of course." His mother thought it was a good idea and he moved in. After about a half year with a lot of oain, my doctor gave me prednisone, and in one month, I was completely better. By that time, Elie had become a permanent resident, and I had become a father for a teenager.

Roberto, Shambil, Joel, and Saul

The elevator was down! The third-, fourth-, and fifth-grade rooms were upstairs and I couldn't get there. I found out that it might be a couple of weeks before it was fixed. What should I do? I went into one of our second-grade classes and offered to help. It was a teacher I knew; she was a fifth-grade teacher the year before. Roberto, Joel, and Shambil were the first students to catch my eye. Roberto was the tallest in the class. He was trying hard to read, and he was kind of scared of math. He was afraid he would do a problem wrong so he wouldn't try. Shambil, on the other hand, was the smartest student in the class. He was bored because it was too easy. He kept asking me to give him harder math, which I did, and he did it right. Joel was about the smallest boy in the class and was one of the cutest kids I have ever seen. His teacher, Ms. Hazen, called Joel her cute patootie. Joel's problem was if things didn't as he wanted or he got something wrong, he would throw a crying tantrum. Shambil was like a little man; he was very mature in his use of language and his ideas. I would sit next to Roberto when he had to do a math paper and keep him going. He would sit, pencil in hand, hardly moving until I said, "Come on, you can do it. Get going!" He then would usually get it right. Joel was incredible; he caught on fast, got almost everything right, and gave you big smiles when he was done. When the elevator was fixed, I still kept coming to their class at their math time, which was when Mrs. Gomez's class had fine arts. Later on in the year, Ms. Hazen separated out a group of the best math students for me to teach. That group included Joel, Shambil, and a couple others. I was able to move faster with my group and even taught them some multiplication I still found some time to keep Roberto's confidence up. Saul was in the second-grade class in the room next to Ms. Hazen. I met Saul at lunch; he was fun to talk with. During the next two years, Saul always gave me a hug when he saw me. He was a very loving boy.

n third grade, I tutored Roberto about an hour a day in math; in ourth, I got him put into Mrs. Gomez's class. I was very pleased o find that Shambil was put into Mrs. Gomez's class as well. It vas great for me to be able to continue where I left off with these wo students. When they graduated, both asked for my e-mail .nd gave me theirs so we could keep in contact.

)uring his third and fourth grades, I would see Joel at lunch, .nd I watched him win the spelling bee and make honor rolls. n fifth grade, I was asked to help with the in-house TV morning .nnouncements. I was in a fifth-grade class to speak to another .tudent about being on the TV team. Sitting at the same table was oel and Saul. I asked them if they would like to be on the TV team .nd got a loud yes. They turned out to be naturals at running the nixer, using the camera, being on air, and everything else we did. thought I knew Joel and Saul very well, but I got to know them . lot better that year.

!very now and then, a student does something out of the blue hat is unexpected but reinforces why I love what I am doing. It vas Take Your Child to Work Day. Joel and Saul met me in the [V studio at about 7:40 AM and asked if I would take them to my vork that day! Joel didn't have a father, and Saul's father had a ob to which he could not bring his child. I got permission from he principal and spent a great day with my two wonderful sons railing behind me. I described to them what I was doing and had hem help me do it. It was one of the best days I have ever had as . volunteer. I will miss Saul and Joel very much. I bet they both nake a big difference with their lives.

Junior

_ast fall, I was waiting in the corridor as a fifth-grade class walked >y. All of a sudden, a boy I didn't know stopped and put out iis hand. His words were something like this: "Hi, my name is unior. I am new here." It wasn't what he said but the way he ;aid it. Right then, I thought he was the politest student I have .ver met. I couldn't talk to him at that point; the line was by me.

Instead, I found out when his class had lunch and went to that lunch.

I had lunch with him and started to get to know him. Some kids with him were bugging me to get out some coins so they could play the coin game I had taught them years ago. Junior quickly got involved in the game and was very good at it. After several lunches with Junior, I found out he was from the Dominican Republic. He had moved here with his mother, stepfather, and two sisters. As the year went by, I tried to have lunch with him a couple of times a week. He surprised me one day with a song he had written; it was about Jesus and him, and it was very good. About a month later, he brought in a longer song he had written, also about Jesus and Junior.

Then one day when I came in, he was sitting by himself in tears. I sat by him and slowly consoled him and tried to talk him out of it. It turned out he had been accused for something he didn't do. I got the crying to stop and even got him to eat most of his lunch. A few weeks later, he was crying again. This time it was about something nasty a girl said to him. Again, I got him back on keel. The crying happened a few more times during the year. He told me I was the only person in the school that could get him to stop crying and thanked me for helping him.

He will now move on to middle school, so who knows whether I will see him again. I felt very honored to know Junior and to be able to help him. I have a feeling he will end up either a minister or a missionary. It will always give me a warm feeling that I was part of his life.

Junior's Song

Oh my Jesus, Oh my Jesus,
Thank you for what you have done for me.

Oh my Jesus, Oh my Jesus,
You and I will always gain victory.

And the poor people out on the street,
Cure them and get them back on their feet.

I want you to shine your light on them tonight,
And when you do I want you to make it bright.

Oh Jesus I love you and I know that in your heart
You love me too, you love me too.

Meanwhile, Back at Plumosa

was asked to come over to Plumosa right after the terrible
principal left to look at some stuff in the computer room that they
didn't know whether to save or toss. It was kind of sad to see all
that stuff I had for my technology clubs and computer classes
sitting exactly where I had left it covered with dust. None of it
had been used. When I heard that Plumosa was going to move
to a new building and become "Plumosa School of the Arts," I
asked the new principal if I could take my technology treasures
to Crosspointe; she said, "Take whatever you want."

Near the middle of May, I went to a music recital at Plumosa.
There were about fifty third—to fifth-grade students playing
string instruments of all sorts and another fifty playing band
instruments. It brought tears to my eyes, seeing Plumosa back on
the road to be the great school it used to be. It made me feel real
good to see things going so well, but it also brought back a lot of
memories. A couple of weeks later, I went to the farewell party
at Plumosa, which was a chance to remember all the good years
of Plumosa. It was also a time to celebrate that in a few months,
a new Plumosa School of the Arts would open on a new campus.
It was great to see teachers and students I hadn't seen for a long
time. It was hard not to cry thinking about those great days I
spent at this school.

One of the nicest things that happened to me was a young man,
about eighteen, came up to me and asked, "Are you Mr. Rosene?"

He then told me the only reason he came was to see me! Wow
What a great and unexpected thing to happen to anyone. He ha
been one of my students many years ago. He had to tell me hi
name; he now had long black hair and, of course, was a lot bigge
He came to tell me he and his sister thought I was the best teache
in Plumosa, and he really liked my technology clubs and all th
stuff I taught him about computers. Out of the blue, I foun
another way I had made a difference, and it was a wonderfu
feeling to be given a compliment like that about ten years afte
the fact.

As I Look Back

About a year and a half ago, I got an invitation to go to a surpris
fiftieth birthday party for Jim Byrnes. Jim and his brothers ha
been instrumental in helping me run Beginnings[34] once it move
to Eliot Church. He has stayed in touch with me ever since. I reall
wanted to go to the party because I knew lots of old Beginning
members would be there, but the trip up north was a stumblin
block. I had been having arthritis problems for several month
and worried about getting on and off a plane and, for that matter
getting in and out of a strange bed. I decided to have Elie com
with me because I knew I would need help.

The party was Friday so we flew up Thursday. I always staye
at a hotel across the street from Eliot Church and planned t
stay through Sunday so I could attend Eliot once more. I knew
I wouldn't be back again. The surprise party was the mos
incredible experience of my life. My arrival at the party surprise
everyone. No one expected I would get there, as I hadn't RSVP'
to the invitation. I felt sure there would be a lot of Beginning
alumni there and I was right. About twenty-five were there wit
their spouses and children.

When Jim showed up, he came over, and we hugged each other
and we both cried. He then told everyone else how much it mean

---

[34.] See part II

o him for me to be there and said most of us wouldn't be here oday if it weren't for Fred. It made me feel like some kind of God! All of the spouses I didn't know and the children had all een told about me and seemed pleased to finally meet me. It eemed like I had known them forever. It is impossible for me o describe how I felt and how great it was to see so many old riends again. I say friends because I always felt all the Beginning ids were friends. I could not have succeeded any other way.

he only person I ever had to send to jail (only five days) was here with his wife and family. The first time I saw him after he ot out of jail, he threw his arms around me and said, "Thank ou. I now know I never want to go to jail again." He had given p drinking and drugs and is leading a great life. There were lots f people who thought he couldn't make it, but he fooled them ll. Thank God I got a chance to help.

Vhen I went to Eliot Sunday morning, someone had alerted many f the members of the youth groups I had run for so many years, nd they all came to church. People also came up to me and said hey were so glad to meet me after hearing so much about me for o many years. Again, I felt very awed at what was happening.

Vhen I got back home, I began to realize I had accomplished a lot nore than I ever dreamed of and a lot more than I ever realized. "hat weekend inspired this book and its title.

You Never Know What's Next

t has been an incredible experience to look back over my :hildhood and youth and remember how inferior I felt and how lopeless I felt when I lost the use of my legs. After my accident, I lever thought about what would be next because I never thought here would be a next. Now I look back and feel very good about ll I have done and all of the lives I have touched. As I wrote this book, I often cried for joy or laughed or became amazed at what had done. Thank God for guiding me and leading me, albeit iometimes forcefully, down the path you had planned for me.

I noticed as I wrote how small actions had major influence on what happened to me—a simple toboggan ride, a request to coach basketball, being taken to see a computer, going to a meeting about Newton youth needs, deciding to retire, being asked to tutor at Plumosa, and meeting a fifth grader who led me to Church of the Palms by simply saying, "I go there!" Behind it all, there must have been a guide leading me to the right place and making sure I made the right choices; I could not have done it without that help.

I realized, as I wrote, how important church has been in my life. As I was growing up, I never really thought of church as being important to my life. It was just something I was supposed to do. On the other hand, it was also a lot of fun and where most of my friends were. When I went off to college, I was the only one in my dorm who went to church. The nearest church to my dorm was Lutheran. The first Sunday I went, the first hymn was "Faith of Our Fathers." That was my favorite hymn. Hearing that hymn made me feel at home. I went to that church all of the time I was at RPI. As I grew older, I became more and more involved with church. When I was hurt, not going to church made me very sad. I vividly remember the first Easter after my accident. I was lying in bed listening to the hymn we always sung on Easter, "Christ the Lord Is Risen Today." The thought in my mind was, *Will I ever be able to listen to this hymn in church again?* At that time, I felt the answer was no!

When I moved to Florida, I tried a few churches, but none hooked me until the Church of the Palms. My life became a lot happier when I found it. Thank God for Elie—he brought me home.

As strange as it may seem, I am sure I would not have had as great a life if I hadn't taken that toboggan ride! It was all in the plan.

Thank you, God. I know I will keep making a difference until you call me home!

Made in the USA
Lexington, KY
30 March 2011